T0091625

AI
Investing

by Paul Mladjenovic

A Wiley Brand

AI Investing For Dummies®

Published by: **John Wiley & Sons, Inc.**, 111 River Street, Hoboken, NJ 07030-5774, www.wiley.com

Copyright © 2024 by John Wiley & Sons, Inc., Hoboken, New Jersey

Published simultaneously in Canada

For general information on our other products and services, please contact our Customer Care Department within the U.S. at 877-762-2974, outside the U.S. at 317-572-3993, or fax 317-572-4002. For technical support, please visit https://hub.wiley.com/community/support/dummies.

Wiley publishes in a variety of print and electronic formats and by print-on-demand. Some material included with standard print versions of this book may not be included in e-books or in print-on-demand. If this book refers to media such as a CD or DVD that is not included in the version you purchased, you may download this material at http://booksupport.wiley.com. For more information about Wiley products, visit www.wiley.com.

Library of Congress Control Number: 2024930804

ISBN 978-1-394-23703-6 (pbk); ISBN 978-1-394-23704-3 (ebk); ISBN 978-1-394-23705-0 (ebk)

SKY10066595_020824

Contents at a Glance

Table of Contents

Introduction

rtificial intelligence (AI) has taken the world by storm, and what better umbrella than a *For Dummies* guide? This book offers friendly and concrete guidance to either the newbie to AI or the intermediate investor, who is also interested in how this dynamic and soon-to-be pervasive topic affects you financially. That may mean investing and wealth-building or related issues ranging from retirement planning to estate planning and college planning. I also cover a wealth of practical resources, strategies, and tools to make sure you're ahead of the pack.

About This Book

AI investing is generally new to the public, and it can be valuable to anyone managing an investment portfolio or who needs information to achieve financial goals, especially with stocks and stock-related funds. This book is laid out so you can go from "What are AI prompts?" to how to use them and which ones work best in varying investing situations.

The first few chapters of this book go into the basics of AI, including its risks and rewards. Later parts go into the panorama of investing and financial topics that AI can help you with. The book doesn't just stop at AI stock investing — it goes deeper since AI affects so much in the world of investing, business, and general finance. No matter what your money concern is, this book has what you need to know written in an easy-to-digest and practical way.

Take a close look at the appendixes because this is the secret treasure of this book. Because AI is changing so quickly, you need to know where to look to keep up, and Part 6 is rich in how-to and where-to resources, educational and otherwise.

A quick note: Sidebars (shaded boxes of text) dig into the details of a given topic, but they aren't crucial to understanding it. Feel free to read them or skip them. You can pass over the text accompanied by the Technical Stuff icon, too. The text marked with this icon gives some interesting but nonessential information about AI investing.

One last thing: Within this book, you may note that some web addresses break across two lines of text. If you're reading this book in print and want to visit one of these web pages, simply key in the web address exactly as it's noted in the text, pretending as though the line break doesn't exist. If you're reading this as an e-book, you've got it easy — just click the web address to be taken directly to the web page.

Foolish Assumptions

In writing this book, I imagined someone pulling a copy off a bookshelf in their local bookstore and scanning it to see whether it's a valuable guide. And I wondered what that person would need to know to find this book interesting. Here are some of the assumptions I came up with about you, the reader:

» You have an interest in artificial intelligence and how it affects you financially.

» You're a consumer or investor and seeking guidance on how AI can increase your prosperity.

» You're worried about AI and how it affects your job or business, and you want to know what to do and how to proceed in this exciting, yet scary, new area.

» You want a convenient source of guidance on resources for the fast-paced world of AI technology.

Icons Used in This Book

In the margins of the book, you'll find these icons helping you out.

Whenever I provide a hint that makes an aspect of AI investing easier or potentially more successful, I mark it with a Tip icon.

The Remember icon marks paragraphs that contain information that you should absolutely take away from this book.

Heed the paragraphs marked with the Warning icon to avoid potential AI investing disasters.

TECHNICAL STUFF

Whenever I get technically inclined, I mark the paragraph with a Technical Stuff icon. If you're not into the nitty-gritty technical details of AI investing, you can skip these nuggets of info.

Beyond the Book

In addition to the material in the print or e-book you're reading right now, this product comes with some access-anywhere goodies on the web. Check out the free Cheat Sheet for info on ways that AI can help you save money and much more. To get this Cheat Sheet, simply go to www.dummies.com and search for "*AI Investing For Dummies* Cheat Sheet" in the Search box.

Where to Go from Here

This book is designed so that you can quickly jump to a specific chapter or section that most interests you. You don't have to start with the first chapter — although if you're new to AI and related investment issues, I recommend that you do so. Understanding the foundation of AI investing helps you better apply the techniques that you discover in the later chapters on the specifics of your investment activity.

You don't have to read this book from cover to cover, but if you're an especially thorough person, feel free to do so! If you just want to find specific information and then get back to work, take a look at the table of contents or the index, and then dive into the chapter or section that interests you. Besides investing and financial issues with AI, I especially suggest that you also review the business and career AI-related information so that you keep up with the professional challenges and opportunities that are unfolding with AI right now.

Keep in mind that success in any endeavor is initially reliant on sound information and guidance, and a *For Dummies* guide is there for you right from the start. *AI Investing For Dummies* will help you forge ahead successfully on your AI-driven path to a brighter future.

1

Artificial Intelligence Basics

Discover what artificial intelligence is and check out some common AI tools.

Get a primer on ChatGPT, the biggest AI tool out there. Look at its features and uses.

Take stock of the risks and rewards of AI.

Chapter **1**

Artificial Intelligence 101

Artificial intelligence, more commonly known as AI: It's all the rage today, and it will likely end up in every corner of modern life. It stokes both excitement and fear. It's changing the business, social, and financial landscape as I write this.

When it comes to AI, the best choice for people is to do what you're doing right now — learning what it is, what it can do, and how you can use it to your advantage in today's competitive economy. Like every major innovation in human history, it can have amazing positive power, and it can have the power to harm. Use it to make yourself stronger. This chapter gets you started on the road to investing with AI.

First Things First: What Is AI?

As a business person and a financial educator, I generally avoid in the scope of this singular book the techie stuff and stick to the how-do-I-use-this-stuff approach. I pride myself on being an educator, and I look at artificial intelligence the same way I look at a laptop computer or a smartphone — like a tool. I may not be able to explain the inner workings of it with much precision, but I know how to use it to achieve my goals or to satisfy my wants and needs.

As for AI, let's do the obvious thing here and ask AI about AI. I use ChatGPT (which is covered in greater detail in Chapter 2). My question (more commonly known as a prompt):

"Please define and explain AI in less than 150 words as if I were an eighth grader."

The response from ChatGPT is in Figure 1-1.

ChatGPT

Artificial Intelligence, or AI, is like giving computers the ability to think and learn on their own. It's a smart computer system that can understand things, make decisions, and even solve problems without being explicitly programmed for each task. Imagine a really smart robot that can figure out how to play a new game or help you with your homework by learning from examples. AI uses data and patterns to make predictions and choices, making it a bit like a computer brain. From virtual assistants to video game opponents, AI is all around us, making machines smarter and more helpful.

FIGURE 1-1:
Asking AI
about AI.

Cool! ChatGPT says it's like a smart robot that can help you with your problems and tasks. That's my kind of answer. Throughout the book I use examples from AI tools, predominately from ChatGPT and also AI-enhanced tools such as Bing Chat (yes, the turbo-charged version of Microsoft's Bing Search engine).

TIP

I wrote this book fully mindful that AI is constantly changing and improving. Make it a point to visit any resource listed throughout this book (especially in Part 6) that is relevant to your concerns (and plenty of valuable resources are included). The resources are both general and specific, but timely, and they are constantly updated to help you keep up with AI's development.

Distinguishing the Two Types of AI

Although I could ask AI to provide an extensive explanation of AI and I could spew all the facets and jargon about it, I'll stick to my terminology about AI in the following sections. The two types of AI are general and specific. Horizontal and vertical would also do.

General AI

The reason I also refer to general AI as "horizontal" is that this type of AI spans the vast digital landscape to produce the response to your inquiry or request. It can be good for starters and for general knowledge.

A good example of this type of AI is the popular ChatGPT (see Chapter 2). Despite its awesome capabilities, I wouldn't use it for an intense, specific purpose. For example, I could use it to learn skills such as creating a web page, but I wouldn't rely on it to learn about brain surgery or cancer. I would go to specialized sources for that or (better) human experts.

TIP

Another general AI tool to add to your arsenal would be AI-enhanced search engines. The last time I looked, you could choose from 18 AI-enhanced search engines, but that number may have changed in the time it took for you to read this! You can find them in Appendix B.

Specific AI

Vertical or specific AI concentrates on a given topic or specialty. Good examples of this are robo-advisors (covered in Chapter 7). Keep in mind that part of the power of AI is that it uses its technological power to learn about what it's working on. Some AI tools specialize in finance, but other tools specialize in healthcare, and so on.

TIP

I think the best example of this is when you need medical treatment or the attention of a doctor. You would first go to a general practitioner (GP). But after that you may need some specialized attention. The GP may know about your heart, for example, but the GP would ultimately need to refer you to a cardiologist. Think of general and specific AI in the same way.

In Chapter 3, different categories of AI are covered; take a look there for some excellent AI directories that can help you find the right AI tool for whatever issue you want to address.

Investing in Stocks with AI's Help

The primary reason you may have gotten this book is because the title includes both "AI" and "investing," and the heart of this combo is covered in Part 2.

REMEMBER

Keep in mind that in this book, as with most of the investing books I author, I point out the crucial distinctions between "investing" and "speculating." To put it simply, investing is putting your money into assets and/or vehicles that have value today and the possibility of much greater value over time. Meanwhile, speculating is essentially like educated gambling, hopefully to make greater gains sooner despite greater risks. Everybody wants to get that amazing stock when it's cheap and obscure and to watch it soar to mind-boggling levels as "ka-ching" is ringing in our brokerage accounts. It could happen with your investing (such as large-cap tech stocks), and you could hit it big with your speculating (such as with small-cap stocks), but you should know the difference.

For investing in large-cap stocks that are neck-deep in AI, head over to Chapter 4. If you're looking for that small company that could soar to the moon, check out Chapter 5. Just keep in mind that many of today's small tech companies won't be around a few years from now, so take heed of the word "fundamentals" (covered in Chapter 8) since that is at the heart of true investing. Speculating, meanwhile, is a stone's throw away from financial gambling, so learn the difference.

For those of you who want to get into AI in a safer way, consider going through exchange-traded funds (ETFs) and/or mutual funds, which are investing in AI through a portfolio approach. See Chapter 6 for details.

Using AI to Try Stock Investing Alternatives

The prior section covered investing in AI-related vehicles. But keep in mind that AI is a versatile tool that can be used across the investing landscape. Part 3 goes into assets from precious metals and commodities to cryptocurrencies and real estate. Getting into these areas will be much easier with AI as your digital research assistant.

TIP

Perhaps the hidden gem for you is Chapter 12. It concentrates on helping you with AI to tackle business and career ventures. For many folks, the rise of AI brings some concerns and uncertainty. Here is where you turn lemons into lemonade, and boost your professional prospects and see AI through the lens of possibilities. Be like me and make an AI-assisted home-based business part of your financial situation (check out my AI resources at www.ravingcapitalist.com/AI/).

Looking at Your Total Financial Picture with AI

Don't just look at the investment landscape. Use AI to kick it up a notch and be holistic with every corner of your financial situation.

As I write this, the national economy and the world's geopolitics are bringing uncertainty everywhere. Be prepared. AI can be used for analyzing the economy (see Chapter 13) so you know what to do whether you are facing a recession, inflation, or both (or worse).

Keep in mind that investing is a part (yes, a large part) of the financial planning process. Get to know the other parts, too. Part 4 goes into retirement planning, budgeting, and much more, so don't ignore these vital parts of your situation. Of course, you need to address the tough stuff like estate planning and taxes (ugh), but AI makes it easier than ever to deal with these issues.

REMEMBER

In some of these areas you'll likely need a human expert, but AI will make the process so much easier, reduce your stress, and increase your knowledge and confidence.

Getting Smart about AI

TIP

For those of you who want to get really informed about AI (beyond the scope of this book), here are some places to turn to that place a heavy emphasis on the world of AI:

>> **AI Practical Guide** (https://aipracticalguide.com/): They have a beginners' guide as well.

>> **IBM's developer blog** (https://developer.ibm.com/): Why not learn the technical side with what is arguably AI's longest participant?

>> **Adult education sites** such as Coursera (www.coursera.com) and Udemy (www.udemy.com): They have some excellent free and low-cost courses on AI.

Appendix A has more AI educational resources.

IN THIS CHAPTER

» **Getting an introduction to ChatGPT**

» **Picking apart AI prompts**

» **Considering the disadvantages of ChatGPT**

» **Checking out alternatives to ChatGPT**

Chapter **2**

A Primer on ChatGPT

Although AI has been evident in recent years through consumer apps like those annoying voices when you call a company's main telephone number and Amazon's Alexa and Google's Siri (and many more applications when you think of them), the dam broke on the public's radar screen about the power and potential of AI when ChatGPT was launched in 2022.

ChatGPT hit one million users in record time and much more quickly than any prior tech launch. Netflix, for example, didn't hit one million users until three years after it launched. In this chapter, I introduce you to using ChatGPT and list some alternatives to consider.

Acquainting Yourself with ChatGPT

ChatGPT was created and launched by Open AI, and it can be accessed at `https://chat.openai.com`. There are two versions at the time of this writing: the free version (GPT version 3.5) and the premium version GPT Plus ($20 per month for version 4). The free version is fine for your AI investing pursuits now so that you can get comfortable interacting with it and exploring its power and potential.

TIP

ChatGPT offers plenty of help. Besides many forums and educational sources online (many are listed in Appendix A), ChatGPT's creator is a great first place to start: `https://help.openai.com/en/`.

Asking ChatGPT to describe itself

Why not have ChatGPT introduce itself? Use the simplest prompt imaginable:

"What is ChatGPT?"

ChatGPT's response when I asked this prompt is in Figure 2-1. This figure is of the interface itself.

 ChatGPT

ChatGPT is a language model developed by OpenAI. It belongs to the GPT (Generative Pre-trained Transformer) family, specifically GPT-3.5. OpenAI, a research organization focused on artificial intelligence, created ChatGPT to understand and generate human-like text based on the input it receives. It has been trained on diverse internet text and is designed to perform various natural language processing tasks.

ChatGPT is known for its ability to generate coherent and contextually relevant responses in conversation-like interactions. Users can input prompts or queries, and the model responds accordingly. It's a powerful tool for a wide range of natural language understanding and generation tasks, making it useful for applications like content creation, text completion, language translation, and more.

It's important to note that ChatGPT doesn't have real-time awareness, and its responses are generated based on patterns it learned during training. Additionally, as of my last knowledge update in January 2022, ChatGPT is a product of OpenAI and is used via OpenAI's API or other interfaces provided by OpenAI.

FIGURE 2-1:
An introduction
from ChatGPT.

TECHNICAL STUFF

As far as the name goes, "Chat" refers to your interaction with it, and the "GPT" refers to "Generative Pre-trained Transformer." Find out more about the meaning of the term "ChatGPT" at www.coursera.org/articles/chatgpt.

Discovering what ChatGPT can help you with

I think that you could be like a kid in a candy store after you start using ChatGPT and getting creative with your prompts. Let's get your creative juicing flowing by giving you some ideas of what you can accomplish with ChatGPT. Consider a prompt like this:

"Please provide a list of ten specific benefits and services that ChatGPT can provide to investors. Please give an explanation and an example of each item."

The first part of ChatGPT's response is in Figure 2-2. Note that number 4 is about portfolio diversification strategies. Right out of the starting gate, you have issues you can address or discuss with your financial advisor. Take each issue and ask AI about them in depth; it will only enhance your knowledge and performance as an investor.

ChatGPT

Certainly, here's an extensive list of 10 specific benefits and services that ChatGPT can provide to investors, each with an explanation and an example:

1. **Market Analysis:**
   * *Explanation:* ChatGPT can analyze market trends and provide insights into investment opportunities.
   * *Example:* "Analyze recent market data and identify emerging trends in the renewable energy sector, highlighting potential investment opportunities."

2. **Stock Price Predictions:**
   * *Explanation:* ChatGPT can generate predictions on stock price movements based on historical data and market conditions.
   * *Example:* "Predict the potential price movement of a specific tech stock over the next quarter, considering recent earnings reports and industry news."

3. **Risk Assessment:**
   * *Explanation:* ChatGPT can assess and quantify risks associated with specific investments.
   * *Example:* "Evaluate the risks associated with investing in a high-volatility cryptocurrency and provide risk mitigation strategies."

4. **Portfolio Diversification Strategies:**
   * *Explanation:* ChatGPT can suggest strategies for diversifying investment portfolios to manage risk.
   * *Example:* "Provide recommendations on how to diversify a stock portfolio, considering various sectors and asset classes."

FIGURE 2-2:
The first few
things ChatGPT
can help with.

Figure 2-3 provides the next batch of items for the investor's consideration. Take item number 7 on dividend stock selection. Dividends are an important part of a long-term stock investing strategy (especially for income investors). You can use AI to locate, analyze, and choose dividend stocks.

Figure 2-4 wraps up the choices with IPOs (initial public offerings) and long-term strategies, both of which can be handled with AI. IPOs are covered in Chapter 5, but now you know that AI can help you choose in a way that was not possible before.

5. **Economic Indicator Analysis:**
   * *Explanation:* ChatGPT can analyze economic indicators and their potential impact on investments.
   * *Example:* "Examine the implications of inflation and interest rate changes on bond investments and recommend adjustments to a fixed-income portfolio."

6. **Investment Research Assistance:**
   * *Explanation:* ChatGPT can assist in researching specific investment options or industries.
   * *Example:* "Research the growth prospects of emerging markets in the technology sector, providing key data and potential risks."

7. **Dividend Stock Selection:**
   * *Explanation:* ChatGPT can help identify dividend-paying stocks for income-focused investors.
   * *Example:* "Suggest a list of dividend stocks with a history of consistent payouts and strong financial health."

8. **Real-Time Market News Updates:**
   * *Explanation:* ChatGPT can provide real-time updates on market news and events.
   * *Example:* "Summarize the latest news affecting the pharmaceutical industry and its potential impact on healthcare stock prices."

FIGURE 2-3:
More things that ChatGPT can assist with.

9. **Initial Public Offering (IPO) Analysis:**
   * *Explanation:* ChatGPT can analyze upcoming IPOs and provide insights into their potential performance.
   * *Example:* "Evaluate the financials and market potential of a company preparing for an IPO, predicting its attractiveness to investors."

10. **Long-Term Investment Strategies:**
    * *Explanation:* ChatGPT can offer advice on long-term investment strategies aligned with financial goals.
    * *Example:* "Propose a long-term investment strategy for retirement planning, considering a mix of growth and income-generating assets."

These examples showcase the diverse range of benefits and services that ChatGPT can offer to investors, helping them make informed decisions, manage risks, and optimize their investment portfolios.

FIGURE 2-4:
ChatGPT can provide plenty of help.

I don't mean to overwhelm you, but to invite you to start getting proficient with a groundbreaking new technology that will only get better and more proficient for those willing to embrace it.

It's All About the Prompt

Your part in using ChatGPT is to enter your question or request, and this is referred to as the "prompt," which makes sense; you're prompting it to generate a response you're seeking.

Yes, you can prompt about anything, but let's keep it in the realm of this book's financial topics. Here's an example in which I prompted ChatGPT about prompts:

> "Please provide a list of 20 useful prompts for financial planning and investing with an explanation and an example of each."

The first part of ChatGPT's response is in Figure 2-5. Using AI to use AI could be the first best approach for investors. Take the item of risk tolerance assessment. Plenty of investors are not that sure about their own tolerance for risk. Using AI to go in-depth here will ultimately mean making choices that will make your path going forward less stressful.

FIGURE 2-5: Some financial planning and investing prompts.

> **ChatGPT**
>
> Certainly! Here's a list of 20 useful prompts for financial planning and investing, each with an explanation and an example:
>
> 1. **Retirement Planning Strategies:**
>   - *Explanation:* Seek advice on planning for retirement and optimizing investment strategies.
>   - *Example:* "Provide personalized strategies for retirement planning, considering a goal of retiring in 20 years with a comfortable income."
> 2. **Tax-Efficient Investing:**
>   - *Explanation:* Inquire about tax-efficient investment strategies to maximize returns.
>   - *Example:* "Suggest tax-efficient investment options to minimize liabilities while maintaining portfolio growth."
> 3. **Diversification Techniques:**
>   - *Explanation:* Request insights into effective diversification strategies across asset classes.
>   - *Example:* "Advise on diversifying my investment portfolio to balance risk and return, considering various sectors and geographic regions."
> 4. **Risk Tolerance Assessment:**
>   - *Explanation:* Assess and understand an individual's risk tolerance for tailored investment advice.
>   - *Example:* "Evaluate my risk tolerance and recommend an investment strategy aligned with my comfort level and financial goals."

Figure 2-6 covers additional financial planning and investing prompts from ChatGPT.

5. **College Savings Plans:**
   * *Explanation:* Seek advice on effective savings plans for funding a child's education.
   * *Example:* "Provide guidance on the best college savings plans and investment options for my child's education fund."

6. **Emergency Fund Planning:**
   * *Explanation:* Discuss the importance of an emergency fund and strategies for building and maintaining it.
   * *Example:* "Outline steps for establishing and managing an emergency fund, including suggested savings targets."

7. **Real Estate Investment Insights:**
   * *Explanation:* Request advice on investing in real estate, considering market trends and potential risks.
   * *Example:* "Analyze the current real estate market and suggest potential investment opportunities, emphasizing long-term growth."

8. **Dividend Investing Strategies:**
   * *Explanation:* Explore strategies for investing in dividend-paying stocks for income generation.
   * *Example:* "Recommend a diversified portfolio of dividend-paying stocks with a focus on consistent payouts and growth potential."

9. **Socially Responsible Investing (SRI):**
   * *Explanation:* Discuss investment options aligned with socially responsible and ethical criteria.
   * *Example:* "Provide insights into socially responsible investment options that align with my values and sustainability goals."

10. **Debt Management Tactics:**
    * *Explanation:* Seek advice on managing and reducing debt while optimizing investment strategies.
    * *Example:* "Offer strategies for managing debt and simultaneously investing for future financial goals."

11. **Market Volatility Preparedness:**
    * *Explanation:* Discuss strategies for navigating market volatility and downturns.
    * *Example:* "Provide tips on staying resilient during market downturns and making informed decisions during times of high volatility."

12. **ETF vs. Mutual Fund Comparison:**
    * *Explanation:* Compare the benefits and drawbacks of investing in ETFs versus mutual funds.
    * *Example:* "Explain the key differences between ETFs and mutual funds and recommend suitable options based on investment goals."

13. **Impact of Interest Rates on Investments:**
    * *Explanation:* Analyze how changes in interest rates may impact different types of investments.
    * *Example:* "Discuss the implications of rising interest rates on bond investments and recommend adjustments to the fixed-income portion of my portfolio."

FIGURE 2-6:
Additional financial planning and investing prompts.

14. **Inheritance and Windfall Planning:**
    * *Explanation:* Offer guidance on managing unexpected financial windfalls or inheritances.
    * *Example:* "Provide a plan for managing a sudden inheritance, addressing tax implications and optimizing investments for long-term growth."

15. **401(k) Allocation Strategies:**
    * *Explanation:* Discuss optimal allocation strategies within a 401(k) retirement account.
    * *Example:* "Recommend a diversified asset allocation strategy for my 401(k) based on my risk tolerance and retirement timeline."

16. **Health Savings Account (HSA) Utilization:**
    * *Explanation:* Explore ways to maximize the benefits of a Health Savings Account for investment purposes.
    * *Example:* "Advise on using an HSA as an investment vehicle for both short-term medical expenses and long-term growth."

17. **Long-Term vs. Short-Term Investment Planning:**
    * *Explanation:* Discuss the benefits and considerations of long-term versus short-term investment planning.
    * *Example:* "Explain the advantages and disadvantages of long-term investment strategies compared to short-term trading, considering my financial goals."

18. **Cryptocurrency Investment Guidance:**
    * *Explanation:* Offer insights into investing in cryptocurrencies, considering risk and potential returns.
    * *Example:* "Discuss the risks and potential rewards of investing in cryptocurrencies, and suggest a balanced approach within my overall portfolio."

19. **Optimizing 529 Plan Investments:**
    * *Explanation:* Provide advice on selecting and optimizing investments within a 529 college savings plan.
    * *Example:* "Suggest suitable investment options within a 529 plan, considering the age of my child and risk tolerance."

20. **Estate Planning and Investment Integration:**
    * *Explanation:* Explore how estate planning and investment strategies can be integrated for wealth preservation.
    * *Example:* "Discuss the integration of estate planning with investment strategies to ensure wealth preservation and seamless asset transition."

These prompts cover a broad spectrum of financial planning and investment topics, offering tailored guidance to individuals based on their unique circumstances and goals.

FIGURE 2-6:
(Continued)

TIP

You find guidance on creating useful investing prompts throughout this book, but here is a simple two-step formula for creating a useful prompt (until you get proficient):

1. **Give the AI tool (such as ChatGPT) a scenario as the first part of your prompt.**

   For example: "I am a 60-year-old single woman with $X amount in my 401(k) plan . . ."

2. **Then give a specific question as the second part of your prompt.**

   For example: "I am considering a growth fund, but I want to compare the pros and cons with a growth-and-income fund."

TIP

When you get proficient with ChatGPT, understand that you can grow with it. ChatGPT has many uses and add-ins so you can get productive. Check out the possibilities here: https://platform.openai.com/examples.

The Limits and Negatives of ChatGPT

REMEMBER

Keep in mind that ChatGPT is far from perfect, and some of its drawbacks and glitches can be problematic. If you're seeking answers to very important questions in your life — money, health, and so on — please consult with human experts where applicable. If you're doing research, then consult with multiple sources.

WARNING

Here are some of the disadvantages of using AI to help with your investing and other financial pursuits:

>> **A limit on knowledge:** ChatGPT 3.5 (the free version) does have a time limitation (January 2022 at the time of writing).

>> **Bias:** If you're asking questions about philosophy, politics, public policy, and related areas in which human bias can be strong, then you may get skewed answers. Note that "garbage in equals garbage out" was first coined when computers became mainstream decades ago, but that saying is just as true (maybe more so) with AI since so many biased humans are involved in both the programming and the data formation.

>> **Incorrect answers:** Until they get the bugs and glitches out, there will be the possibility of errors and poor and/or inaccurate answers and responses. Again, check multiple sources — especially if the topic is very sensitive or important to you.

>> **Cannot provide personal advice:** Because AI tools for the most part do not (yet!) have access to your personal data, refrain from asking very personal questions. Yes, you can give it scenarios and example problems and issues, but just understand that AI is not developed yet to give you mindful, sentient guidance similar to human experts.

>> **Other issues with AI:** I won't seek to be comprehensive about all the failings and shortcomings of AI, but at this point why not ask ChatGPT or other AI this pointed question? Since it isn't emotional and won't take the question personally, it's remarkably open about its own problems and shortcomings.

Looking at ChatGPT Alternatives

Before you think it's ChatGPT 24/7/365 around here, keep in mind that there are alternatives for your consideration. Who knows? Maybe a week or a year from now, one of the following sites surpasses ChatGPT. In fact, some of these already have done better than ChatGPT in some tasks:

>> **AnonChatGPT:** For those who want to use ChatGPT anonymously to preserve their privacy, this is a good consideration. For more details, go to https://anonchatgpt.com/.

>> **Bing Chat:** Microsoft Edge's Bing search engine coupled with the power of ChatGPT competes with Google's Bard. Check it out at www.bing.com/chat. I have been using Bing Chat, and I like the AI enhancements. Some of its capabilities are superior to ChatGPT.

>> **ChatPDF:** One of the drawbacks of ChatGPT (the free version 3.5 at least) is that it can't review or summarize PDFs. With PDFs so ubiquitous both online and probably on your hard drive, ChatPDF (www.chatpdf.com/) can be very useful.

>> **Copy.ai:** Found at www.copy.ai/, many users feel that Copy.ai is better than ChatGPT for summarizing and writing in general.

>> **Google Bard:** You didn't think that Google was just going to sit on the sidelines, right? Check out Bard at https://bard.google.com/. It has the power of Google behind it so it has plenty of capabilities. It is also free (as of this writing) and can access live and real-time internet data. This is a big advantage over ChatGPT's time limitation (the last update was January 2022 for the 3.5 version).

TIP

Sites such as Writesonic (https://writesonic.com/), **Lifewire** (www.lifewire.com/), and other sites listed in Appendix A regularly review and compare various AI tools. Writesonic, for example, did a post titled "Top 30 ChatGPT alternatives that will blow your mind in 2023 (Free & Paid)" found at https://writesonic.com/blog/chatgpt-alternatives/.

TIP

To get proficient with ChatGPT, it can be good to be part of a like-minded group to ask questions, share ideas, and so on for ChatGPT. Consider joining the forum of users at Discord (https://discord.com/invite/openai).

Flip to Chapter 3 for details on different inputs and outputs of various AI tools (audio to text, text to image, and the like). For more ChatGPT educational resources, head over to Appendix A.

Chapter **3**

Spanning the AI Landscape: Different Inputs and Outputs

The purpose of both your investment pursuits and your AI secret weapon are ultimately to make your future years as financially comfortable as possible. Using AI now makes it easier to plan your future.

In this chapter, I focus on grouping AI technology according to the user's perspective and needs. As I write this, hundreds of AI tools and apps are available, and by the time you read this, there will likely be thousands. The good ones will survive, but many will go into the dustbin of technological history.

I lay out this chapter as an "input-to-output" mode. You provide the input (your wants, needs, issues, and so on), and AI will provide the output (responses in text, audio, graphic images, programming, and so forth).

First Things First: Text-to-Text with Chatbots

When the most well-known chatbot, ChatGPT, exploded on the scene in late 2022, the public was getting a taste of what was to come. This is the use of AI like an information genie. Don't just ask it three questions — ask numerous questions of this genie.

REMEMBER

ChatGPT (covered in greater detail in Chapter 2) is an AI tool designed to interact with you and provide responses to your questions and requests (prompts). The most obvious interaction is asking a simple question and then getting an answer moments later. Part of the genius of this chatbot (and its competitors) is that it is interactive and keeps track of your questions so that it acts seamlessly as a dutiful and patient all-knowing robot.

It role-plays with you. If you ask for an answer "as if you were a fifth grader," it obliges. If you want the answer as if it were told to you by Darth Vader or Tarzan or Donald Duck, you got it.

You ask or request in text format, and the response comes in text format. But that's just the start:

>> **Language power:** The chatbot (in this case, ChatGPT) is fluent in languages. If you copy and paste a 500-word paragraph in Spanish, in seconds it translates the text into English or another requested language. Now we learn that AI can teach us something useful.

>> **Learn a new skill:** Given how competitive the economy can be, the more you know, the better chances you have to be employable or to serve your clients if you run a business. AI can teach you a new skill — quickly in the comfort of your home and without expensive courses or tutors. What skill do you need to know? Ask for a step-by-step lesson plan and have AI give you all the details that you need; you can learn a skill in days instead of weeks or months.

>> **Do programming for you:** What's that? Do you want to design a webpage in HTML or Python? Let AI do it. Do you need to create formulas in that Excel spreadsheet that your boss needs by tomorrow? No worries, AI will do it for you. Ask a detailed question and request a step-by-step answer, and in seconds you can complete that task.

>> **What do you imagine you need?** Need a poem for your 30th wedding anniversary (yep, that was me in October; the missus was impressed). Create a resume in seconds? Business plan? Marketing checklists? The uses are endless.

Keep in mind that AI is a perfect tool for investors. If you want to create a specially designed spreadsheet to help you analyze your finances or a public company's finances, or do your retirement planning projections, AI can do it for you. I enjoy using AI to help me find research and analyze investments online that could fit my criteria or my future goals. The rest of this book focuses on text-to-text, so you'll have plenty of examples to get you rolling.

Other AI Inputs and Outputs

Don't just rely on text-to-text for your pursuits. The following formats can help you in other creative ways that can greatly benefit you professionally (with your business or career) or your investing pursuits.

Document-to-text

I think that document-to-text AI is one of the most useful AI functions. We live in the information age — at times we seem to be drowning in information and data. We need to extract useable, succinct meaning from voluminous documentation.

A good example of this type of service is ChatPDF (www.chatpdf.com). This is a good example of a site that can help you analyze or summarize a lengthy PDF to make your research a lot easier to do. More tools like this can be found in Appendix B.

TIP

A function that I think can be very useful for investors and speculators is the ability for an AI tool to review and summarize online documents such as research reports, investment posts, and other detailed documents.

Audio-to-text

I do videos on economics, investing, business, and related topics. In recent months, I've used an AI tool to help me transcribe my spoken words into texts that I can use in multiple ways (such as training materials or e-books for clients and/or students).

It's amazing and useful for me to record my lecture (using a digital voice recorder or my smartphone) as a WAV or MP3 file. Then, I upload that to a service I use (such as Otter at www.otter.ai) and get a well-done transcript completed in minutes and ready for my use.

For investors, audio-to-text AI can turn investing classes and lectures into transcripts.

Text-to-image

There was a time when you needed a graphic designer to do a specific image for your needs, but that was . . . uh . . . hours ago! Now you can provide a specific description of what you want (the text input) and plug it into the AI tool designed for "text-to-image" and get it done for free or low-cost.

Whatever your graphic image needs, here are the top AI tools for your consideration:

>> MidJourney (www.midjourney.com)

>> DALL-E 3 (https://openai.com/dall-e-3)

>> Leonardo.AI (www.leonardo.ai)

TIP

Imagine what you can do if you are into graphic design or need imagery for a variety of personal and business needs. Specifically for investing and financial purposes, you can use text-to-image AI for

>> **Business uses:** If you're running a business in an area like graphic design or you have a website for any kind of business, creating images with AI will be very useful. You can describe the type of image you want (the "text") and AI will produce an image — and usually many images — according to your description. If you're creating a webpage and you need an image of an "ice cream cone," for example, you can create it in seconds. But don't stop there! If you want "an ice cream cone that is chocolate and strawberry with rainbow sprinkles in a waffle cone," it can be done in seconds.

>> **Financial uses:** If you want to know how well a given stock, asset, or other investment vehicle has performed over a given period of time against a standard such as the Dow or the S&P 500, you can describe it to the AI tool, which can create a chart so you can judge the performance of your particular choice.

Text-to-video

Need to create a video? Whether for personal or business pursuits, AI can create stunning video from your descriptions or your text (such as an article or post). Here are top AI tools for this task:

>> Pictory.ai (www.pictory.ai)

>> Hour One (www.hourone.ai)

>> Flexclip (www.flexclip.com)

Sometimes a simple picture is more powerful and useful than a mountain of dry data. A good example of this is at the site Visual Capitalist (www.visualcapitalist.com/). Since AI is excellent at sifting, analyzing, and presenting data, taking it just one more level (to a simple visual) can be useful for investment decision-making.

One analyst I know sees the value of how one investment vehicle (junk bonds) was an amazing precursor to the value of another investment vehicle (stocks in the S&P 500). When junk bonds went up, the S&P 500 followed; when junk bonds declined, S&P 500 declined as well. He found this in a chart (a visual!), and that chart was the culmination of extensive data that.

TIP

Using the AI tools mentioned in this chapter (and in Appendix B), have AI extract data for two or more interrelated markets and vehicles and see whether one correlates to another. How closely are interest rates correlated to economic cycles (such as bull markets and recessions)? How closely is gold related to the inflation rate? This is where AI can shine as an alert system for your investing and trading strategies.

Finding Even More Tools with a Few Helpful Resources

The AI tools I mention earlier in this chapter are examples of the power of AI that you can use for your own pursuits. By the time you read this, more great tools will become available. Most are either free or available for a trial period or for a low cost.

TIP

When you write a book in the midst of a fast-moving phenomenon like AI, you're bound to miss some details and developments. But no worries! This book helps you in real time because of the top-rated resources I list here and in Part 6:

>> **AI Tool Report:** This site is maintained and updated by the folks that do the AI Tools report (www.aitoolreport.com/), which has more than 475,000 subscribers (at the time of writing).

>> **AI Tool Guru:** This is another useful directory (https://aitoolguru.com/), and the layout helps you easily search based on your category or concern.

>> **Future Tools:** Matt Wolfe's AI site (www.futuretools.io/); Matt's AI YouTube channel is listed in Appendix A with other AI educational resources.

Lots more AI tools and resources are in Appendixes A and B. For general investing resources, check out Appendix C.

AI Stock Investing

Discover the major players in the AI investing space.

Find out about AI-related small cap stocks and IPOs (more formally known as initial public offerings).

Diversify your portfolio using exchange-traded funds (ETFs) and mutual funds.

Get the low-down on robo-advisors and how they can complement your actual human investment advisors.

Examine the essentials of fundamental and technical analysis and how they can work together as you make investments.

Chapter **4**

Large-Cap AI Stocks

Right out of the starting gate here in Part 2 of the book, let's nail down all the major ways you can invest directly in artificial intelligence. First, here are the major ways you can invest directly in AI:

» The major companies involved with AI (covered in this chapter)

» Smaller (growth-oriented) companies involved in AI (covered in Chapter 5)

Second, here are diversified ways to invest directly in AI, both covered in Chapter 6:

» AI-related exchange traded funds (ETFs)

» AI-related mutual funds

Keep in mind that you can also profit indirectly in AI by checking out those companies and industries/sectors that benefit from the uses and benefits of AI; those companies are covered in Chapter 6.

Getting a Sense of AI's Place in the Big Picture

It's like a movie that gets replayed over and over. Internet stocks soared during the late 1990s and then crashed during 2000–2002. Real estate and housing stocks soared during 2003–2007 and then crashed in 2008. Marijuana stocks soared in 2018 and then crashed. Bitcoin and other cryptocurrencies soared and then crashed several times from 2010 to 2022.

Fast forward to early 2023; AI-related stocks soared, and here we are about to head into 2024 (at the time of writing), and we ask, "Will there be a crash?"

When the market is enamored by a given class of stock or other investment asset, investors and speculators plow into it with abandon. Your email is chock full of marketing messages from brokers and investment gurus as they push their hot choices and wealth-building strategies. In this regard, AI is no different. No matter what stocks are in favor, the cycle of ups and downs tends to endure. Yes, AI will endure, and it's here to stay, but tried-and-true investment principles from long ago continue to endure in today's market and will continue for the foreseeable future.

REMEMBER

Just because a stock or a group of stocks corrects or crashes, that doesn't mean that the "game is over" and that you have to look elsewhere. If the aggregate demand is there for a given product or service (such as AI), then the long-term prospects for that stock or group of stocks will continue to be bright. But you still have to do your homework and separate the stocks that have long-term growth prospects intact from those stocks that have a shaky or dubious future. The fundamentals matter in both the AI-related stocks and whatever group of stocks follow with whatever their dazzling prospects are.

No, AI is not a fad or a temporary development. It has "legs" and will likely be a growing, long-term component of the financial and economic landscape. But this is where you dust off the books on your shelf that focus on investment fundamentals (such as the latest edition of *Stock Investing For Dummies* by yours truly, published by Wiley); they will come in handy for making sound choices in a new and exciting field. Read the rest of this chapter for solid choices and principles so that AI is a fruitful part of your portfolio.

Understanding Market Capitalization Basics

REMEMBER

I refer to the stocks in this chapter as "AI stocks" because of the concentration of their AI activity and as a convenience reference for me, but some of these are familiar technology firms that in days gone by (and today as well) are not technically pure plays in AI. Stocks such as Apple and Microsoft are big players in AI, but we've always known them for other tech pursuits such as smartphones and internet-related technology.

REMEMBER

In this chapter, I cover "large-cap" and "mega-cap" stocks while I cover "small-cap" stocks in Chapter 5. Just in case you need to know, the "cap" is a reference to capitalization, which refers to a public company's market size. *Capitalization* means a number of shares times the share price. If you have a public company that is $20 per share and the total shares outstanding is 100 million shares, then the market capitalization is $2 billion, which may sound like a lot but is actually a small-cap stock. Here is the general breakdown:

>> **Micro-cap:** Companies with a market capitalization under $1 billion

>> **Small-cap:** Companies with a market capitalization under $10 billion

>> **Mid-cap:** Companies with a market capitalization of $10 to $50 billion

>> **Large-cap:** Companies with a market capitalization from $50 billion to $100 billion

>> **Mega-cap:** Companies with a market capitalization above $100 billion

Technically, those are not "hard and fast" numbers. Someone will tell me I'm a billion off here and there (my luck, it will be an AI tool).

WARNING

Many market observers tend to look at the market size of a company (market capitalization) as a rough profile of safety. All things being equal, a $100 billion company is considered safer than, for example, a $100 million company. But don't be lulled into a sense of security just because of market size.

At their peak, notable companies such as WorldCom, Lehman Brothers, Enron, and others were huge, large-cap stocks but went into bankruptcy. Also, during market meltdowns (such as the internet/tech crash of 2000–2001 and the crisis of 2008), many large-cap stocks saw their capitalization shrink by double- and triple-digit billions. Market size isn't always a reliable plus, especially during market crises tied to economic downturns.

REMEMBER

In the world of stocks (especially over the long term), all roads lead back to fundamentals. A small company with strong fundamentals is a safer bet than a huge company with poor/bad fundamentals such as net losses, growing debt, and so on.

AI Companies: The Major Players

When ranked as the largest companies on the planet, here are the notable AI players:

» **Apple (AAPL):** As of December 2023, Apple was the largest company on the planet at a market cap of $3.0 trillion. It's the quintessential tech mega-cap stock well known for consumer electronics like the iPhone and MacBook. and it's a leader in software, tech services, and innovation such as AI.

» **Microsoft (MSFT):** A mega-cap global software titan, Microsoft is the creator of Windows OS and the Office suite, with a major presence in cloud computing and enterprise solutions.

» **Nvidia (NVDA):** This is another mega-cap stock that is a graphics processing unit (GPU) innovator. Nvidia drives progress in gaming, AI, and data visualization. It has played a huge role in recent AI technology advancement.

» **IBM (IBM):** Perhaps the oldest company in this list, it's one of the few with a significant dividend (meaning regular quarterly payouts to shareholders).

» **Google (GOOGL):** The ubiquitous internet giant is synonymous with online searches and offers diverse services from advertising to Android, while being a global leader in internet technologies and innovation.

Here's where you can use AI to do research on major tech companies. What say you, AI (in this case, Bing Chat)? My prompt:

"In the AI field, please list the 10 largest companies with a brief description of each."

The response from Bing Chat is in Figure 4-1.

Certainly! Here are the 10 largest companies in the AI field, along with a brief description of each:

1. **Microsoft**: Microsoft is a technology company that develops and licenses software, services, and hardware. It is known for its Windows operating system and Office productivity suite. Microsoft has been investing heavily in AI and machine learning, and has developed several AI-powered products, including the Cortana virtual assistant and the Azure Machine Learning platform [1].

2. **IBM**: IBM is a multinational technology company that provides hardware, software, and consulting services. IBM has been a leader in AI research for decades, and has developed several AI-powered products, including Watson, an AI-powered question-answering system, and IBM Cloud, a cloud computing platform that offers AI and machine learning services [1].

3. **Google**: Google is a technology company that specializes in internet-related services and products. Google has been investing heavily in AI and machine learning, and has developed several AI-powered products, including Google Assistant, Google Translate, and Google Photos [2].

4. **Amazon**: Amazon is an e-commerce and cloud computing company that offers a wide range of products and services. Amazon has been investing heavily in AI and machine learning, and has developed several AI-powered products, including Alexa, an intelligent personal assistant, and Amazon Rekognition, a facial recognition service [1].

5. **Facebook**: Facebook is a social media and technology company that provides a platform for people to connect and share information. Facebook has been investing heavily in AI and machine learning, and has developed several AI-powered products, including DeepFace, a facial recognition system, and FBLearner Flow, a machine learning platform [1].

6. **Apple**: Apple is a technology company that designs, develops, and sells consumer electronics, computer software, and online services. Apple has been investing heavily in AI and machine learning, and has developed several AI-powered products, including Siri, an intelligent personal assistant, and Core ML, a machine learning framework for iOS apps [1].

7. **Intel**: Intel is a multinational technology company that designs and manufactures microprocessors and other computer components. Intel has been investing heavily in AI and machine learning, and has developed several AI-powered products, including the Intel Nervana Neural Network Processor, a chip designed specifically for deep learning [1].

FIGURE 4-1:
Top companies in the AI field, according to AI.

AI stocks have inherently all rainbows and endless profits, as far as the eye can see. Certainly, a look like that can do it. On the exciting news of AI stocks, but you need to be aware of both the good and the potential bad. In the 1920s, when

8. **Nvidia**: Nvidia is a technology company that designs and manufactures graphics processing units (GPUs) for gaming and professional markets. Nvidia has been investing heavily in AI and machine learning, and has developed several AI-powered products, including the Nvidia Tesla V100, a GPU designed for deep learning [2].

9. **Baidu**: Baidu is a Chinese technology company that specializes in internet-related services and products. Baidu has been investing heavily in AI and machine learning, and has developed several AI-powered products, including DuerOS, an intelligent personal assistant, and Apollo, an open-source autonomous driving platform [2].

10. **Samsung**: Samsung is a South Korean multinational conglomerate that specializes in electronics, appliances, and other products. Samsung has been investing heavily in AI and machine learning, and has developed several AI-powered products, including Bixby, an intelligent personal assistant, and Samsung ARTIK, an IoT platform that offers AI and machine learning services [1].

I hope this helps!

Learn more ∨ | 1 ⚙ spiceworks.com | 2 FC fastcompany.com | 3 companiesmarketcap.com

FIGURE 4-1:
(Continued)

1 of 30 ●

TIP

How convenient to have AI help us with AI companies! Here are some prompts to help you digger a little deeper before you make any investment decision:

» "Compare [company X] with [company Z] in a side-by-side table format with the following fundamentals: three years of profit growth, three years of sales growth, and three years of growth in their respective net shareholder equity."

» "Analyze and summarize the income statement and balance sheet of [company x] in the following 10K report" (you can use ChatPDF for this).

» "Compare financial metrics such as P/E ratio, P/S ratio, and profit growth among the five leading large-cap AI stocks. Highlight differences to assist in evaluating investment opportunities."

Checking Out the Pros and Cons of AI Stocks for Investors

AI stocks aren't necessarily all rainbows and endless profits as far as the eye can see. Certainly a book like this can focus on the exciting pluses of AI stocks, but you need to be aware of both the good and the potential bad. In the 1920s, when automobiles were "the hot technology," there were hundreds of auto companies, and investors plowed money into most of them. However, most auto companies (and their stocks) headed into the dustbin of investing history. For investors, it's all about the fundamentals, as you find out in the following sections.

The pros

For conservative, long-term investors seeking growth, investing in large-cap AI stocks either directly or through a fund (see Chapter 5) is fine. For large-cap AI stocks, here are the pros.

Growth

REMEMBER

As a widespread development, AI is in its early stages so growth looks promising for it. Well-positioned AI stocks should perform well over time. I think that if your horizon is intermediate (2–5 years) and/or longer, AI stocks do deserve a place in your portfolio.

A good historical example is NVIDIA. In the 12-month time frame of September 2022 to October 2023, the stock went from about $115 per share to about $414 — a blistering gain of 266 percent in just a year. Of course, not every AI-related stock will do this well in such a short period of time, but it's a good example of the right stock during the right time (market demand for AI-related investments).

Income

Dividend-paying stocks deserve a spot in every conservative stock portfolio, especially for those interested in growing income. Most AI-related stocks aren't typically known as dividend payers.

Speak to your human advisor (and, of course, research with your AI tool) about the strategy of doing a covered call option. For those concerned about generating income with their stock portfolio (especially with large-cap stocks that have little or no dividend income), covered call option writing could deliver thousands in income, which would come in handy during your retirement years.

TIP

Get the full details with AI. Use prompts such as "What is covered call option writing?" and "What are the pros and cons of covered call writing?" A good educational source on using options is www.optionseducation.org.

The cons

No matter how hot or sexy the topic, the downside of investing in AI stocks is real for two reasons:

>> The first risk is if the stock has poor fundamentals and has risen due to the market's ebullience over a hot topic. Many dot-com stocks soared during 1998–2000 only to crash and burn during 2001–2002. But the fundamentally strong stocks rebounded and went on to greater success (such as Amazon, eBay, Cisco, and so on).

>> The second risk is if the company is indeed strong fundamentally, but market enthusiasm has driven the stock's price to a higher yet unsustainable level. The company is fine, but the stock price is at risk due to "overbought" conditions. At moments such as this, keep an eye on valuation metrics such as the P/E ratio (price-to-earnings ratio). The higher the P/E ratio, the more overpriced the stock is and the more it is at risk for a pullback or correction.

An example of a generally safe P/E ratio is the range of 25–40. However, if you see a P/E ratio north of that range, then it has entered overpriced territory. Find out more about the P/E ratio in Chapter 8.

The Indirect Way to AI Profits: Investing in Impacted Companies

Keep in mind that investing in AI companies directly isn't the only game in town. AI impacts many industries both positively and negatively. Think about what traditional businesses gain benefits from AI.

For research on current developments on AI coupled with investing concerns, check out Appendix B for resources that will keep you on top as AI continues to change the investing landscape.

Let's ask Bing Chat about industries that will benefit from AI:

"What are the top three industries that will benefit from AI technologies and why?"

The response from Bing Chat is in Figure 4-2. It provides a great starting point for your investment research. Once you know which industries receive an outsize benefit from AI, the next step is to locate the top stocks, analyze them (their fundamentals), and make your investment decision.

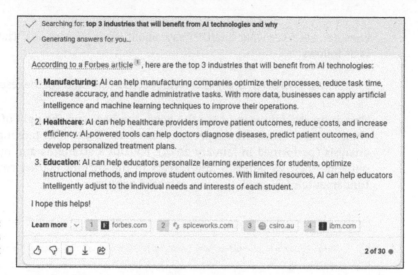

FIGURE 4-2:
Some industries
that may benefit
from AI.

Armed with the response in Figure 4-2, the next step is to drill down on your chosen industry. (Bing Chat's listing has links to more detailed reports.) Once you find the industry's leading companies, use the prompts and steps described in the next section.

TIP

When you're convinced that industry *X* will be a good investment opportunity, use your AI tools to research the top stocks. An alternate and potentially safer way to invest would be to see whether there is an ETF for that industry or sector. More on ETFs is in Chapter 6.

Using AI to Analyze Large-Cap Stocks

AI can perform a number of useful functions in your stock analysis. Here are two examples to consider.

Doing a SWOT analysis

A SWOT analysis is a Strengths, Weaknesses, Opportunities, and Threats (SWOT) assessment. It gives you, in a nutshell, the main "pluses and minuses" of a given public company. Consider this example: NVIDIA is a powerhouse in the AI vertical, and if you're going to consider it for your portfolio, it's a good prompt for you to consider. Let's see what ChatGPT says about this in Figure 4-3. The prompt I used is as follows:

"Please do a SWOT analysis of NVIDIA Corporation and put the results in a table."

This is an efficient way to see the good, the bad, and the ugly of your potential choice. And AI can delve deeper into each issue if you like. Judging by this SWOT analysis (performed in January 2024), NVIDIA's strengths and opportunities do outshine their weaknesses and threats in the current market conditions. If the fundamentals are good, this is a potential winner.

ChatGPT

Certainly! Below is a simplified SWOT analysis for NVIDIA Corporation presented in a table format:

Strengths	Weaknesses
1. Dominance in GPUs	1. Concentration on GPUs
2. Innovation in AI	2. Dependence on gaming
3. Diverse product line	3. Vulnerability to trends
4. Strong financials	

Opportunities	Threats
1. AI and Data Centers	1. Competition in AI
2. Autonomous Vehicles	2. Market cyclicality
3. Edge Computing	3. Supply chain disruptions
4. Healthcare applications	4. Regulatory challenges

Strengths:

1. Dominance in GPUs: NVIDIA is a leader in graphics processing units (GPUs), crucial in gaming, AI, and data processing.
2. Innovation in AI: Strong focus on AI with advanced technologies like deep learning.
3. Diverse product line: Offers GPUs, hardware, and software solutions for various industries.
4. Strong financials: Consistently robust financial performance.

Weaknesses:

1. Concentration on GPUs: Heavy reliance on GPUs for revenue.
2. Dependence on gaming: A significant portion of revenue comes from the gaming industry.
3. Vulnerability to trends: Susceptible to rapid changes in technology trends.

FIGURE 4-3:
A SWOT analysis courtesy of AI.

Opportunities:

1. AI and Data Centers: Increasing demand for AI and data processing in various sectors.
2. Autonomous Vehicles: Growth potential in the development of autonomous driving technology.
3. Edge Computing: Expanding opportunities in edge computing solutions.
4. Healthcare applications: AI applications in healthcare offer new revenue streams.

Threats:

1. Competition in AI: Intense competition in the AI space from tech giants.
2. Market cyclicality: Vulnerability to economic downturns affecting discretionary spending.
3. Supply chain disruptions: Dependence on global supply chains poses risks.
4. Regulatory challenges: Increasing scrutiny and regulations in the technology sector.

Please note that this SWOT analysis is a simplified overview, and a more in-depth analysis may require detailed research and consideration of additional factors.

FIGURE 4-3:
(Continued)

Summarizing financial data

TIP

Stock investing research data can be voluminous, and your eyes could go bleary reading so much information. Use AI to give you the essential points you need. Here are some examples:

» Stock research reports (whether in PDF, in DOC format, or on a webpage) can be analyzed and summarized for your convenience.

Sample prompt: "Summarize the key findings from the attached stock research report (in PDF format) for [company name]. Highlight financial performance, growth opportunities, potential risks, and any analyst recommendations. Provide a clear overview to aid in decision-making."

» Public documents from the Securities and Exchange Commission (SEC) such as 10K reports have a ton of information, but AI can summarize this.

Sample prompt: "Analyze the SEC Form 10K filing for [company name]. Summarize financial statements, risk factors, and management discussion. Identify significant events or changes disclosed in the report and provide insights relevant to investment decision-making."

» Company documents such as annual reports can also be a heavy read; use AI to analyze them for you.

> Sample prompt: "Conduct a comprehensive analysis of [company name]'s annual report for the latest fiscal year. Summarize financial metrics, strategic initiatives, and risk factors. Highlight any notable events or developments disclosed, offering insights relevant to investment decisions."

For AI software that can help you with the preceding tasks, check out Appendix B for AI tools and Appendix C for investment-related information.

Chapter 5

Small-Cap AI Stocks and IPOs

I n Chapter 4, I cover investing in large-cap and mega-cap AI-related stocks. In this chapter, I cover speculating with small-cap AI-related stocks and initial public offerings (better known as IPOs).

Keep in mind that investing and speculating are two distinctly different approaches. Simply put, investing is analyzing assets for value that increases over the long term. Speculating is making bets about the asset's direction (up or down) in the near term. The safer of the two is investing, but some folks bought this book because they are looking for the big bucks. Hey, who wouldn't want to buy that hot yet obscure small-cap AI-related tech stock expecting it to zoom 1,000 percent upward so you can buy that luxury penthouse unit you have been eyeing! But you need to know some important stuff first, and this chapter is here to help.

TIP

Here are some resources that can help you with this chapter's topics:

» *Penny Stocks For Dummies* by Peter Leeds (Wiley)

» *High-Level Investing For Dummies* by Paul Mladjenovic (yours truly), published by Wiley

» AI Directory (www.aidirectory.org/)

Beginning with the Basics of Small-Cap Stocks

As I explain in Chapter 4, *capitalization* refers to a public company's market size. Capitalization means a number of shares times the share price, and a small-cap stock is offered by a company with a market capitalization under $10 billion. Given that, let's find out about the pros and cons of small-cap stocks.

In this case, I asked Bing Chat with the simple prompt of "pros and cons of small-cap stocks," and Figure 5-1 has the response.

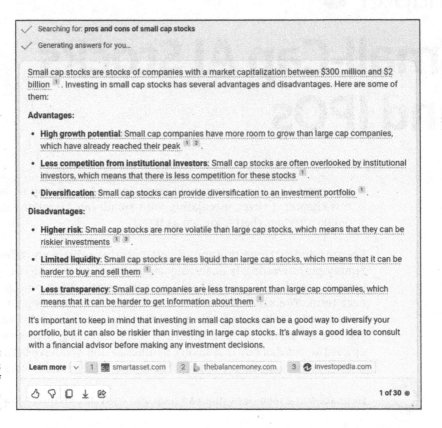

✓ Searching for: **pros and cons of small cap stocks**

✓ Generating answers for you...

Small cap stocks are stocks of companies with a market capitalization between $300 million and $2 billion [1]. Investing in small cap stocks has several advantages and disadvantages. Here are some of them:

Advantages:

- **High growth potential**: Small cap companies have more room to grow than large cap companies, which have already reached their peak [1] [2].
- **Less competition from institutional investors**: Small cap stocks are often overlooked by institutional investors, which means that there is less competition for these stocks [1].
- **Diversification**: Small cap stocks can provide diversification to an investment portfolio [1].

Disadvantages:

- **Higher risk**: Small cap stocks are more volatile than large cap stocks, which means that they can be riskier investments [1] [3].
- **Limited liquidity**: Small cap stocks are less liquid than large cap stocks, which means that it can be harder to buy and sell them [1].
- **Less transparency**: Small cap companies are less transparent than large cap companies, which means that it can be harder to get information about them [1].

It's important to keep in mind that investing in small cap stocks can be a good way to diversify your portfolio, but it can also be riskier than investing in large cap stocks. It's always a good idea to consult with a financial advisor before making any investment decisions.

Learn more ∨   1 ▦ smartasset.com   2 ▦ thebalancemoney.com   3 ▦ investopedia.com

👍 👎 ▢ ⬇ ↪   1 of 30 ●

FIGURE 5-1: The pros and cons of small-cap stocks, according to AI.

The most important "pro" for small-cap stocks is the higher growth potential, while the most important "con" is the greater risk. You maximize the former and minimize the "con" with greater knowledge and information. At this point you use AI to drill down on both points and focus on the fundamentals (profit, low debt, and so on).

The list of pros and cons in Figure 5-1 is sufficient for starters. I like Bing Chat because each line item is hyperlinked to get more details. Every investor (in this case we really mean speculator) is attracted to the positives, but good research is necessary to reveal the weaknesses and potential risks.

TIP

Here is where you dive in with AI. Here are some small-cap stocks prompt to consider:

>> "Do a thorough fundamental analysis of [small-cap choice], focusing on key financial indicators such as revenue growth, earnings per share (EPS), debt levels, and cash flow. Assess the company's balance sheet, income statement, and cash flow statement to ensure financial stability and sustainable growth."

>> "Determine the company's financial strength and value using the most accepted financial ratios such as the price/earnings (PE) ratio, price-to-book-value (P/B) ratio, and price-to-sales (P/S) ratio."

>> "Provide a full assessment of the real and potential risks of [small-cap choice]. This includes the company's market risks and threats present from the company's competitors."

Finding AI-Related Small-Cap Stocks

The good news is that AI-related small-cap stocks aren't hiding. No need to rifle through dark attics or cluttered closets. Most will post press releases at the prominent financial sites, such as

>> Bloomberg (www.bloomberg.com)

>> MarketWatch (www.marketwatch.com)

>> Seeking Alpha (www.seekingalpha.com)

>> Real Clear Markets (www.realclearmarkets.com)

And also corporate publicity sites such as

>> PR News Wire (www.prnewswire.com)

>> Business Wire (www.businesswire.com)

>> Globe Newswire (www.globenewswire.com)

TIP

Of course, use your AI-enhanced search engine. You can find them using the resources in Appendix B. Lastly, another place to find AI opportunities is AI Directory (www.aidirectory.org). You can use AI Directory to find stocks by name or category.

Choosing Small-Cap AI Stocks

After you locate some AI small-cap stock opportunities, the next step is how to choose them. Let's ask Bing Chat the next question:

"How do you choose a successful small-cap stock? Please provide in bullet point style with an explanation of each step."

Figure 5-2 is the response. Now you have the main issues listed clearly. At this point, go to the individual items. Use Bing's footnotes to find out more, or do a new prompt about a given line item. If the line is about the company's management team, then use a prompt such as "How can I evaluate the company's management team? Please provide guidelines and detailed explanations."

✓ Searching for: **how to choose successful small cap stocks**

✓ Generating answers for you...

Here are some steps to consider when choosing a successful small-cap stock:

- **Research the company**: Look for companies with strong financials, such as high cash flows, revenues, and profits after tax. It's also important to select companies with low debt on their balance sheet [1].
- **Analyze the industry**: Analyze the industry in which the company operates. Look for industries that are growing and have a positive outlook [1].
- **Check the management team**: Check the management team of the company. Look for a management team with a proven track record of success [1].
- **Assess the competition**: Assess the competition in the industry. Look for companies that have a competitive advantage over their peers [1].
- **Evaluate the stock price**: Evaluate the stock price of the company. Look for companies that are undervalued compared to their peers [1].
- **Consult with a financial advisor**: It's always a good idea to consult with a financial advisor before making any investment decisions. They can provide you with personalized advice based on your investment goals and risk tolerance [1].

Please note that investing in small-cap stocks can be riskier than investing in large-cap stocks. It's important to do your due diligence and consult with a financial advisor before making any investment decisions.

FIGURE 5-2:
Choosing a
small-cap
AI stock.

You've heard the adage "When it's raining, sell umbrellas." Obvious, right? Anyway, the idea, when applied to small-cap stocks, is simple. Buy a quality small-cap stock in an industry or vertical that's on fire (market demand or interest is up).

REMEMBER

Choose a strong company in a growing industry. This is marrying the "micro" to the "macro." You've already chosen the growing industry, the "macro" (AI), and now you need to choose one (or more) stocks of companies with good fundamentals and good prospects (the "micro"). Good fundamentals include profitability, strong and/or rising sales, a good balance sheet, and so on. "Good prospects" mean that the macro environment is very favorable; market demand for that particular good/service/technology/idea is strong today and looks favorable for the foreseeable future.

Guesswork isn't necessary. AI can help you fill in the blanks. A good AI-enhanced search engine such as Bing Chat or Google Bard will do. AI can

>> Analyze and summarize stock reports (such as PDFs)

>> Analyze and summarize reports from the SEC (such as 10K reports)

>> Explain each term and concept

>> Analyze financial data to gain meaning (profitability, and so on)

TIP

A good prompt to get you rolling here would be this:

"Provide a comprehensive list of concerns to analyze regarding small-cap stocks in a bullet point format with a detailed explanation of each step."

Introducing IPOs

Whenever we buy stocks, we buy them in what is technically called *the secondary market*. But the stock first emerges in what is technically called the *primary market*. Don't assume in this case that primary means large or dominant. No, here we use the word "primary" as in first or initial.

REMEMBER

When a company goes public, as in going through the process of offering shares to the investing public, it is called the *initial public offering* (IPO). Keep in mind that there are two types of IPOs:

>> **A private company going public:** In many cases, a company has been operating for years as a private entity and then goes public. A good example is United Parcel Service (UPS). It was operating for many years before the management team decided to go public. This type of IPO is a safer bet than the next option.

>> **The brand-new startup IPO:** This is the stuff of dreams. The ambitious entrepreneur or business partners have a great idea, and they put together a business plan and proceed to an investment banking firm or the investment banking division of a prominent brokerage firm. The bankers, accountants, and lawyers put together the offering. The shares get sold through a marketing syndicate of brokerage firms.

Then hopefully the business plan works out, and a successful launch occurs. The primary offering may be 10 million shares at $25 per share, for example.

When all the shares are sold, the $25 million received (10 million times $25 per share) is divided between the fees for the investment banking firm, the member organizations that are part of the marketing syndicate, and related expenses (legal, accounting, and so on), and a net amount (say $18–20 million) goes to the newly launched enterprise to fund their operations.

WARNING

More brand-new start-up IPOs fail than succeed, so if you're participating in this type of IPO, you aren't investing; you are *speculating*. In this type of launch, there is no assurance or sign of profitability. The profit comes from the rigors of the marketplace — meaning specifically the business marketplace of competing products and services.

The safer speculation is the prior category — the existing private company that has already had its products and services achieve market acceptance, making the IPO a less risky proposition for investors.

TIP

To find upcoming IPOs, check out Nasdaq's IPO Calendar: https://www.nasdaq.com/market-activity/ipos.

Keep in mind that AI companies either are already operating (with small-cap stocks) or are private companies seeking to "go public" (become an IPO), so AI tools can help you find them and analyze them. Use the resources in this chapter coupled with the resources in Appendix C.

Surveying Safety and Hedging Strategies for Small Caps and IPOs

Successful investing (and speculating) is not just about what you invest in but also how you invest. It's easy for you to just go buy some AI-related (or not) stock in your brokerage account, hold it, and keep your fingers crossed that it turns out okay for you.

REMEMBER

Successful long-term investors, no matter how different their personalities and priorities, generally stick to an approach that helps them maximize the good (capital gains and/or income) while minimizing the bad (limiting losses through hedging and defensive strategies). They participate in bull markets, but they tend to be ready for bear markets. So should you.

The following sections cover defensive and hedging points that you should address, and AI is an excellent tool to help you here.

Stop-loss orders

The stop-loss order is a brokerage order that helps you limit the downside risk of your stock while placing no limits on the upside. If you have a $25 stock and you're concerned about the downside, you can place, for example, a stop-loss order 10 percent below the current stock price (in this case, $22.50, which is 10 percent or $2.50 lower than $25).

Then you choose a timeframe for this order. It can be a *day order*, which means the order expires at the end of the current market day (usually 4 p.m. EST), or it can be a *Good 'til cancelled* (GTC) order, which can be in effect much longer such as 60 days, 90 days, or longer (depending on the brokerage firm).

A good example of a prompt you can use is this:

> "Show me how to place a stop-loss order that is a GTC or good 'til cancelled order at a stock brokerage website, and do so in a step-by-step manner with an explanation of each step."

Trailing stops

A trailing stop is my favorite type of order. It takes the stop-loss order a step further. A trailing stop is an active stop-loss order that can trail the stock's price rise automatically. As the stock price rallies, the trailing stop keeps adjusting upward.

The higher the stock price goes, the higher the trailing stop is moved. Then when the moment comes that the stock reverses and heads downward, the trailing stop stays firm (as with stop-loss orders) to minimize the downside.

Your homework is to use AI to analyze this type of order, which I think every investor/speculator should get familiar with. Start with a prompt such as this:

> "How do I place a trailing stop order, and what are all the considerations I should take into consideration before I place it? Give a detailed explanation of each consideration."

Option strategies

Options can be a superb addition to your overall strategies. Here are three ways they can help you:

>> Add speculative firepower (when you buy call and/or put options).

>> Add income to your portfolio (as with covered call option writing or writing put options).

>> Protect or hedge your positions. You can buy puts for downside protection.

I love call and put option strategies because they offer something for everyone. At a minimum, you should get familiar with the defensive option strategies (such as protective puts, covered calls, and so on) in order to discover how to protect your portfolio in times of market uncertainty and/or chaos.

I am just whetting your appetite for options here, but please do some research and due diligence with your AI tools. For more information, head over to Appendix C for leading information sources on general investing.

Chapter **6**

Diversifying with ETFs and Mutual Funds

E
arlier in Part 2, I discuss direct investing in AI-related stocks, either the stocks of large-cap, established players involved with AI (see Chapter 4) or in small-cap, growth-oriented AI stocks (see Chapter 5). Although directly investing in stocks has many benefits, many (most?) investors may need a greater measure of safety and diversification.

That's where exchange-traded funds (ETFs) and mutual funds come into play. A winning stock in sector X will likely do much better than ETF Z that covers the same sector. The ETF has many stocks, likely in the range of 35–80 issues. Yes, it will have winning stocks, but it will also have laggards (or losers) as well. Meanwhile, if you have a losing single stock in a growing sector, you'll underperform against the ETF covering the same sector due to diversification.

The overall point is clear: Individual stocks will tend to do much better, or much worse, than an ETF. The ETF will be safer than a losing stock but not do as well as an individual winning stock.

For those folks who prefer active management (versus the static portfolios typical of most ETFs), mutual funds will be a better choice. For those whose money is in retirement funds like 401(k)s, where only mutual funds will do, this chapter will help you too.

In short, ETFs and mutual funds have powerful benefits for the investor and belong in many (if not most) portfolios. Get the scoop on AI-related ETFs and mutual funds in this chapter.

Comparing ETFs and Mutual Funds

ETFs and mutual funds (MFs) have many similarities but a few differences, too, as you find out in the following sections.

Something in common: Diversification

Both ETFs and MFs generally have diversified portfolios. An S&P 500 ETF and an S&P 500 mutual fund (very likely an index fund) will perform very similarly in the same market conditions (bullish, bearish, and/or neutral). This makes sense since their portfolios would closely mirror the stocks that compose the S&P 500.

Both ETFs and MFs also have plenty of subcategories that can be similar. A health-care sector ETF and a healthcare sector mutual fund will generate similar overall results over time given the overall performance of major healthcare stocks. The same can be said for energy sectors, consumer staples, consumer discretionary, and so forth.

Also, both ETFs and MFs have specialized categories in different asset classes. There are U.S. Treasury bond ETFs as well as U.S. Treasury bond MFs. So far, so good!

Static portfolios versus actively managed portfolios

REMEMBER

Although ETFs and mutual funds are similar in that they both give you diversification (a primary benefit of funds in general), the key difference is in the management style of the portfolio involved:

>> ETFs tend to have "static" portfolios, which means they tend to buy a portfolio of issued stock and will do very little active buying, selling, and holding. Basically they are holding the stocks. The only time they may adjust their portfolio is in the case of stock mergers, takeover situations, and other relatively infrequent events.

>> Mutual funds, on the other hand, are actively managed, meaning they regularly adjust the portfolio as they see fit. Not a week or month goes by without some buying and selling of stock.

Shares versus cash purchases and sales

ETFs are bought and sold similarly to stocks. Just as you buy shares of a stock, you can buy shares of an ETF. You can buy as little as 1 share or in odd lots (1–99 shares) or round lots (100 shares or more). More brokers are allowing the ability to buy fractional shares as well.

Meanwhile, MFs are bought and sold in cash amounts and there may be minimum amounts involved, depending on the mutual fund management firm. This method is also referred to as "open-ended."

TIP

For long-term investors in venues such as retirement funds, stick to mutual funds that have a good long-term track record (going back 5 years or longer) with a time horizon over an extended period of time (say 5–10 years or longer). Also, consider total reinvestment (having interest, dividends, and capital gains reinvested back into the fund).

Meanwhile, I love ETFs, and I think they merit a place in many types of portfolios and investing approaches. ETFs have some great benefits that are typically tied to stocks such as the following:

>> You can place protective orders on ETF shares through your brokerage account. You can place stop-loss orders or trailing stop orders (more on these brokerage orders is in Chapter 5).

>> Using covered call options is a great technique to generate additional income from a stock position (provided you have 100 shares or more); covered call options can be a great income-producing strategy.

>> Hedge with protective put options. ETFs are optionable, which add a whole new dimension to your capabilities with ETFs. Protective puts, for example, can help you during periods of market corrections or the occasional crash.

TIP

Because call and put options are versatile tools and can be good accompaniments to individual stocks and ETFs, consider reading up on their benefits. Two books to consider are *Options Trading For Dummies* by Joe Duarte and *High-Level Investing For Dummies* by Paul Mladenovic (that's me!), both published by Wiley.

Looking at the Pros and Cons of ETFs and Mutual Funds with AI's Help

It's hard to give you all the pluses and minuses of ETFs and MFs, but then again that's easily done by you when you unleash the power of AI.

ETFs

Let's get the "tale of the tape" going with AI. Here's a prompt about the advantages and disadvantages of ETFs:

"Please provide a list of pros and cons for ETFs in a bullet point style and be detailed."

ChatGPT's response is in the following text.

Exchange-Traded Funds (ETFs) have gained significant popularity as investment vehicles due to their unique characteristics. Here's a detailed list of pros and cons of ETFs in a bullet point style:

Pros:

1. Diversification:

Pro: ETFs typically hold a basket of assets (e.g., stocks, bonds, commodities) providing investors with instant diversification.

Pro: Diversification can help spread risk and reduce the impact of poor-performing individual assets.

2. Liquidity:

Pro: ETFs trade on stock exchanges throughout the trading day, offering high liquidity. Investors can buy or sell shares at prevailing market prices.

3. Low Costs:

Pro: ETFs often have lower expense ratios compared to mutual funds, making them a cost-effective investment option.

Pro: Their passive nature (index-tracking) means lower management fees.

4. Transparency:

Pro: ETFs disclose their holdings daily, enabling investors to see exactly what assets they own.

Pro: Transparency helps in better understanding and monitoring of investments.

5. Flexibility:

Pro: Investors can use various trading strategies with ETFs, including buying on margin, short selling, and trading options.

Pro: ETFs cover a wide range of asset classes, sectors, and geographic regions, allowing for tailored investment choices.

6. Tax Efficiency:

Pro: ETFs often have tax advantages due to the creation and redemption process, which can minimize capital gains distributions.

7. Intraday Trading:

Pro: ETFs can be bought and sold throughout the trading day, allowing investors to react to market developments and adjust positions as needed.

8. Dividend Reinvestment:

Pro: Many ETFs offer automatic dividend reinvestment, helping to compound returns over time.

Cons:

1. Trading Costs:

Con: While ETF expense ratios are generally low, investors may incur trading commissions when buying and selling shares.

2. Bid-Ask Spread:

Con: ETFs have a bid-ask spread, which represents the cost difference between buying and selling prices. In highly traded ETFs, this spread is often minimal, but it can be wider for less liquid ETFs.

3. Tracking Error:

Con: ETFs may not perfectly replicate the performance of their underlying index due to tracking error, which can result from factors like fees and trading costs.

4. Lack of Active Management:

Con: While passive management is a pro for cost-efficiency, it can be a con for investors seeking active management and potential outperformance.

5. Overconcentration:

Con: Some ETFs may be highly concentrated in a particular sector or group of stocks, increasing risk if that segment underperforms.

6. Lack of Individual Control:

Con: ETF investors have no say in the selection of specific holdings within the fund, as they do in individual stock investing.

7. Intraday Volatility:

Con: The intraday trading feature can lead to higher price volatility compared to mutual funds, which only have one daily price.

8. Dividend Variability:

Con: Dividend payments from ETFs can vary, potentially making them less suitable for income-focused investors.

REMEMBER

It's important to consider these pros and cons in the context of your investment goals, risk tolerance, and overall portfolio strategy when deciding whether ETFs are the right choice for your investment needs.

Mutual funds

OK, AI, let's have it on MFs. I used the following prompt with ChatGPT:

"Please provide a list of pros and cons for traditional mutual funds in a bullet point style and be detailed."

ChatGPT's response is in the following text.

Certainly, here's a detailed list of the pros and cons of traditional mutual funds:

Pros:

1. Diversification:

Mutual funds pool money from many investors to buy a diversified portfolio of stocks, bonds, or other securities. This spreads risk, reducing the impact of a single investment's poor performance.

2. Professional Management:

Mutual funds are managed by professional fund managers who make investment decisions on behalf of investors, using their expertise to make informed choices.

3. Liquidity:

Mutual fund shares can be easily bought or sold, providing liquidity. Investors can generally redeem their shares at the fund's net asset value (NAV) at the end of each trading day.

4. Convenience:

They are user-friendly and accessible, offering investors an easy way to invest without needing to make individual investment choices.

5. Automatic Investment Options:

Many mutual funds offer systematic investment plans (SIPs) that allow investors to make regular, automated contributions, helping with dollar-cost averaging.

6. Regulation and Oversight:

Mutual funds are regulated by the U.S. Securities and Exchange Commission (SEC) and other governing bodies, which provides a level of investor protection.

Cons:

1. Fees and Expenses:

Most mutual funds charge various fees, including management fees, administrative costs, and loads (sales charges), which can eat into your returns.

2. Lack of Control:

Investors have limited control over specific investments within the fund. Decisions are made by the fund manager, and you may not agree with all their choices.

3. Tax Inefficiency:

Mutual funds can generate capital gains distributions that result in tax liabilities for investors, even if they didn't sell their shares.

4. Minimum Investment:

Some mutual funds may have minimum investment requirements, limiting access for small investors.

5. Closed-End Trading:

Mutual fund shares are bought and sold at the NAV at the end of the trading day, which can be a disadvantage in rapidly changing markets compared to ETFs which are traded throughout the day.

6. Lack of Transparency:

Mutual funds are required to disclose their holdings periodically, typically on a quarterly basis, which means investors may not always have up-to-the-minute information on the fund's portfolio.

7. Overdiversification:

Some mutual funds can become overdiversified, holding too many securities, which can dilute the impact of strong-performing stocks or bonds.

Investors should carefully consider their investment goals, risk tolerance, and the specific mutual fund's features before investing. The choice between mutual funds and other investment options like ETFs or individual stocks depends on individual circumstances and preferences.

All these features are great, especially for those who are employees and have pension plans and other retirement vehicles that usually only provide mutual fund choices. My personal preference is an ETF, but I know many folks who have neither the time, energy, ability, or patience to manage a portfolio, so mutual funds are as good an option now as they were when they were initially offered to the public decades ago.

Noting Some Top AI-Related ETFs

And now for your AI-driven research pleasure, Table 6-1 is a list of the most prominent AI-related ETFs (at the time of writing). Envelope and drumroll please!

TABLE 6-1   ## AI-Related ETFs

ETF Name	Symbol
AdvisorShares Let Bob AI Powered Momentum ETF	LETB
AI Powered Equity ETF	AIEQ
ALPS Disruptive Technologies ETF	DTEC
ARK Autonomous Technology & Robotics ETF	ARKQ
ARK Next Generation Internet ETF	ARKW
BTD Capital Fund	DIP
Capital Link Global Fintech Leaders ETF	KOIN
Clockwise Core Equity & Innovation ETF	TIME
Defiance Quantum ETF	QTUM
Direxion Daily Robotics, Artificial Intelligence & Automation Index Bull 2X Shares	UBOT
Fidelity MSCI Information Technology Index ETF	FTEC
First Trust Dow Jones Internet Index Fund	FDN
First Trust Indxx Innovative Transaction & Process ETF	LEGR
First Trust Nasdaq Artificial Intelligence & Robotics ETF	ROBT
Franklin Exponential Data ETF	XDAT
Gabelli Automation ETF	GAST
Global X Artificial Intelligence & Technology ETF	AIQ

ETF Name	Symbol
Global X Autonomous & Electric Vehicles ETF	DRIV
Global X E-commerce ETF	EBIZ
Global X Future Analytics Tech ETF	AIQ
Global X Robotics & Artificial Intelligence ETF	BOTZ
Innovator Deepwater Frontier Tech ETF	LOUP
Invesco AI and Next Gen Software ETF	IGPT
Invesco NASDAQ Internet ETF	PNQI
iShares Expanded Tech Sector ETF	IGM
iShares Exponential Technologies ETF	XT
iShares Global Tech ETF	IXN
iShares Robotics and Artificial Intelligence Multisector ETF	IRBO
iShares U.S. Consumer Focused ETF	IEDI
iShares U.S. Tech Independence Focused ETF	IETC
iShares U.S. Technology ETF	IYW
Neuberger Berman Disrupters ETF	NBDS
Optimize AI Smart Sentiment Event-Driven ETF	OAIE
Pacer BlueStar Engineering the Future ETF	BULD
QRAFT AI Enhanced U.S. Large Cap ETF	QRFT
QRAFT AI-Enhanced U.S. Large Cap Momentum ETF	AMOM
QRAFT AI-Enhanced US Next Value ETF	NVQ
ROBO Global Robotics & Automation Index ETF	ROBO
Roundhill Generative AI and Technology ETF	CHAT
SPDR S&P Kensho New Economies Composite ETF	KOMP
Spear Alpha ETF	SPRX
WisdomTree Artificial Intelligence and Innovation Fund	WTAI
WisdomTree International AI Enhanced Value Fund	AIVI
WisdomTree U.S. AI Enhanced Value Fund	AIVL

Researching ETFs with AI

Investors often have to read a lot of investment data and research before they make a decision on which stocks, ETFs, and/or mutual funds to add to their portfolio. Fortunately, AI is your huckleberry. You can ask ChatGPT, for example, to summarize a web page to make it easier for you to analyze your potential choice.

When I searched for a good dividend income ETF, I found a suitable choice at ETF Database (https://etfdb.com/). So I decided to ask AI to make my analysis a little easier. I asked my question, and I provided the page URL. Check out my prompt:

> "Please summarize this in less than 250 words and list the 10 most important points in a numbered list: https://etfdb.com/etf/SPYD/#etf-ticker-profile."

ChatGPT's response is in Figure 6-1.

Cool! Just what I needed. You see in Figure 6-1 that the result was great. It summarized very nicely and listed the most pertinent facts and features of that particular ETF. Before AI, you needed to pore over tons of text (written or PDF), but distilling it with AI's help makes for a faster decision for you (or your advisor). This should be your next task: when you find a detailed public post on a financial topic you're interested in, use my earlier prompt as a template or starting point for your (faster!) research.

ETFdb.com (run by VettaFi) is certainly one of the top ETF news, views, and data sources online that has been my go-to source for ETF answers and issues for years. It has both free and premium (paid) aspects, but the free version is just fine for most investors, and when you couple it with AI, you have a powerful combo.

I also did a search on the AI-enhanced Bing search engine with the following prompt:

> "What is the largest AI-related ETF?"

I got the result in Figure 6-2. You see that Bing Chat provided a succinct response about the largest AI-related ETF and some runners-up along with hyperlinks for more details. Because Bing Chat is real-time (or pretty close), it's better than ChatGPT (given its time constraint on data only up until January 2022). Now I can take this information and keep drilling down to find all the necessary data of that specific fund. I can take the ETF's name and symbol and continue getting relevant information at places such as VettaFi's ETFdb.com.

You
Please summarize this in less than 250 words and list the 10 most important points in a numbered list: https://etfdb.com/etf/SPYD/#etf-ticker-profile

 ChatGPT
The provided link leads to an ETF (Exchange-Traded Fund) profile for the SPYD ETF (SPDR Portfolio S&P 500 High Dividend ETF) on ETFdb.com. Here are the 10 most important points about the SPYD ETF from the profile:

1. **ETF Overview**: SPYD is an ETF designed to track the performance of the S&P 500 High Dividend Index.
2. **Dividend Focus**: This ETF focuses on high dividend yields, making it attractive for income-seeking investors.
3. **Dividend Yield**: The ETF typically offers a competitive dividend yield compared to traditional S&P 500 ETFs.
4. **Investment Strategy**: SPYD invests in stocks from the S&P 500 that have historically paid high dividends.
5. **Diversification**: It offers exposure to a diversified portfolio of U.S. large-cap stocks.
6. **Sector Allocation**: The ETF's holdings are spread across various sectors, including financials, energy, and utilities.
7. **Low Expenses**: SPYD is known for its relatively low expense ratio, which can be cost-effective for investors.
8. **Liquidity**: It is a highly liquid ETF, making it easy for investors to buy and sell shares.
9. **Performance History**: Investors can review the historical performance of the ETF, including returns and volatility.
10. **Dividend History**: The ETF's profile provides details on its dividend payment history, including dividend distribution dates and amounts.

In summary, the SPYD ETF is designed for income-focused investors seeking exposure to U.S. large-cap stocks with a history of high dividend payments. It offers diversification, competitive dividend yields, and cost efficiency, making it a potentially attractive option for those looking to generate income from their investments.

FIGURE 6-1:
Summarizing information on an AI-related ETF.

TIP

If you're looking for an attractive AI-related stock to invest in directly, why not cut down your research and analysis time by checking out the top stock holdings of a successful ETF? For example, check out Global X Robotics & Artificial Intelligence ETF (symbol BOTZ) at `https://etfdb.com/etf/BOTZ/#holdings`. You can see BOTZ's top 15 holdings. You can also see what percentage of the ETFs total portfolio that particular stock is.

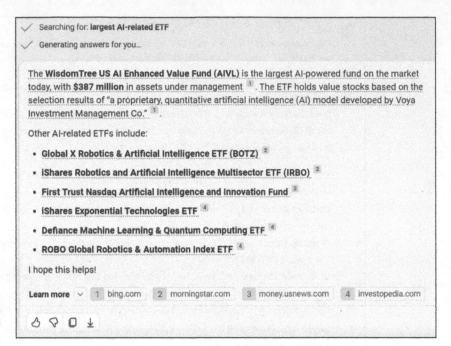

FIGURE 6-2:
Asking AI about
the largest
AI-related ETF.

You can safely assume that the ETF management team did their homework on those top holdings (and probably used AI to help them). It isn't merely a potential "list of attractive choices" or some guru's overhyped "top picks" listing. You know that the fund actually invested their money here.

Now you can benefit from this and use AI to dig deeper into the stocks that you find attractive. Of course, you can also discuss this with your human advisor, too.

Focusing on AI-Related Mutual Funds

For those who want exposure to artificial intelligence investing in the coming months and years but are concerned about risk and volatility that can be a part of regular stock investing, going the fund route can be a more appropriate path. Why pick the top AI stocks when you can simply choose a fund and let those expert portfolio managers make (and monitor) the individual stock choices?

The following is a list of the most prominent AI-related mutual funds:

>> AlphaCentric Robotics and Automation Fund: https://mutualfunds.com/funds/gnxcx-alphacentric-global-innovations-fund-c/

>> BlackRock Technology Opportunities Fund: https://mutualfunds.com/funds/bstsx-blackrock-technology-opportunities-svc/

>> BNY Mellon Technology Growth Fund: https://mutualfunds.com/funds/dtgcx-dreyfus-technology-growth-c/

>> Fidelity Advisor Technology Fund: https://mutualfunds.com/funds/fatix-fidelity-advisor-technology-i/

REMEMBER

The world of AI-related mutual funds is very fluid in the current environment, whether there will be more mutual funds concentrated on AI or not, but more conventional mutual funds will likely rotate a portion of their portfolios into AI-related positions to increase their exposure to this growing area.

For more information on researching AI-related mutual funds, see the prior section; the same tips apply.

Reviewing Resources for Investing in ETFs and Mutual Funds

Lastly, use your AI skills coupled with the following resources to nail down some good fund-investing strategies. For ETFs, try the following:

>> ETF.com (www.etf.com)

>> ETFGuide.com (www.etfguide.com)

>> ETF Database by VettaFi (www.etfdb.com)

>> ETF Trends (www.etftrends.com)

>> Morningstar ETF ratings (www.morningstar.com/5-star-etfs)

>> Seeking Alpha on ETFs and Funds (https://seekingalpha.com/etfs-and-funds)

For Mutual Funds, try the following:

» Kiplinger's Mutual Funds center (https://www.kiplinger.com/investing/mutual-funds)

» Morningstar's Mutual Funds site (https://www.morningstar.com/funds)

» MutualFunds.com (www.mutualfunds.com)

» SEC's Mutual Fund search: (https://www.sec.gov/edgar/searchedgar/prospectus)

Check Appendix C for more investing resources.

Chapter **7**

Robo-Advisors

From the world of AI to your brokerage account. The robo-advisor — the subject of this chapter — is really an AI enhanced with investing knowledge. It's used for both investment research and for actually implementing some investment-related tasks. It may not replace actual brokers, but brokers' assistants may be worried.

Defining What a Robo-Advisor Does

After the invention of the personal computer, the internet, and the smartphone, AI is the current game-changing innovation for the financial markets. But first, let's get a bead on what it is from our AI friend (ChatGPT) with the first obvious question (prompt):

"What is a robo-advisor?"

ChatGPT's response is in Figure 7-1. Keep in mind that you are the portfolio manager (or another human is). AI is merely a very efficient assistant. Letting it "manage your portfolio" is like having a self-driving vehicle manage your cross-country road trip. You should oversee everything (at least until you have a comfort level with your robo-advisor). Given that, a robo-advisor will be very useful to you once you master the settings. It should inform you what's going on with a position in your portfolio before it implements a trade.

ChatGPT

A robo-advisor is a digital platform or software that provides automated, algorithm-driven financial planning services with little to no human supervision. These platforms are designed to offer investment management and financial advice with the goal of optimizing and automating the investment process.

Key characteristics of robo-advisors include:

1. **Automation:** Robo-advisors use algorithms and computer models to automate various aspects of financial planning and investment management. This includes tasks such as portfolio construction, asset allocation, and rebalancing.
2. **User-Friendly Interface:** Robo-advisors typically have user-friendly interfaces that allow individuals to easily input their financial information, risk tolerance, and investment goals. The platform then uses this information to create a customized investment portfolio.
3. **Low Costs:** One of the advantages of robo-advisors is their cost-effectiveness compared to traditional financial advisory services. They often have lower fees because they minimize the need for human intervention.
4. **Diversification:** Robo-advisors aim to create well-diversified portfolios by allocating investments across different asset classes based on the user's risk profile. This diversification helps manage risk.
5. **Goal-Based Investing:** Users can set specific financial goals, such as saving for retirement, buying a home, or funding education. Robo-advisors create and manage portfolios with these goals in mind.
6. **Automated Rebalancing:** Over time, the allocation of assets in a portfolio may deviate from the target due to market movements. Robo-advisors automatically rebalance portfolios to bring them back in line with the desired asset allocation.
7. **Risk Assessment:** Robo-advisors assess the user's risk tolerance through a series of questions, and the algorithm generates a portfolio that aligns with the identified risk level.
8. **24/7 Accessibility:** Users can access their investment accounts and monitor performance at any time through the robo-advisor's online platform or mobile app.

While robo-advisors offer convenience and cost-effectiveness, they may not be suitable for individuals who require more personalized advice or have complex financial situations. Some investors prefer a hybrid approach, combining the automation of robo-advisors with occasional consultations with human financial advisors for more tailored guidance.

FIGURE 7-1:
Traits of a robo-advisor according to AI.

Debating the Pros and Cons of Robo-Advisors

After you have a handle on what a robo-advisor does, you may wonder about the advantages and disadvantages of using one as you invest in stocks (both related to AI and not). Back to ChatGPT with a prompt:

> "What are the pros and cons of robo-advisors? Please provide an answer in a bullet point style with an explanation of each."

First, the pros according to ChatGPT are in Figure 7-2. A number of benefits show that robo-advisors have (directly or indirectly) cost benefits for investors. Human input and service in the stock brokerage world get expensive, and the more you're involved coupled with AI technology, the more efficient the cost and the more streamlined your service. I think that seasoned investors are the best candidates for using a robo-advisor.

Although all the robo-advisors have lots of minor differences, the listing in Figure 7-2 is generally good.

WARNING

And now the negatives from ChatGPT are in Figure 7-3. When you cut out human service, you also cut out the ability to ask questions that can be more nuanced and layered, which is often not possible with machine language technology. Also, robo-advisors are not "set it and forget it" — if you give it parameters to trade and monitor your portfolio, your preferences could easily change along with market conditions and other factors that could change without warning. Robo-advisors are excellent at research and acting like your financial virtual assistant, but don't rely on its judgment.

ChatGPT

Certainly, here are the pros and cons of robo-advisors in a bullet-point style with explanations for each:

Pros:

1. **Cost-Effective:**
   - *Explanation:* Robo-advisors typically have lower fees compared to traditional financial advisors, making them a cost-effective option for investment management.
2. **Accessibility:**
   - *Explanation:* Robo-advisors are user-friendly and accessible, allowing individuals with varying levels of financial knowledge to start investing easily.
3. **Diversification:**
   - *Explanation:* Automated algorithms create well-diversified portfolios, spreading investments across different asset classes to manage risk effectively.
4. **Automation and Efficiency:**
   - *Explanation:* The entire investment process is automated, saving time and effort for investors. This includes portfolio construction, rebalancing, and dividend reinvestment.
5. **Goal-Based Investing:**
   - *Explanation:* Robo-advisors allow users to set specific financial goals, and algorithms tailor investment portfolios to align with these goals.
6. **Continuous Monitoring:**
   - *Explanation:* Robo-advisors monitor portfolios continuously and automatically rebalance them to maintain alignment with the user's risk tolerance and goals.
7. **No Emotional Decision-Making:**
   - *Explanation:* Automation reduces the impact of emotional biases in investment decisions, as robo-advisors operate based on predefined algorithms and market data.
8. **Low Minimum Investment Requirements:**
   - *Explanation:* Many robo-advisors have low or no minimum investment requirements, making investing accessible to a broader range of individuals.
9. **Educational Resources:**
   - *Explanation:* Some robo-advisors provide educational resources and tools to help users understand basic investment concepts and financial planning.

FIGURE 7-2:
The advantages of robo-advisors.

FIGURE 7-3: The disadvantages of robo-advisors.

Digging into Robo-Advisors' Main Features

Let's drill down and look at the main features of robo-advisors. In this case, I add some commentary from a human financial professional (me!). Here is the prompt:

> "What are the top 12 main features of robo-advisors? Provide answer in bullet point style with a detailed explanation of each."

ChatGPT's response is in the following text (and my comments are in italics).

Here are the top 12 main features of robo-advisors, presented in a bullet point style with detailed explanations for each:

1. Automated Portfolio Management:

Explanation: Robo-advisors use algorithms to create and manage investment portfolios tailored to your financial goals, risk tolerance, and time horizon. The process is automated, reducing the need for constant human intervention.

Comments: Walk slowly with this first. You don't want to give the robo-advisor the greenlight and on Monday morning find out half your portfolio was sold. Many firms can guide you on how to set this and how to make sure you can review recommendations before actual trades are done.

2. Risk Assessment and Profiling:

Explanation: Robo-advisors assess your risk tolerance through a questionnaire, helping to determine an appropriate asset allocation that aligns with your comfort level and financial objectives.

Comments: This will be an important consideration. Ask customer service about what levels of risk tolerance there are so you can choose close to your personal profile.

3. Diversification:

Explanation: Robo-advisors diversify your investments across a range of asset classes, such as stocks, bonds, and ETFs. Diversification helps spread risk and optimize returns.

Comments: Find out what they mean about diversification. And double-check with secondary sources about diversification needs, such as your human advisor and/or other AI tools.

4. Goal-Based Investing:

Explanation: You can set specific financial goals, such as retirement, buying a home, or saving for education. Robo-advisors customize your portfolio and investment strategy to achieve these goals.

Comments: Again, understanding your personal goals will come first before any robo-advisor can help you reach them.

5. Automated Rebalancing:

Explanation: Robo-advisors periodically review your portfolio and rebalance it by buying or selling assets to maintain your desired asset allocation. This ensures your investments stay aligned with your objectives.

Comments: Here you must be careful since having any automated service "rebalance a portfolio" could mean transactions you aren't happy with. Check what controls are available to you.

6. Tax Optimization:

Explanation: Some robo-advisors offer tax-efficient strategies, such as tax-loss harvesting, to reduce tax liabilities by offsetting capital gains with losses.

Comments: To a long-term investor, tax optimization means harvesting any tax losses, holding quality investments for the long term (longer than a year and a day to qualify for favorable long-term capital gains tax treatment), and other strategies. Double-check with your tax advisors.

7. Low Minimum Investments:

Explanation: Many robo-advisors allow you to start investing with relatively low minimum deposits, making them accessible to individuals with smaller budgets.

Comments: This I like! You could even afford to have two accounts with two different robo-advisors. Think of the possibilities . . .

8. Accessibility:

Explanation: Robo-advisors are accessible through websites and mobile apps, allowing you to monitor your investments and financial planning tools at your convenience.

Comments: Since it is technology-driven, it can be on 24/7 — either on your laptop or smartphone. Tracking your investments and getting some quick answers is easier than ever.

9. Transparency:

Explanation: These platforms provide clear information about your investments, performance, and fees, ensuring transparency and informed decision-making.

Comments: Big plus here!

10. Personalization:

Explanation: Robo-advisors take your financial objectives, risk tolerance, and individual circumstances into account, tailoring investment strategies to your specific needs.

Comments: You can adjust the settings to calibrate the robo-advisor to your preferences.

11. Educational Resources:

Explanation: Many robo-advisors offer educational resources, including articles, webinars, and tools to help investors make informed decisions and understand the investment process.

Comments: Another big plus — endless education to choose from.

12. Mobile Accessibility:

Explanation: Most robo-advisors have mobile apps, allowing you to manage your investments on the go, track performance, and receive notifications about your portfolio.

Comments: This feature dovetails nicely with item 10.

These features make robo-advisors a convenient and cost-effective way to invest, particularly for individuals who want automated, goal-based, and diversified investment solutions. The level of customization and additional features can vary among different robo-advisor platforms, so it's important to choose one that aligns with your specific needs and preferences.

REMEMBER

As technology keeps improving, your ability to leverage AI gets better, and your investing confidence and results can keep improving over time as well.

The Bottom Line: Choosing a Human Advisor or a Robo-Advisor

REMEMBER

The honest answer to the question "Human advisor or robo-advisor?" is "it depends." Not so much on the human advisor or the robo-advisor; it depends on how well you know yourself:

>> If you're uncertain about investing in general and worried about the twists and turns that will arise in the weeks and months ahead of you, then consider a human advisor.

>> If you are a very experienced investor and can generally manage and navigate your own portfolio, then a robo-advisor is worth a shot.

What if you are on the fence about it — not sure about doing it but intrigued about using a robo-advisor? Fortunately for you, this isn't an "all or nothing" issue.

If you're using human advisors to handle the bulk of your investable assets, why not open a small account (say $5,000 or less) with a highly rated robo-advisor?

WARNING

Please don't do it if you're inexperienced and the $5,000 is your entire nest egg. But if you have, say, $1 million or more in investable assets, and risking $5,000 will not change your lifestyle (or have you jumping out a window), then it isn't such a bad consideration.

I actually think that a greater value (besides hopefully growing your account) is what you will learn. The robo-advisor could end up being a valuable second source or opinion that could help you better interact with your human advisor.

Listing a Few Top Robo-Advisors

TIP

Several major financial sites regularly survey consumers' use and popularity with robo-advisors. Here are a few current robo-advisors along with their websites:

>> Ally Invest Managed Portfolios (https://www.ally.com/invest/managed-portfolios/)

>> Axos Invest (https://www.axosinvest.com/)

>> Betterment (https://www.betterment.com/)

>> Ellevest (https://www.ellevest.com/)

>> E*TRADE Core Portfolios (https://us.etrade.com/what-we-offer/our-accounts/core-portfolios)

>> Fidelity Go (https://www.fidelity.com/go)

>> M1 Finance (https://www.m1finance.com/)

>> Schwab Intelligent Portfolios (www.schwab.com/intelligent-portfolios)

>> SigFig Wealth Management (https://www.sigfig.com/)

>> SoFi Invest (https://www.sofi.com/invest/)

>> StashAway (https://www.stashaway.sg/)

>> Vanguard Personal Advisor Services (https://investor.vanguard.com/advice/personal-advisor)

>> Wealthfront (https://www.wealthfront.com/)

Keep in mind that most major financial websites do their own reviews and surveys about robo-advisors and other issues (such as reviews and surveys on stockbrokers).

Chapter **8**

Fundamental and Technical Analysis

I nvesting — and I mean real investing for the long haul — boils down to the fundamentals. But trading and speculating are intended for the short term, and traders and short-term speculators tend to rely to a greater extent on the technical. You can summarize it like so:

» Long-term investors should overwhelmingly be involved with fundamental analysis.

» Short-term traders and speculators are primarily involved with technical analysis.

Another way to look at it is that fundamental analysis is about the "what" while technical analysis is about the "when." This book focuses for the most part on investing, so fundamental analysis is the primary approach you should consider. This chapter covers both fundamental and technical analysis, and I touch on AI along the way.

Fundamental Analysis

Fundamental analysis looks at the underlying company instead of the stock. It focuses on the company's income and expenses (the income statement), its assets and debt (the balance sheet), cash flow considerations, and market conditions (such as the company's competitors, industry, market share, and so on).

REMEMBER

The point here is that when you buy a stock, you're really buying a company. If the company is doing well now and for the foreseeable future, the stock's price will tend to rise (appreciate). If the company is doing poorly now and for the foreseeable future, it tends to result in a declining stock price. Since stock investing tends to be a long-term pursuit (measured over the years), it pays to watch the fundamentals of the underlying company so that your stock continues to grow in value.

Key fundamental factors

When you use AI to drill down on important concepts, focus on those in the following sections.

Profitability

Profitability is the top consideration in the world of fundamental analysis. A company's profit provides the basis of the answers to the most important questions such as these:

>> "Is this company succeeding?"

>> "Will it continue to stay in business?"

>> "Will it have money for tomorrow's bills or be able to fund future growth?"

Everything else in the company's financial picture flows from that. Profit is the single most important factor in a successful company. I could even make the case that it is the single most important factor in a successful economy.

TIP

So make AI focus on profitability first as you research stocks to buy. Ask questions such as "What is [company X's] profitability for the last three years? Provide the answer as a percentage of total sales for each year."

Solvency

While profitability is the main going concern in the company's income statement (gross income less gross expenses), solvency is the primary concern with the company's balance sheet (total assets less total liabilities equals shareholder equity).

Shareholder equity is just the corporate way of saying net worth. Solvency is the issue that if you liquidate the company's assets, you will be able to pay off 100 percent of its liabilities (with some left over for the owners).

The point is that if you invest in a company whose total liabilities are greater than their total assets, that is certainly a danger signal. Long-term investors always want a positive and healthy balance sheet where total assets always exceed total liabilities and where the difference (the net worth or net equity) is trending upward.

But what say you, AI? Here is a sample prompt to get you rolling, but keep in mind that this prompt should be with an AI tool that has access to current data on publicly traded companies:

> "Analyze the potential solvency issues of a publicly traded company such as [company X] using key financial indicators and solvency ratios."

For AI tools that can help with this type of prompt, check out either Bing Chat and/ or the tools in Appendix B.

Multi-year consistency

One good year of profits is fine, but three or more years is better — much better. That goes for other measures of the company. Consistency over multiple years makes for a more reliable investment choice for your portfolio and for the long term.

Your prompts here should be with AI tools that are current with public company data (such as Bing Chat, robo-advisors, and so on). Ask AI for at least three years of data (five years is better) so that you can see a discernible pattern that is useful for your long-term picture.

The company's market and competition

A company's market and competition are essentially external to the company's financial situation, but they have a strong bearing on the company's long-term viability and how well it's competing in the marketplace. Ask AI about the company's industry and about its main competitors. For example, ask your AI tool about the top three to seven companies in a given industry and rank them for market share. Consider prompts such as this:

"For [industry X], please list the top five companies in a table format with rankings for company size and market share over a three-year period."

TIP

Ask AI to do a SWOT analysis. SWOT stands for Strengths, Weaknesses, Opportunities, and Threats. You can first ask, of course, "Please explain what a SWOT analysis is and how to do it." Then do this analysis of the company itself and also of its main competitors. A good sample prompt is this:

"Please provide a SWOT analysis of the three largest companies in [industry X] with explanations of each, and rank the companies in each item."

Fundamental analysis and AI

Yes, fundamental analysis is at the heart of sound, long-term investing. But let's turn to AI's take on it. Here is where the analysis comes in. Here is the ChatGPT prompt I used:

"What are the ten most important metrics for stocks in fundamental analysis? Please explain each one."

The response from ChatGPT is in the following text:

Fundamental analysis of stocks involves evaluating a company's financial health and performance by analyzing various metrics. Here are ten of the most important metrics used in fundamental analysis, along with explanations for each:

1. Earnings Per Share (EPS):

Explanation: EPS represents a company's profitability on a per-share basis. It's calculated by dividing the company's net income by the number of outstanding shares. EPS is a fundamental measure of a company's ability to generate profits for its shareholders.

2. Price-to-Earnings (P/E) Ratio:

Explanation: The P/E ratio compares a company's stock price to its earnings per share. It reflects how much investors are willing to pay for each dollar of earnings. A higher P/E ratio may indicate greater growth expectations but also higher valuation.

3. Price-to-Book (P/B) Ratio:

Explanation: The P/B ratio compares a company's stock price to its book value per share (total assets minus total liabilities). It's a measure of how the market values a company in relation to its net assets. A low P/B ratio may suggest a potentially undervalued stock.

4. Dividend Yield:

Explanation: Dividend yield represents the annual dividend income a company pays out to shareholders as a percentage of its stock price. It's essential for income-focused investors and provides insight into the company's dividend policy and financial stability.

5. Return on Equity (ROE):

Explanation: ROE measures a company's profitability relative to its shareholders' equity. It's calculated by dividing net income by shareholders' equity. A high ROE indicates efficient use of equity capital to generate profits.

6. Debt-to-Equity Ratio:

Explanation: The debt-to-equity ratio evaluates a company's leverage by comparing its total debt to shareholders' equity. It shows the proportion of financing provided by creditors versus shareholders. A high ratio may indicate higher financial risk.

7. Free Cash Flow (FCF):

Explanation: FCF represents the cash generated by a company's operations after deducting capital expenditures. It's a measure of a company's ability to generate cash for debt repayment, dividends, and investments. Positive FCF is a sign of financial health.

8. Operating Margin:

Explanation: Operating margin measures a company's profitability from its core operations. It's calculated by dividing operating income by total revenue. A higher margin indicates efficiency in managing costs and generating profits.

9. Growth Rates (e.g., Revenue Growth, Earnings Growth):

Explanation: Assessing a company's historical and projected growth rates in revenue and earnings provides insight into its growth prospects. Companies with consistent growth may be more attractive to investors.

10. Current Ratio:

Explanation: The current ratio assesses a company's short-term liquidity by comparing its current assets (e.g., cash, accounts receivable) to its current liabilities (e.g., accounts payable, short-term debt). A ratio above 1 indicates the company can cover its short-term obligations.

These fundamental metrics help investors assess a company's financial position, profitability, valuation, and overall health. It's important to note that these metrics should be used in conjunction with qualitative analysis and consideration of the company's industry, competitive positioning, and future growth prospects to make well-informed investment decisions.

My two cents: Because both fundamental analysis (and technical analysis, covered later in this chapter) is data-intensive, AI will be very useful in distilling and summarizing the data so that it provides you with useful guidance for your decision-making needs.

TIP

Since fundamental analysis is so important to long-term investing, I go into greater details in my book *Stock Investing For Dummies* (Wiley). Keep in mind that specialized AI tools for fundamental analysis can be found in Appendix B and the use of robo-advisors is covered in Chapter 7.

Technical Analysis

REMEMBER

As I mention earlier in this chapter, technical analysis is more useful for the short term, and it's focused on timing: when to get in and when to get out. It is typically not a long-term "buy and hold" approach, and this is why I refer to technical analysis as a timing strategy since it's focused on the "when" as in when to get in (buy stock) and when to get out (sell the stock).

It's quite common for a trader or short-term speculator to get in and out of a stock multiple times during a relatively short timeframe (say, less than a year) because they want to take advantage of the ups and downs and the general ebb and flow of the stock's price movement.

Given that, the following sections discuss some important technical analysis points to watch for.

A spotlight on RSI

The relative strength index (RSI) is a technical analysis metric that helps you figure out whether a particular stock (or other tradeable asset or vehicle) is overbought or oversold. The conditions here help you to time the trade to find an optimal exit point (sell) or entry point (buy).

The RSI gauges recent price action and share volume to provide (hopefully) a useful, actionable number. If a stock's RSI is at or above the number 70, it's considered overbought. If a stock's RSI is anywhere near or below 30, it's considered oversold.

If a stock is overbought, that means that the stock's price may have gone up too far and/or too quickly (too many buyers) and its price is poised for a pullback or correction. For those who were considering buying the stock and looking for an optimal buying moment, they would consider getting in when the stock is oversold.

So the RSI obviously has value for short-term movements, but how about for long-term investors? For a long-term investor, if the fundamentals look good and you were considering buying that stock *anyway* (regardless of short-term price gyrations), and the stock is oversold (again, near, at or below 30), then you have a good buying opportunity.

If, for example, you've held a stock for many years and you were considering getting out (selling your stock) and you see it has a high RSI (near, at or above 70), then you have a good selling opportunity.

Resources on using RSI are available (and not just on AI). Investopedia (www.investopedia.com) has great info on it, as do the sources at the end of this chapter and in Appendix C.

Technical analysis and AI

Technical analysis is one area where I think AI can be very valuable. Since technical analysis is very data-driven (share price, trading volume, and so on), AI makes a great tool. Here's a good first prompt:

> "What are the ten most important metrics for stocks in technical analysis? Please explain each one."

ChatGPT's response is in the following text:

> Technical analysis of stocks involves evaluating price and volume data to make trading decisions. Here are ten of the most important technical indicators and metrics used in technical analysis, along with explanations for each one:
>
> **1. Moving Averages (e.g., Simple Moving Average — SMA, Exponential Moving Average — EMA):**
>
> **Explanation:** Moving averages smooth out price data over a specified period, helping identify trends. The SMA gives equal weight to each data point, while the EMA gives more weight to recent prices.

2. Relative Strength Index (RSI):

Explanation: RSI measures the magnitude of recent price changes to assess overbought or oversold conditions. Values above 70 may indicate overbought, while values below 30 may indicate oversold.

3. Moving Average Convergence Divergence (MACD):

Explanation: MACD is a trend-following momentum indicator that calculates the difference between two moving averages (usually 12-period and 26-period) and plots a signal line (9-period). It helps identify trend changes and potential buy or sell signals.

4. Bollinger Bands:

Explanation: Bollinger Bands consist of a middle band (usually the 20-period SMA) and two outer bands that represent volatility. The bands expand and contract based on price volatility, helping identify potential reversals or breakouts.

5. Volume:

Explanation: Volume measures the number of shares or contracts traded during a given period. Changes in volume can confirm trends, indicate potential reversals, or suggest increased investor interest.

6. Stochastic Oscillator:

Explanation: The stochastic oscillator identifies overbought and oversold conditions based on the closing price relative to the price range over a specified period. It consists of two lines: %K and %D.

7. Average True Range (ATR):

Explanation: ATR measures market volatility by calculating the average range between the high and low prices over a specified period. It helps assess the potential for price movements.

8. Fibonacci Retracement Levels:

Explanation: Fibonacci retracement levels identify potential support and resistance levels based on key Fibonacci ratios (e.g., 38.2%, 50%, 61.8%) from a previous price move. Traders use these levels to identify potential reversal points.

9. Ichimoku Cloud:

Explanation: The Ichimoku Cloud is a comprehensive indicator that provides information about support and resistance levels, trend direction, and potential buy or sell signals. It consists of five lines and a cloud.

10. Average Directional Index (ADX):

Explanation: ADX measures the strength of a trend, whether it's bullish or bearish. A rising ADX indicates a strong trend, while a falling ADX suggests a weakening trend.

These technical indicators and metrics are used by traders to analyze price trends, momentum, volatility, and potential buy or sell signals. It's important to note that technical analysis should be used alongside other forms of analysis, and no single indicator should be relied upon in isolation for trading decisions.

Time to get rolling with your AI prompts and research. Since technical analysis is all about data (prices, trading volume, and so on) and patterns (charts and the like), AI will be very useful. And the fact that it can explain technical analysis jargon in either simple terms ("explain it to me as if I were a fifth grader") or extensive "drill down" terms makes AI a great partner in these trading venues. Given the preceding list, the first thing I would likely use AI to explain to me in simple terms is what a "Ichimoku Cloud" is!

TIP

A good companion to your AI-driven technical analysis is the book *Technical Analysis For Dummies* by Barbara Rockefeller (Wiley).

3

AI Stock Investing Alternatives

Use AI to invest in hard assets (like precious metals) and commodities.

Analyze bonds and other debt-related investments with the help of AI.

Survey AI strategies for real-estate investing.

Start a business or boost your career with AI.

Chapter 9

Hard Assets and Commodities

H old the phone! A chapter on hard assets and commodities in a highfalutin book on AI investing?! Yes!

Virtually all the purposes of money and related financial assets (such as stocks, bonds, cash, cryptocurrencies, and so on) are for current and future needs. Those needs ultimately include food, clothing, transportation, lodging, and more "stuff." As humanity keeps growing, our wants and needs grow with that. And most of the time, the needs and wants are met with commodities.

Commodities and hard assets are areas to which all investors should have at least *some* exposure because this is the essence of investing: putting your money in those things (supply) that will be met by human wants and needs (demand). And yes, AI will help you in your investing approach.

In this chapter, I want investors to think both about AI and a diversification away from stocks, bonds, and other paper/digital assets. Why? Because a truly diversified portfolio does have some exposure in assets that aren't dependent on counterparty risk as well as assets that are more dependent on "human need" versus "human wants." In other words, the types of stuff covered in this chapter are good, investable complements in a diversified portfolio.

Here I break down this "stuff" into two basic segments: precious metals like gold and silver (examples of hard assets) and the general commodity complex (examples include oil, corn, and copper). Yes, real estate is considered a "hard asset," but it's treated elsewhere in the book; see Chapter 11.

No matter how successful AI and other technologies become, they will always depend on commodities. Smartphones, laptops, flat-screen TVs, electric vehicles, and anything that runs AI or other software needs silver, base metals, silicon, and so on. What's that? All modern software and technology also need electricity? Yes, and electricity needs commodities such as oil, gas, coal, and the like.

Understanding Investing versus Speculating

In a chapter such as this, most financial professionals would tell you that the vehicles covered (precious metals and commodities) are very speculative and that most investors should avoid them altogether.

That was very true years ago when the most common way to participate in them was through the futures market, which is very risky and volatile. However, through quality stocks, exchange-traded funds (ETFs), and mutual funds, commodities investing has become more realistic and possible in many investing approaches.

For vehicles that are covered in this chapter, it's important to understand the distinction between investing and speculating:

>> **Investing:** Investing means you're putting your money into assets that you understand and that have long-term value.

>> **Speculating:** For the purposes of this book, speculating is a form of financial gambling. It's betting on the short-term price movements of a given asset.

There is nothing wrong with speculating, but it's risky. Speculating is not only about the investment or asset itself, but it is also about the person doing the speculating. If you're putting your money into an asset that you don't fully understand (especially the downside risks), then you're speculating. If you don't realize that a given asset or investment in a given market can plummet just as easy as it can rise, then you're speculating.

Another aspect to consider is your financial condition. If you're speculating with $10,000 in commodities futures, and you have a $1 million net worth, then you aren't speculating (not dangerously). But if you're speculating with $2,000 and your net worth is $10,000, now that is bad.

REMEMBER

Understand your personal limits, especially if losses are a real possibility and could be life-changing. Speculating is fine when you are experienced and the amount won't severely impair your lifestyle.

Comparing the Risks of Precious Metals and Commodities

Many AI-related books are pouring onto your physical and digital bookshelves, and few of them (if any) are covering hard assets and commodities. So, why am I choosing to cover them?

REMEMBER

Diversification is a prime goal for any portfolio, especially in times such as now (war, inflation, debt bubbles, geopolitical crises, and so on), and the primary directive of diversification is *lowering overall risk*. In a world such as ours, you cannot eliminate all forms of risk, but you can eliminate or reduce many types of risk (financial risk, purchasing power risk, and so on) and mitigate it so that you're still safe and prosperous at the end of the day.

The following sections go over different types of risks as they relate (and don't relate) to precious metals and commodities.

What precious metals don't have: Counterparty risk

We face many forms of risk both as investors and as participants in our society and economy at large. For this section, I want to focus on a risk many financial pros may not realize (or focus on), which is *counterparty risk*.

Counterparty risk exists in assets whose value is reliant on a counterparty. This risk is present in all paper assets (stocks, bonds, currencies) and their digital equivalents. For example:

>> **Stocks:** Stocks are only as good or secure as the value of the underlying company. This is why good long-term investors (including those who look at

AI-related stocks, which are covered in Chapters 4 and 5) always study the fundamentals of the underlying company. XYZ stock (a common stock usually found in stock investing books) is only as secure and as successful as XYZ the underlying company. You look at the company's profits, assets, market opportunities, and so on. If the company is losing money, drowning in debt, and so on, then the company will go bankrupt and the stock will ultimately become worthless. The stock is only as good as the counterparty (the underlying company).

>> **Bonds (and other forms of debt):** This counterparty risk should be obvious. If the counterparty (the issuer of the debt such as a company or government entity) defaults on that debt, then the bond or other debt-related vehicle either loses value or becomes worthless. Bonds depend on the financial ability and the willingness of the underlying entity (the debtor) to pay back the principal and associated interest.

>> **Currencies:** Yes, currencies have counterparty risk. If you have 100 units of a given currency (dollars, euros, yen, and so on), then you will assume those 100 units have value. But what happens when the issuer (typically a national government's central banking authority) overproduces that currency? It has been very common throughout history that central banks tend to overproduce a currency (monetary inflation), and the currency loses value to the point that it becomes worthless. In that case, those 100 units of the currency become as valuable as zero units of the same.

REMEMBER

Precious metals don't have counterparty risk. They have their own intrinsic value, which means their value isn't dependent on a third party such as a company or government agency. Given that, they tend to earn a spot in most portfolios since they have had sustainable value for thousands of years, and they retain their value even in times of economic decline or chaos. Keep in mind that this does not necessarily mean that precious metals don't have market risk — their prices can fluctuate — but the point here is that precious metals have never gone to zero due to some counterparty (such as a government or corporate entity). For more details and guidance on precious metals, check out the resources mentioned later in this chapter.

Commodities in general don't have counterparty risk since, say, a bushel of corn or a barrel of oil has its own intrinsic value. However, given the type of investment or vehicle, other risks may apply. The stock of an agricultural company that produces soybeans, for example, may have counterparty risk in the same way other publicly traded stocks have. More on general commodities appears later in this chapter.

Other risks associated with stocks and other conventional vehicles

In the previous section, I focus on counterparty risk because that type of risk is rarely mentioned in investment books and forums, but here I mention the risks with stocks and other conventional investment vehicles that all investors should be aware of:

>> **Financial risk:** This is the most obvious risk, which is that the specific underlying company tied to your stock will go bankrupt at some point. This is why we focus on fundamentals (covered in Chapter 8). In 2023, there was an explosion of AI-related stocks; keep in mind that AI isn't a guarantee of profit. You'll see some (many?) of these companies go out of business. The same risk exists with bonds.

>> **Interest rate risk:** Many assets and vehicles may have interest rate risks. What if interest rates rise and that particular asset is dependent on low interest rates? In 2022 some prominent banks plummeted in value as interest rates rose because their investments were earning a low interest rate; meanwhile, for new deposits and certificates of deposit (CDs), they were paying a higher interest rate, and that created unsustainable losses.

Many investments are affected when interest rates are rising, such as fixed-interest rate bonds, which lose value in that scenario. If, for example, you have a 3 percent bond and interest rates reach 4 percent (and are still rising), the incentive is to sell your 3 percent bond and seek a bond (or other investment) with a higher rate of return. Real estate also is affected (see Chapter 11 for more information).

>> **Inflation risk (also called purchasing power risk):** The value of investments such as fixed-interest rate bonds decline in a period of rising inflation. The reason is that if a bond is earning interest of 3 percent and inflation — through measurements such as the Consumer Price Index (CPI), covered in Chapter 13 — is at 4 percent and rising, then holders of the 3 percent bond have a market incentive to sell it and seek investments with a higher rate of return.

Other types of risk exist, so use AI tools (such as ChatGPT, covered in Chapter 2) to research the risk profile of any investment you are considering. If you are using a financial advisor, then discuss any risks that a given investment carries or is exposed to.

Risks with precious metals

So, do precious metals have any risks? Let's ask ChatGPT about this. See Figure 9-1.

ChatGPT

Investing in precious metals like gold and silver can offer diversification and act as a hedge against economic uncertainties, but it also comes with risks. Here are some key risks associated with buying precious metals:

1. **Price Volatility:**
   * Precious metal prices can be highly volatile. The values of gold and silver can fluctuate based on various factors, including economic conditions, geopolitical events, interest rates, and market sentiment. Investors should be prepared for price swings that can impact the value of their investments.

2. **Market and Economic Conditions:**
   * Economic factors, such as inflation rates, interest rates, and overall market conditions, can influence precious metal prices. Changes in these conditions may affect the demand for gold and silver as safe-haven assets and impact their market prices.

3. **Lack of Income Generation:**
   * Unlike dividend-paying stocks or interest-bearing bonds, precious metals do not generate income. Holding gold or silver does not provide investors with regular interest or dividend payments, and the return on investment is primarily dependent on price appreciation.

4. **Storage and Insurance Costs:**
   * Physical possession of precious metals requires secure storage, and storing large quantities can incur additional costs. Investors may need to pay for safe deposit boxes or invest in secure storage facilities. Additionally, insuring precious metal holdings may involve additional expenses.

5. **Counterparty Risk:**
   * Some investors choose to hold precious metals through financial instruments such as exchange-traded funds (ETFs) or certificates. In such cases, there is counterparty risk associated with the financial institution or issuer of the instrument. If the issuer faces financial difficulties, it could impact the value of the investment.

6. **Government Policies and Regulations:**
   * Changes in government policies, including tax regulations and restrictions on precious metal transactions, can impact the market. For example, import/export restrictions or changes in taxation may affect the flow and pricing of precious metals.

7. **Market Manipulation and Fraud:**
   * Like any financial market, precious metals markets may be susceptible to manipulation and fraud. Investors should be cautious of unscrupulous schemes or fraudulent activities that can target those looking to buy or sell precious metals.

FIGURE 9-1:
The risks of buying precious metals, according to AI.

8. **Currency Risk (for Non-U.S. Investors):**
   - Precious metals are priced in U.S. dollars, so investors outside the United States may face currency risk. Fluctuations in exchange rates between their local currency and the U.S. dollar can impact the returns on their precious metal investments.

9. **Industrial Demand and Supply Factors:**
   - Silver, in particular, has significant industrial applications. Changes in industrial demand, supply disruptions, or shifts in technology that reduce the need for silver in certain industries can affect its price independently of its role as a precious metal.

10. **Speculative Nature:**
    - The value of precious metals is often influenced by speculation and investor sentiment. Speculative trading activity can lead to short-term price volatility that may not necessarily be aligned with fundamental economic factors.

Investors should carefully assess their investment goals, risk tolerance, and the role they envision for precious metals within their overall portfolio. Diversification strategies that include various asset classes can help manage risks associated with any single investment. Consulting with financial advisors and staying informed about market conditions are essential components of responsible investing in precious metals.

FIGURE 9-1:
(Continued)

This is a good list of potential risks related to gold or silver. In general, precious metals don't normally produce income; they are intended as assets that can hold their value or have the potential for capital gain (or loss if sold in a declining market). Given that, market risk will be present.

By the way, Figure 9-1 does mention "counterparty risk" but that is a reference to the dealer involved and not the metal(s) itself.

WARNING

Buying physical gold and/or silver bullion (for example, through bullion coins such as gold eagles or silver eagles issued by the U.S. Mint at www.usmint.gov) is the safest way to hold gold and silver and store them yourself. But many precious metals investors opt to have storage done by the dealer. That can be fine, but just do your research and due diligence regarding the dealer's reputation, solvency, reliability, and so forth.

Risks with commodities

While we're at it, let's ask ChatGPT about the risks with commodities. I used this simple prompt:

"What are the risks of investing in commodities?"

I'll show ChatGPT's answer in text (so I can comment in italics).

Investing in commodities can be a valuable addition to a diversified investment portfolio, but it also carries certain risks that investors should be aware of. Here are some of the key risks associated with investing in commodities:

1. Price Volatility: Commodities are known for their price volatility. Factors like supply and demand imbalances, geopolitical events, weather conditions, and currency fluctuations can lead to rapid and substantial price movements.

Comments: This risk is primarily referencing speculating in the commodity futures market. Investors can reduce this as a risk factor when investing in quality large-cap, commodities-related stocks and commodity ETFs.

2. Lack of Income: Unlike stocks or bonds, commodities typically do not generate income in the form of dividends or interest payments. Investors rely on price appreciation for potential returns.

Comments: This is true, but there are stocks and ETFs that pay dividends.

3. Storage Costs: Investing in physical commodities, such as gold or oil, may require storage solutions. Storage costs can erode returns, especially for investors holding significant quantities of physical commodities.

Comments: Keep in mind that storage costs can be a long-term consideration, which is why many holders choose to find a more personal and discreet storage approach (such as a home safe).

4. Counterparty Risk: When trading commodity futures contracts or using commodity-related financial products, investors are exposed to counterparty risk. This risk arises if the counterparty (e.g., a futures broker or financial institution) defaults.

Comments: This may be a distant possibility in the futures market, but it is likely not plausible. Futures are speculating anyway, so it is safer to stick with commodities ETFs.

5. Liquidity Risk: Some commodities may have less liquidity compared to more traditional investments like stocks or bonds. This can make it challenging to enter or exit positions at desired prices.

Comments: Liquidity is a risk with futures trading on thinly traded commodities. Investors and speculators are best advised to avoid those risky markets.

6. Rolling Costs: Investors in commodity futures contracts must periodically roll over their positions to avoid physical delivery. The costs associated with rolling positions, including transaction fees, can impact returns.

Comments: Again, investors are best advised to stay away from futures trading. Commodities ETFs are a better way to go for beginners.

7. Regulatory Risks: The commodity markets are subject to government regulations that can change over time. New regulations or tax policies can affect the cost and ease of trading commodities.

8. Geopolitical Factors: Geopolitical events, such as trade disputes or conflicts in commodity-producing regions, can disrupt supply chains and impact commodity prices.

9. Currency Risk: Many commodities are priced in U.S. dollars. Changes in exchange rates can affect the cost and returns of investing in commodities, especially for investors using other currencies.

10. Weather and Natural Disasters: Agricultural commodities, in particular, are vulnerable to weather conditions and natural disasters like droughts, floods, or hurricanes. These events can significantly affect supply and prices.

11. Environmental Concerns: Some commodities, such as oil and coal, face increasing scrutiny due to environmental concerns. Regulations and shifts in consumer preferences toward cleaner energy sources can affect the demand for certain commodities.

12. Ethical and Social Considerations: Investors may have ethical or social considerations when investing in certain commodities. For example, concerns about the environmental and social impact of mining operations can influence investment decisions.

Comments: This is your personal choice.

13. Contango and Backwardation: In commodity futures markets, contango (higher future prices than current prices) and backwardation (lower future prices than current prices) can impact returns for investors rolling over futures contracts.

Comments: Both are important concepts in the world of commodity futures markets. Use AI to drill down on these conditions since it will greatly help traders and speculators.

To manage these risks, investors often diversify their portfolios across various asset classes, including stocks, bonds, real estate, and cash. When investing in commodities, they may also consider using commodity ETFs or mutual funds that provide exposure to commodity price movements without the need for direct commodity ownership. Additionally, conducting thorough research and staying informed about market dynamics and global events is essential for commodity investors.

Comments: Nice conclusion — now go make some money.

Handling Hard Assets (Primarily Precious Metals)

"Hard assets" refers to investable, tangible assets that you and I can actually hold; they are not paper or digital. Although "hard assets" can embrace a colorful assortment of tangible investments such as real estate, collectibles, and precious metals, they are most often a reference to precious metals such as gold and silver.

Keep in mind that "precious metals" also encompasses metals such as platinum and palladium, but the marketplace tends to focus on the two metals that have a long history (dating back thousands of years!) of being a reliable "store of value" and a "means of exchange": gold and silver.

Gold and silver are typically treated as a separate category from general commodities because these two assets have a unique history and place in the global marketplace. Yes, gold and silver do have one side of them that are similar to generic commodities. Both are used in jewelry, for example, and silver has literally hundreds of applications as an industrial metal. It's used in solar panels, smartphones, consumer electronics, healthcare, and so on.

The difference with gold and silver is also that they have been used as money for thousands of years — both as a store of value and as a means of exchange. As a form of currency, both have actually outlasted virtually every man-made currency to date. It is probably not an exaggeration to say that they could very likely outlast today's currencies as well.

In the following sections, you discover methods for investing in precious metals, how AI can help with your investments, and handy resources for more information.

Ways to invest in gold and silver

If you do decide to add gold and/or silver (or other precious metals) to your portfolio, here are the primary ways to do so:

>> **Physical coins/bars:** This is the safest way to add gold and silver to your portfolio. Physically, these precious metals come in coins, bars, medals, or ingots. There are two ways to invest in the physical: bullion and numismatic.

If you're new to physical gold and silver, stick to bullion coins issued by the U.S. Mint (www.usmint.gov). Stay away from numismatic coins until you're more experienced and more knowledgeable; there is too much risk in

WARNING

numismatic coins due to a wide range of issues such as the condition of the coin, authenticity, and so forth.

>> **Futures:** Futures is not about investing; it is about speculating. Futures trading is fast-paced, very volatile, and very risky.

>> **Stocks:** Certainly less risky than futures, yet stocks still have long-term growth potential. There are plenty of great stocks in the world of precious metals, and this is a good way to add that exposure in a typical portfolio. Although Chapters 4 and 5 are geared toward AI stocks, much of the resources and strategies can help any stock investor.

Stock investing beginners and novice investors will benefit from my book *Stock Investing For Dummies* (published by Wiley).

>> **ETFs and mutual funds:** Compared to the preceding choices, this is the more conservative investing approach. Exchange-traded funds (ETFs) and mutual funds are the way to go. For more information on these vehicles, check out Chapter 6.

AI strategies and precious metals

Here are some ways AI can assist investors with hard assets like gold and silver:

>> **Market analysis:** AI can analyze historical price data, market trends, and news sentiment to provide real-time market insights for informed investment decisions.

>> **Price prediction:** AI algorithms can forecast gold and silver prices, helping investors identify optimal entry and exit points for trades.

>> **Risk assessment:** AI models can assess the risk associated with investing in precious metals by considering factors such as geopolitical events and economic indicators.

>> **Portfolio diversification:** AI can recommend optimal allocation of precious metals within a diversified investment portfolio to manage risk.

>> **Pattern recognition:** AI can identify technical patterns in price charts, helping investors recognize potential breakout or reversal points.

>> **Optimized asset allocation:** AI can recommend adjustments to a portfolio's gold and silver holdings based on changing market conditions and risk profiles.

>> **Market alerts:** AI-powered systems can send real-time alerts to investors when significant price movements or news events occur.

>> **Historical performance analysis:** AI can analyze historical performance data of precious metals, helping investors understand their long-term potential and risks.

>> **News summarization:** AI can summarize and prioritize news articles related to gold and silver, saving investors time in staying informed.

TIP

Need some help in crafting some appropriate prompts to get you rolling? Why not use ChatGPT to help you with creating useful prompts to get your juices flowing? I just asked, "Please provide five sample prompts that would be very useful to precious metals investors." Give it a shot!

Precious metals resources

TIP

For more information and research on precious metals, head over to the following resources:

>> World Gold Council (www.gold.org)

>> The Silver Institute (www.silverinstitute.org)

>> Precious Metals Investing (www.preciousmetalsinvesting.com)

>> *Investing in Gold & Silver For Dummies* by Paul Mladjenovic (published by Wiley)

>> *Precious Metals Investing For Dummies* by Paul Mladjenovic (published by Wiley)

Considering Commodities

Setting aside precious metals, which is really a category different from conventional commodities, this section now gets to the "stuff" of everyday life. Everyone needs to eat, drive a car, turn on their lights, and a thousand other daily, functional pursuits of life. This is what makes commodities an important part of an investor's portfolio. After a tour of commodities here, I note ways to invest and how AI can help you do it.

REMEMBER

Keep in mind that most folks think in terms of futures (and futures options) to speculate with these commodities, but you can participate in each of the following commodities through ETFs, which is a safer, investing-oriented approach to including them in your portfolio. For a full introduction to commodities, check out the latest edition of *Commodities For Dummies* by Amine Bouchentouf (Wiley).

Comparing commodities and futures

Very often "futures" and "commodities" are used interchangeably. But please understand the crucial distinction. Commodities are the "stuff," but futures are the stuff in a specific, marketable format.

If, for example, you have a bushel of corn, that is a commodity. But futures in corn are commodities in a tradeable security such as a contract.

Let's ask ChatGPT a simple prompt:

> "What is the specific difference between futures and commodities?"

Figure 9-2 is ChatGPT's response focusing on futures.

 ChatGPT

"Futures" and "commodities" are related financial terms, but they refer to different concepts in the context of financial markets.

Futures:

1. **Definition:**
   - **Futures** are financial contracts that obligate the buyer to purchase, or the seller to sell, a specific quantity of an asset (the underlying asset) at a predetermined price on a specified future date. These contracts are standardized and traded on organized futures exchanges.

2. **Underlying Assets:**
   - Futures contracts can be based on various underlying assets, including commodities (such as gold, oil, or agricultural products), financial instruments (such as stock indices or interest rates), or other assets (such as foreign currencies).

3. **Purpose:**
   - Futures contracts are often used for hedging or speculative purposes. Hedgers use them to manage or mitigate the risk of price fluctuations in the underlying asset, while speculators seek to profit from price movements.

4. **Standardization:**
   - Futures contracts are standardized in terms of contract size, expiration date, and other specifications. This standardization facilitates trading on organized exchanges, such as the Chicago Mercantile Exchange (CME) or the Intercontinental Exchange (ICE).

5. **Leverage:**
   - Futures trading often involves leverage, allowing traders to control a larger position with a smaller amount of capital. While leverage can amplify returns, it also increases the risk of significant losses.

FIGURE 9-2: AI Information on futures.

And then ChatGPT's commodities portion of the answer is in Figure 9-3.

Commodities:

1. **Definition:**
   * **Commodities** refer to raw materials or primary agricultural products that are traded on exchanges. Commodities can be broadly categorized into two types: hard commodities (physical goods like gold, oil, and wheat) and soft commodities (agricultural products like coffee, cotton, and soybeans).

2. **Physical Goods:**
   * Commodities represent tangible goods that are typically interchangeable with other goods of the same type. They are considered fungible, meaning one unit is equivalent to another.

3. **Market Characteristics:**
   * The commodities market is where these raw materials are bought and sold. It includes spot markets (for immediate delivery) and futures markets (for future delivery).

4. **Supply and Demand:**
   * The prices of commodities are influenced by factors such as supply and demand dynamics, geopolitical events, weather conditions, and global economic trends.

5. **Diversification:**
   * Investors often use commodities as a diversification strategy within their investment portfolios. The idea is that commodities may not always move in sync with traditional financial assets like stocks and bonds.

In summary, "futures" refer to financial contracts with standardized terms that obligate the buyer or seller to trade an underlying asset at a future date and price. "Commodities," on the other hand, refer to the physical goods or raw materials that are traded on markets, including futures markets. Commodities can serve as the underlying assets for futures contracts, but not all futures contracts are based on commodities—some are linked to financial instruments or other assets.

FIGURE 9-3: AI information on futures.

And, finally, the key differences according to ChatGPT are in Figure 9-4.

REMEMBER

As you can see from the preceding figures, commodities and futures can be different animals even when, at their core, they have the same essential content. That should tell you that in today's diverse marketplace, there can be many different vehicles and strategies involved with the same essential asset. Use AI to discover the pros and cons as well as strategies to incorporate an asset according to your needs. You can participate with precious metals or commodities either directly through venues such as the futures market, but you can also participate through vehicles such as stocks, ETFs, mutual funds, and other sources.

 You
In a paragraph of 200 words or less, what are the key differences?

 ChatGPT
Futures and commodities are distinct concepts in financial markets. Futures are standardized financial contracts obligating the buyer to purchase or the seller to sell a specific quantity of an underlying asset at a predetermined price on a specified future date. While commodities can serve as underlying assets for futures contracts, they encompass tangible goods or raw materials traded in markets. Commodities include hard commodities like gold and oil, as well as soft commodities like coffee and cotton. Futures contracts, on the other hand, can be based on various assets beyond commodities, such as financial instruments or stock indices. Futures are traded on organized exchanges, featuring standardized terms and often involving leverage. They serve purposes of hedging against price fluctuations or speculative trading. In contrast, commodities are physical goods with intrinsic value, subject to supply and demand dynamics, geopolitical events, and global economic trends. Investors often use commodities for portfolio diversification, recognizing their distinct role as tangible assets within the broader financial landscape.

FIGURE 9-4: Differences between commodities and futures.

Looking at different types of commodities

Every specific commodity you see listed in the following sections can be traded either directly (through futures or ETFs) or indirectly (publicly traded companies).

TIP

Keep in mind that when something catches the imagination of the investing public, think about what commodities will be needed. Electric vehicles (EVs), for example, have in recent years have become the focus of both government and corporate funding. The environmental downside of EVs is that they require huge amounts of rare metals. Investing in EVs may be risky, but a less risky way to benefit from EVs is to consider investing in those commodities that EVs will ultimately need.

Agricultural commodities

The world eats this stuff every day, and investing in it with the help of AI is a good consideration. In this segment, we discuss the sustenance of life.

While there is a futures market for each of the following commodities (and most of the items listed in later sections), you can invest in them through other routes:

>> Wheat

>> Corn

>> Soybeans

>> Rice

>> Cotton

>> Coffee

>> Sugar

>> Cocoa

One way to invest in an agricultural commodity without going the speculative route of futures is through ETFs. A good prompt to try is to ask AI to describe an ETF with a particular symbol. I used the following prompt as an example:

"Please describe the ETF with the symbol DBA."

Figure 9-5 has ChatGPT's answer.

Livestock and meat

These commodities are related to animal farming and meat production:

>> Cattle

>> Hogs

>> Feeder cattle

>> Lean hogs

Oilseeds

These are seeds primarily used for oil production:

>> Soybeans

>> Canola

>> Sunflower seeds

ChatGPT

As of my last knowledge update in January 2022, the ETF with the symbol "DBA" is the Invesco DB Agriculture Fund. However, keep in mind that information might have changed since then, and it's important to verify the details with up-to-date sources.

The Invesco DB Agriculture Fund (DBA) is an exchange-traded fund (ETF) that seeks to track the performance of the DBIQ Diversified Agriculture Index Excess Return. This index is composed of futures contracts on some of the most widely traded agricultural commodities, including corn, wheat, soybeans, and sugar.

Key points about DBA:

1. **Objective:** The fund aims to provide exposure to the agricultural sector, allowing investors to participate in the price movements of key agricultural commodities.
2. **Holdings:** DBA holds futures contracts, and the performance of the fund is linked to the price changes in these agricultural commodities.
3. **Diversification:** By holding a basket of agricultural commodities, DBA provides investors with a level of diversification within the agricultural sector.
4. **Risk and Volatility:** Investing in commodity ETFs like DBA involves exposure to the price volatility of the underlying commodities, which can be influenced by factors such as weather conditions, global demand, and geopolitical events.
5. **Expense Ratio:** Investors should also consider the expense ratio, which represents the percentage of fund assets used for administrative and other expenses. It's important to compare this ratio with similar funds.

FIGURE 9-5: You can ask AI about a commodity-related ETF.

Tropical products

These commodities are typically grown in tropical regions:

- Coffee
- Cocoa
- Rubber
- Palm oil

Dairy products

These include various dairy-based commodities:

- Milk
- Butter
- Cheese

Energy commodities

This area deserves a spot in many portfolios as energy is a primary driver in the overall national and global economy:

» Crude oil

» Natural gas

» Heating oil

» Gasoline

» Coal

» Propane

Industrial (base) metals

These are base metals that are primarily used in construction and industrial applications:

» Copper

» Aluminum

» Zinc

» Nickel

» Lead

» Tin

These metals are not considered "precious" because they are not typically bought for their own intrinsic value; they are valuable due to industrial utility and manufacturing uses.

Exotic metals

These include precious and rare metals that are less commonly traded:

» Rhodium

» Iridium

» Ruthenium

These metals typically have utilitarian value and are not considered standard "precious metals" since they are not widely used as investment vehicles in the same way as, say, gold and silver.

Rare earth metals

These are a group of 17 elements with specialized uses in technology and manufacturing. Examples are neodymium, dysprosium, europium, and terbium. Use AI to research these earth metals if you're interested in finding out more details.

For investors, the category of rare earth metals is similar to exotic metals in that it is a relatively obscure and thinly traded area of the world of metals. For those investors who are interested, it is better to research the world of small-cap mining stocks, and AI can help you do the research.

Checking out commodities investing vehicles

After you have done your homework and are deciding to add commodities to your portfolio, the next step is to see what types of vehicles are appropriate and available:

WARNING

>> **Futures and options:** These areas should be considered speculative and are best done later after you have accrued enough knowledge and experience. Meanwhile, do your research with AI and at sites such as www.cftc.gov and www.cmegroup.com (more details are at the end of this chapter).

>> **Stocks:** Water is a critical commodity (who disagrees?), yet as boring as it sounds, water stocks have been among the top stock market performers since the year 2000. Many company stocks have been stable and reliable performers over the years. Use AI to find large-cap stocks in those commodities that are in strong demand. For more info on stocks, check out Chapters 4 and 5.

>> **ETFs and mutual funds:** For both precious metals and commodities, ETFs and mutual funds are the easiest and least risky way for investors to add exposure to these areas. You can find a number of broad-based ETFs at www.etfdb.com.

Of course, do your due diligence (or speak with your financial advisor) since you have many good ETFs in the commodities area to choose from. Find out more about ETFs in Chapter 6.

Using AI to get the scoop on commodities

After you are keenly interested in commodities, here are some AI tactics and strategies to consider:

>> **Explanations of markets and concepts:** The first use of AI is explaining concepts, markets, and investing vehicles. For beginners, this is the best use.

>> **Supply and demand analysis:** Since AI can process vast amounts of data, use it to assess the most recent supply and demand for a given commodity. Supply and demand should be the most important factors guiding your investment and/or speculative decisions. For this, it becomes obvious:

- Growing demand coupled with stable or low supply is bullish for the price of that commodity.

- Likewise, if demand is stable but supply is shrinking, that is also bullish.

- If demand is falling but supply is stable, that is bearish.

- If demand is falling and supply is rising, that is very bearish.

TIP

Understanding supply and demand is critical for many products and services in the general economy, but it's also critical in many markets including the stock market and other financial markets. Use AI to drill down on this critical dynamic, and your investing success will be more ensured.

>> **Technical analysis:** AI can help you with understanding and tracking short-term price movements. Understanding concepts such as "overbought" and "oversold" will enhance your trading success. Find out more about technical analysis in Chapter 8.

>> **Weather forecasting:** AI-driven weather models can provide insights into how weather conditions may impact agricultural commodities like corn and wheat, aiding in trading decisions.

>> **Market sentiment analysis:** AI can analyze news articles, social media, and financial reports to gauge market sentiment and its potential impact on commodity prices.

>> **Trading strategies:** AI can develop and optimize trading strategies for commodities, considering factors like technical indicators, market trends, and risk tolerance.

>> **Portfolio diversification:** AI can recommend the optimal allocation of commodities within a diversified investment portfolio to manage risk. AI tools such as robo-advisors are well suited for this (more details are in Chapter 7).

>> **Trading automation:** AI-driven trading algorithms can execute commodity trades automatically based on predefined criteria and market signals.

>> **Trade alerts:** AI-powered systems can send real-time alerts to investors when specific price thresholds or trading opportunities are reached.

>> **Historical performance analysis:** AI can analyze historical performance data for commodities, helping investors assess their long-term potential and risks.

>> **Correlation assessment:** AI can assess the correlation between commodities and other asset classes, aiding in risk management and portfolio construction.

>> **Energy market insights:** For energy commodities like oil, AI can analyze geopolitical events, production levels, and OPEC decisions to inform trading strategies.

>> **Customized investment strategies:** AI can create personalized investment strategies based on an investor's financial goals, risk tolerance, and time horizon, optimizing commodity holdings within the broader portfolio.

Consider turning some of the preceding points into AI prompts to dig deeper for answers. You can even have AI help you craft prompts to do this. Here is a sample prompt for ChatGPT:

"Discuss the cyclical nature of commodity markets. Examine historical price cycles for a chosen commodity, considering factors like economic cycles, seasonal patterns, and industry trends. How can investors identify and leverage these cycles for more informed investment decisions?"

Yep, that's a mouthful, but you get the idea.

AI-driven capabilities provide investors with valuable insights, automation, and data-driven decision-making tools to navigate the commodities market, manage risk, and seize investment opportunities effectively. The AI tools that can help you are found in Appendix B.

Reviewing resources on commodities

Want even more information on commodities? Check out the following:

>> Commodity Futures Trading Commission (www.cftc.gov). Great site covering the rules of the futures and futures options market. For you, they have great resources and education for beginning speculators.

>> CME Group (www.cmegroup.com). This is the industry trade group, and their site is rich with information and education on futures trading for both beginners and experienced speculators.

>> *Commodities For Dummies* by Amine Bouchentouf (published by Wiley).

Chapter **10**

Bonds, Bank Investments, and Digital Currencies

I t's a common foundational point that financial planners seek diversification for most portfolios. Even if a portfolio was 100 percent stocks, the prudent investor would be counseled to have different categories and/or subcategories of stock. If you were heavy into tech stocks and you were in your retirement years, for example, an experienced financial planner or investment advisor would tell you to decrease your heavy exposure in the technology sector and shift money to sectors such as utilities and consumer staples.

If you were that retiree, the emphasis would be to lessen exposure to growth-oriented investments (such as tech stocks) and allocate those funds into income-producing assets such as dividend stocks, bonds, and bank CDs (formally certificates of deposit).

In this chapter, I cover bonds and bank investments (for investors), and for speculators, I cover cryptocurrencies (including the Federal Reserve's upcoming digital currencies). While Chapter 9 covers "real stuff" in terms of hard assets and items you can physically touch and use (commodities), this chapter covers the digital and/or paper assets that people use.

Bonds and Bank Investments

All bonds are debt instruments. To an investor, a bond is considered an asset in their portfolio, and they are technically considered the "creditor." To the issuer of that debt (usually a corporate or governmental entity), a bond is a liability, and they are technically the "debtor."

Bank investments cover those debt instruments issued by a bank such as certificates of deposit, savings accounts, and money market accounts. They typically come with deposit insurance such as that from the FDIC (Federal Deposit Insurance Corporation). These types of accounts are viewed as being generally safe and a good place to hold your cash, both as diversification away from other riskier vehicles (such as stocks and mutual funds) and as a temporary "parking spot" for your funds until the money is needed for other uses, such as paying off debt or for investment purposes.

Bonds and bank investments are considered generally safe ways to add diversification to your general investing approach. The following sections cover bonds and bank investments in more detail.

Bonds

In 2023, investors saw interest rates rise to historic levels. This was part of the efforts of the U.S. Federal Reserve to fight inflation. The end result is that many debt instruments are yielding better returns than they have in many years.

This is a different scenario from what it looked like a few short years ago. Anyone investing in bonds at that time would have seen losses as interest rates and inflation rates rose sharply.

For AI, the question you should ask after "What is bond investing?" should be "What happens to bonds when interest rates and/or inflation rates go up (or down)?" Of course, if interest rates go down (and inflation, too), then your bonds would go up in value and be worth a fortune.

The following sections discuss points to ask AI about when it comes to bonds.

Bond issuers and types

There are several ways of looking at bond categories:

» Bond categories in terms of issuer classification

» Bond categories in terms of bond types

For example, there are several categories of issuers:

>> Federal government (issued by the Treasury Department)

>> Municipal government (state and local)

>> Corporate

TIP

In terms of safety, Treasury bonds (from the federal government) are considered the safest category on the planet.

Bonds can usually be one of the following types:

>> Fixed rate

>> Adjustable rate

Bonds usually have a fixed interest rate, but that can be problematic in a period of rising interest rates and rising inflation rates. Both will have a detrimental effect on the value of fixed-interest rate bonds. Meanwhile, in times of rising interest rates, adjustable rate bonds are a safer way to go.

REMEMBER

The bottom line is that you should use AI to help you understand which bond categories and types are most suitable for your personal profile. Some prompts to consider are the following:

>> "I am retired and also risk-averse. What types of bonds are suitable for me?"

>> "I have $100,000 and I want to invest in bonds, but I am not sure how to structure my purchases so I can get the most interest but minimize potential risks. Please provide a sample portfolio with explanations for each aspect."

>> "What are the pros and cons of municipal bonds? Give me a breakdown of each category of municipal bonds with a detailed explanation of each pro and con for each category."

Bond ratings

Bonds that are issued are graded (rated) on their quality. The higher the quality, the safer for your portfolio. But let's ask AI! Consider this prompt:

"Give me bond ratings in a bullet point style with an explanation of each."

ChatGPT's response is in Figure 10-1.

ChatGPT
Bond Ratings:

1. **AAA (Triple-A):**
   * Explanation: Bonds with the highest credit rating, indicating the lowest risk of default. Issuers are considered extremely stable, and the likelihood of timely payment is very high.

2. **AA (Double-A):**
   * Explanation: High-quality bonds with a very low risk of default. Slightly lower than AAA, but still considered to have a strong capacity to meet financial obligations.

3. **A:**
   * Explanation: Bonds with an upper-medium credit rating. While still considered investment-grade, there is a slightly higher risk compared to AA or AAA-rated bonds.

4. **BBB:**
   * Explanation: Bonds are of medium credit quality. They are considered investment-grade but may be more susceptible to economic downturns or adverse changes in financial conditions.

5. **BB:**
   * Explanation: Non-investment grade or speculative bonds. While currently meeting payment obligations, there is a higher risk of default compared to investment-grade bonds.

6. **B:**
   * Explanation: High-risk or speculative bonds. Financial conditions can be variable, and there is a notable risk of default, though interest payments are still being made.

7. **CCC:**
   * Explanation: Bonds with a substantial risk of default. Issuers may struggle to meet their payment obligations, and the financial situation is precarious.

8. **CC:**
   * Explanation: Highly vulnerable bonds. Default is a real possibility, and the financial condition of the issuer is weak.

9. **C:**
   * Explanation: Bonds of poor standing, with a high risk of default. The issuer is often in a distressed financial situation.

10. **D:**
    * Explanation: Issuer has defaulted on its debt obligations. Bonds in this category are in default, and investors may face losses.

Bond ratings are assigned by credit rating agencies such as Moody's, Standard & Poor's (S&P), and Fitch Ratings. These ratings help investors assess the creditworthiness and risk associated with investing in a particular bond or issuer. Higher-rated bonds generally offer lower yields but come with lower default risk, while lower-rated bonds may provide higher yields but with increased risk.

FIGURE 10-1:
Different bond ratings according to AI.

Bond ratings range from AAA, AA, and A all the way down to D. Treasury bonds are considered the safest (AAA rating) and are best for those who are worried about safety in terms of the financial security of the issuer. The drawback is that Treasury bonds typically don't have higher rates than corporate bonds. But there is a trade-off. Corporate bonds give you higher interest rates, but they are not considered safer than Treasury securities.

Questions about bonds to ask AI

After you're set on bonds as an addition to your portfolio, drill down and ask about quality, bond rating, category, and type. Here are some example prompts about these concepts:

» "Please provide a list of bond categories in order of least risky to most risky with an explanation for each item."

» "Analyze and compare yields of government, corporate, and municipal bonds. Identify factors contributing to yield variations and potential opportunities for bond investors."

» "Assess the performance of fixed-interest corporate bonds versus adjustable-rate savings bonds in today's inflationary environment."

» "In a period of high inflation and high interest rates, how have investment-grade bonds performed versus low-rated, junk bonds?"

Bond resources

TIP

Here are some bond investing resources that you can start reviewing:

» Bonds Online (www.bondsonline.com)

» Treasury Direct (www.treasurydirect.gov)

» Best Bond Market Blogs and Websites (https://finance.feedspot.com/bond_market_blogs/)

Bank investments

With bank "investments," there are the following choices, all of which play a role in your overall wealth-building strategy:

» **Checking accounts:** These accounts provide a means of transacting, ranging from paying bills to funding investments.

>> **Savings accounts:** These accounts are a safe place to accumulate funds either for investment or for emergency fund purposes.

>> **Money market accounts:** These accounts provide a higher interest rate for a greater ability to accumulate funds for investment purchases.

>> **Certificates of deposits (CDs):** A CD is a fixed-term, interest-bearing bank account that offers you a higher interest rate in exchange for you locking in money for a specified time (such as six months, one year, or longer).

REMEMBER

Bank investments aren't the best suited for long-term growth, but they are excellent places to park your cash as you wait for opportunities.

Use Bing Chat and/or Google Bard to research and rank the top ten bank investments by currently available interest rates so you can shop for the best yields.

Cryptocurrencies

If you aren't familiar with cryptocurrencies, they were the craze just before AI. Simply stated, cryptocurrencies are decentralized digital or virtual currencies that use cryptography for security. They operate on a technology called blockchain, enabling secure, transparent, and peer-to-peer transactions outside traditional banking systems. Many (most?) investors still have uncertainties about cryptocurrencies, but those can be overcome with knowledge.

WARNING

Cryptocurrencies are a speculative consideration. Only consider them as opportunities for growth but with added risk.

Given that, use AI to guide you along the way. Here's my first prompt about cryptocurrencies to ChatGPT:

"What are cryptocurrencies?"

ChatGPT's response is in Figure 10-2.

As you can see in Figure 10-2, cryptocurrencies do have advantages over regular currencies. A huge advantage is that the supply is limited and (so far) cryptocurrencies are not being overproduced into oblivion — a condition that has happened far too often with conventional currencies that are managed (mismanaged?) by government central banks. Having a small portion (say, less than 5 percent) of your money in cryptocurrencies for the sake of diversification isn't a bad idea. Think long and hard about cryptocurrencies and whether they are worth putting your money in. Keeping a greater presence in traditional investment vehicles may be a better consideration until you gain knowledge and experience.

ChatGPT

Cryptocurrencies are digital or virtual currencies that use cryptography for security and operate on decentralized networks, typically based on blockchain technology. Unlike traditional currencies issued by governments and central banks, cryptocurrencies are decentralized and often operate on a technology called blockchain, which is a distributed ledger enforced by a network of computers, often referred to as nodes.

Key characteristics of cryptocurrencies include:

1. **Decentralization:** Cryptocurrencies operate on a decentralized network of computers, eliminating the need for a central authority like a government or financial institution. This decentralization is typically achieved through blockchain technology.
2. **Blockchain Technology:** Blockchain is a distributed ledger that records all transactions across a network of computers. It ensures transparency, security, and immutability of transaction data. Each "block" in the chain contains a list of transactions, and once a block is filled, it is linked to the previous block, forming a chain.
3. **Cryptography:** Cryptocurrencies use cryptographic techniques to secure transactions, control the creation of new units, and verify the transfer of assets. Public and private keys are essential elements in ensuring the security of cryptocurrency transactions.
4. **Limited Supply:** Many cryptocurrencies have a fixed supply or a predetermined issuance schedule, which can influence factors like inflation and scarcity. For example, Bitcoin has a maximum supply capped at 21 million coins.
5. **Anonymity and Pseudonymity:** While transactions are recorded on the blockchain, the identities of the participants involved in transactions are often pseudonymous. Users are identified by their cryptographic addresses rather than personal information.
6. **Global Accessibility:** Cryptocurrencies can be transferred and accessed globally without the need for intermediaries like banks. Transactions can be conducted 24/7, and funds can be sent and received across borders with relative ease.
7. **Volatility:** Cryptocurrency markets are known for their price volatility. The value of cryptocurrencies can experience significant fluctuations over short periods, presenting both opportunities and risks for investors.
8. **Use Cases:** Cryptocurrencies can serve various purposes, including as a medium of exchange, a store of value, and a unit of account. Some cryptocurrencies also enable the execution of smart contracts, self-executing contracts with the terms of the agreement directly written into code.

Bitcoin, created in 2009, was the first decentralized cryptocurrency, and since then, numerous other cryptocurrencies have been developed, including Ethereum, Ripple (XRP), Litecoin, and many more. Each cryptocurrency operates on its own underlying technology and may have unique features and use cases. The cryptocurrency ecosystem continues to evolve, with ongoing developments and discussions about its role in the broader financial landscape.

FIGURE 10-2: Defining cryptocurrencies.

TIP

For more assistance on this topic, check out the latest edition of *Cryptocurrency Investing For Dummies* by Kiana Danial (Wiley). Here are some great sites for learning about and researching cryptocurrencies:

>> Coinbase (www.coinbase.com)

>> CoinGecko (www.coingecko.com)

>> CoinMarketCap (www.coinmarketcap.com)

>> Crypto.com (www.crypto.com)

Central Bank Digital Currencies (CBDCs)

At the time of writing, there have been lots of rumbling about Central Bank Digital Currencies (CBDCs), and consumers and investors should get very familiar with (wary about?) them. CBDCs have the potential to be serious considerations for everyone.

In short, CBDCs are a digital form of a country's official currency issued by its central bank, offering a digital alternative to physical cash.

First, let's ask AI about what they are. I used this prompt:

"What are Central Bank Digital Currencies?"

Figure 10-3 shows ChatGPT's response. I like that ChatGPT went beyond just an explanation and provided a definitive list of features so you get a more complete understanding. I read the features and it seems to me that there aren't many pluses for consumers, but if society is forced to adopt this, consumers better learn as much as possible to find utility and value for themselves. Check out the resources at the end of this chapter to get informed.

ChatGPT

Central Bank Digital Currencies (CBDCs) are digital forms of a country's national currency issued and regulated by the central bank. Unlike cryptocurrencies such as Bitcoin or Ethereum, CBDCs are not decentralized and are issued and backed by a central authority, typically a country's central bank or monetary authority. CBDCs are considered a digital evolution of traditional fiat currencies.

Key features and aspects of Central Bank Digital Currencies include:

1. **Centralized Control:**
   - CBDCs are centralized digital currencies, meaning they are issued and regulated by the central bank or monetary authority of a country. This distinguishes them from decentralized cryptocurrencies like Bitcoin.
2. **Legal Tender:**
   - CBDCs are recognized as legal tender, just like physical banknotes and coins. They have the same status as traditional forms of money.
3. **Digital Representation of Fiat Currency:**
   - CBDCs are digital representations of a country's national currency. For example, 1 CBDC unit might be equivalent to 1 unit of the traditional fiat currency.
4. **Backed by the Central Bank:**
   - CBDCs are backed by the central bank, providing them with the same level of trust and confidence as physical currency. The central bank ensures the stability and value of the digital currency.
5. **Regulatory Compliance:**
   - CBDCs operate within the existing regulatory framework of a country, ensuring compliance with financial and monetary regulations.
6. **Integration with Traditional Banking System:**
   - CBDCs are designed to work seamlessly with existing financial infrastructure, including banks and payment systems. They can be used for various transactions, both between individuals and between financial institutions.
7. **Different Models:**
   - There are different models of CBDCs, including retail CBDCs and wholesale or interbank CBDCs. Retail CBDCs are meant for the general public, while wholesale CBDCs are designed for use among financial institutions.
8. **Privacy and Traceability:**
   - CBDCs can be designed with varying levels of privacy and traceability. Central banks need to strike a balance between privacy concerns and the need to prevent illicit activities such as money laundering.

FIGURE 10-3:
Defining CBDCs.

FIGURE 10-3:
(Continued)

9. **Potential Impact on Monetary Policy:**
   - The introduction of CBDCs may have implications for monetary policy. Central banks could have more direct control over the money supply and interest rates, potentially influencing economic conditions.
10. **Financial Inclusion:**
    - CBDCs have the potential to enhance financial inclusion by providing a digital form of currency that is accessible to a broader population, including those without access to traditional banking services.

Several countries and central banks are exploring or piloting CBDCs, with some already in the advanced stages of development. The motivations for introducing CBDCs vary and may include enhancing payment efficiency, reducing costs, and adapting to the evolving digital economy. The development of CBDCs is a significant area of interest and research in the field of central banking and monetary policy.

Figure 10-4 provides some benefits of CBDCs.

Of course, I had to ask ChatGPT the next question:

"What are the risks and negatives of CBDCs for consumers and investors?"

Figure 10-5 shows ChatGPT's response. The benefits listed are primarily and clearly for the government, but the benefits for consumers are vague.

WARNING

The public wasn't clamoring for a new way to track every penny of their financial picture (but the government loves this idea). It sees great value in watching (and potentially controlling) your transactions. Be wary: Find out as much as you can about CBDCs. You can use AI, of course, and the resources at the end of this chapter.

The bottom line is that CBDCs hold special risks for consumers and investors, so use AI to help you understand and navigate with them.

Here are a few additional resources to check out:

» Federal Reserve's CBDC FAQs (www.federalreserve.gov/cbdc-faqs.htm)

» Corporate Finance Institute's CBDC guide (https://corporatefinance institute.com/resources/cryptocurrency/central-bank-digital-currency-cbdc/)

» Nomad Capitalist's guide to CBDCs (https://nomadcapitalist.com/global-citizen/the-ultimate-guide-to-cbdcs/)

ChatGPT

While the specific benefits of Central Bank Digital Currencies (CBDCs) can vary based on their design and implementation, here are three potential key advantages for investors:

1. Enhanced Liquidity and Settlement Efficiency:

* CBDCs could contribute to enhanced liquidity in financial markets by facilitating faster settlement of transactions. The use of blockchain or distributed ledger technology may streamline settlement processes, reducing the time required for clearing and settlement. This increased efficiency can benefit investors by providing quicker access to funds and improving overall market liquidity.

2. Reduced Counterparty Risk:

* The transparency and immediacy of transactions enabled by CBDCs on distributed ledger technology may help reduce counterparty risk. Investors engaging in transactions may experience a lower risk of default, as the real-time settlement and clear record-keeping on the blockchain can enhance trust and security in financial transactions.

3. Access to Digital Securities and Innovative Financial Products:

* CBDCs can pave the way for the issuance and trading of digital securities on blockchain platforms. Investors may gain easier access to a broader range of assets, including tokenized stocks, bonds, and other financial instruments. Additionally, the introduction of CBDCs may stimulate innovation in financial products and services, offering investors new opportunities to diversify their portfolios and engage in novel investment strategies.

It's important to note that these benefits are illustrative, and the actual impact of CBDCs on investors will depend on various factors, including the specific features of each CBDC, regulatory frameworks, and the evolution of financial markets. Investors should closely monitor developments in the CBDC space and consider how these digital currencies align with their investment goals and strategies.

FIGURE 10-4:
The benefits
of CBDCs
according to AI.

ChatGPT

The introduction of Central Bank Digital Currencies (CBDCs) could have both benefits and risks for consumers and investors. While CBDCs offer potential advantages, it's essential to consider the potential downsides and risks associated with their use:

Risks and Negatives for Consumers:

1. **Privacy Concerns:**
   * CBDCs may raise privacy concerns as transactions could be traceable by central authorities. Consumers might be uncomfortable with the idea of their financial transactions being monitored, potentially infringing on personal privacy.

2. **Cybersecurity Threats:**
   * As digital assets, CBDCs are susceptible to cybersecurity threats such as hacking, fraud, and identity theft. Consumers may face risks related to the security of their digital wallets and the potential loss of funds.

3. **Dependence on Digital Infrastructure:**
   * The reliance on digital infrastructure means that consumers would need access to reliable internet connectivity and digital devices to use CBDCs. This may pose challenges for those in areas with limited technological access.

4. **Operational Issues:**
   * Technical glitches, system outages, or disruptions in digital infrastructure could impact the accessibility and availability of CBDCs, leading to potential operational issues for consumers.

5. **Financial Exclusion:**
   * Certain segments of the population, such as those without access to digital technology or those uncomfortable with digital transactions, may face challenges in adopting CBDCs, potentially exacerbating financial exclusion.

Risks and Negatives for Investors:

1. **Impact on Traditional Banking Sector:**
   * Investors in traditional banking institutions may see a reduction in the profitability of these institutions as CBDCs could lead to disintermediation, with individuals preferring to hold digital currency directly with the central bank.

2. **Interest Rate and Monetary Policy Risks:**
   * If CBDCs result in the effective lower bound on interest rates, as individuals may prefer holding CBDCs over bank deposits, investors could face challenges in the traditional monetary policy environment.

3. **Market Structure Changes:**
   * The introduction of CBDCs could alter the dynamics of financial markets, impacting the roles of traditional financial intermediaries and payment service providers. Investors in these sectors may need to adapt to changing market structures.

FIGURE 10-5:
The drawbacks of CBDCs according to AI.

4. **Increased Regulatory Scrutiny:**
   * Investors in the cryptocurrency and fintech sectors may face increased regulatory scrutiny as CBDCs are introduced. Regulatory changes could impact the business models and operations of these entities.

5. **Currency Exchange Risks:**
   * For investors engaged in cross-border transactions or currency exchange services, the adoption of CBDCs may introduce new complexities and risks associated with evolving regulatory environments and currency conversion mechanisms.

6. **Technology and Obsolescence Risks:**
   * Investors in technology firms and infrastructure related to CBDCs may face risks associated with rapid technological advancements. Obsolescence of existing technologies or the need for frequent updates could impact investment viability.

7. **Volatility and Market Uncertainty:**
   * The introduction of CBDCs may lead to increased market volatility and uncertainty, particularly in the cryptocurrency and traditional financial markets, as participants adjust to the new digital currency landscape.

It's important to note that the specific risks associated with CBDCs can depend on the design and implementation details of each central bank's digital currency initiative. Policymakers and regulators need to carefully address these risks to ensure the smooth integration and acceptance of CBDCs within the financial ecosystem. Investors and consumers alike should stay informed about the developments and implications of CBDCs in their respective financial landscapes.

FIGURE 10-5:
(Continued)

IN THIS CHAPTER

» **Determining whether real estate investing is right for you**

» **Keeping in mind two big real estate considerations**

» **Investing in real estate directly or indirectly with AI's help**

» **Thinking about REITs and REIT ETFs**

» **Coming up with prompts and looking at real estate resources**

Chapter **11**

Real Estate Investing

T he most common type of "hard asset" that is considered a diversification away from paper (and digital) assets is real estate. Whether you own a house, condo, and/or rental properties, real estate is a major part of many folks' financial picture. For everyone who is already a real estate investor, there are many more who want to be. Fortunately, AI can be a powerful addition to their real estate investing approach, as you find out in this chapter.

Knowing Whether You Have What It Takes to Be a Real Estate Investor

Some folks have the right attributes or qualities to be great entrepreneurs or to succeed in a given career, but some real estate investors are successful and some are . . . uh . . . not. Just because you're interested in real estate may not be enough for you to succeed. Then again, AI has the potential to improve your chances of success.

Let's ask AI a question in our first real estate prompt:

"What are the most important qualities of a successful real estate investor? And what type of person should not be a real estate investor?"

Figure 11-1 provides ChatGPT's answer to the first question and gives you the most common things you should be aware of in terms of potential success. You can review that list and see where you are weakest, then use AI to "drill down" and find out more to prepare yourself accordingly.

ChatGPT

Successful real estate investors often possess a combination of financial acumen, market knowledge, and personal characteristics. Here are some important qualities that contribute to success in real estate investing:

1. **Financial Literacy:** Successful investors understand financial concepts, such as cash flow, return on investment, and risk management. They are adept at analyzing deals, assessing potential profits, and managing finances effectively.

2. **Market Knowledge:** A deep understanding of the local real estate market is crucial. Successful investors keep track of market trends, property values, and economic indicators that can impact real estate.

3. **Risk Management:** Real estate investing involves risks, and successful investors are skilled at identifying and mitigating these risks. They have a risk management strategy and are prepared for market fluctuations.

4. **Networking Skills:** Building a network of contacts, including real estate professionals, other investors, and potential partners, can provide valuable insights, opportunities, and support.

5. **Patience and Long-Term Vision:** Real estate is often a long-term investment. Successful investors are patient and have a strategic, long-term vision. They understand that real estate values may appreciate over time.

6. **Negotiation Skills:** Negotiation is a key part of real estate transactions. Successful investors are skilled negotiators who can secure favorable deals, whether buying or selling properties.

7. **Adaptability:** The real estate market is dynamic and can change rapidly. Successful investors are adaptable and able to adjust their strategies based on market conditions.

8. **Discipline:** Discipline is essential for sticking to investment strategies, financial plans, and timelines. Successful investors avoid impulsive decisions and stay focused on their goals.

9. **Legal and Regulatory Knowledge:** Real estate transactions involve legal and regulatory aspects. Successful investors have a basic understanding of real estate laws and regulations to ensure compliance and protect their interests.

10. **Problem-Solving Skills:** Real estate investing comes with challenges. Successful investors are effective problem solvers, finding solutions to issues that may arise during the acquisition, management, or sale of properties.

FIGURE 11-1: Qualities of a successful real estate investor.

Figure 11-2 gives you ChatGPT's answer to the second question. Not everyone is geared for maximum success in a given enterprise or pursuit. Let AI give you the potential "land mines" before you proceed to minimize the pain — or help you understand that your chances of success are better elsewhere.

FIGURE 11-2: Who shouldn't be a real estate investor.

Given the information in Figures 11-1 and 11-2, are you up to the task? The great thing is that if you fall short on an item or two, you can use AI to fill in that weakness. You can literally use AI to thoroughly educate yourself. Many times, the weakness can be overcome with more knowledge, and AI is your instant teacher.

Noting Two Major Real Estate Considerations

REMEMBER

Before I get into the nitty-gritty of real estate investing and how AI can help you, let me remind you about the two universal truths of real estate investing:

>> **Location, location, location:** Yep, you saw that one coming. Whatever real estate you're investing in, the location is indeed a major consideration. Neighborhoods, towns, and so forth change all the time; good places go bad; bad places come back in style; but location is the first thing to research with AI.

>> **What type of real estate?** Real estate is very diverse. There are all types of real estate. The most successful investors get proficient with a type of real estate, and they stick to this vertical investment. What's that? You're successful with condos? Stick with condos. You're successful with office buildings for medical professionals? Great! But stick with that specific type of real estate. Become very expert and specialized so success is easier to achieve.

WARNING

Real estate investors get in trouble because they haven't done their homework with both location and with the type of real estate. The condo investor decides to invest in a manufacturing facility without realizing that it is an entirely different type of investment and requires more expertise. The bottom line is to stick to what you know.

Getting into Direct Real Estate Investing

The most common, traditional transaction for an investor is to find and acquire a real estate property (typically with a mortgage and a down payment) and then rent it out. Over time, the income from the renter(s) will pay the mortgage payment and real estate expenses such as real estate taxes, insurance, repairs, depreciation, and so forth.

WARNING

Direct real estate investing is considered the riskiest path. It requires knowledge and the necessary capital for a down payment and the ability to take on debt (mortgage).

But let's ask our AI friend about the advantages and disadvantages of direct real estate investing. Consider a prompt like the following:

> "What are the pros and cons of direct real estate investing? Please answer in bullet point style with an explanation of each line item."

First, the "pros" according to ChatGPT are in Figure 11-3. This is your chance to see whether direct real estate investing is in sync with your personal wealth-building goals.

And the cons according to ChatGPT are in Figure 11-4.

TIP

AI can help you avoid issues with the "cons" of real estate investing. In the issue regarding "legal and regulatory challenges," for instance, AI can help you with understanding and summarizing legal documents. ChatPDF (www.chatpdf.com) is a tool that helps you review an entire legal PDF document and give you analysis and summarization.

ChatGPT

Pros of Direct Real Estate Investing:

1. **Potential for High Returns:**
   * Explanation: Real estate has the potential for strong returns, especially through property appreciation and rental income.
2. **Control over Investment:**
   * Explanation: Investors have direct control over property decisions, including renovations, tenant selection, and overall management.
3. **Tax Benefits:**
   * Explanation: Real estate investors may benefit from tax advantages, such as mortgage interest deductions, property depreciation, and capital gains tax treatment.
4. **Diversification:**
   * Explanation: Real estate provides diversification within an investment portfolio, helping to spread risk across different asset classes.
5. **Leverage Opportunities:**
   * Explanation: Investors can use leverage by financing a portion of the property purchase, potentially amplifying returns if property values rise.
6. **Income Generation:**
   * Explanation: Rental income can provide a steady cash flow, serving as a source of passive income for investors.
7. **Inflation Hedge:**
   * Explanation: Real estate values often rise with inflation, providing a natural hedge against the eroding purchasing power of money.
8. **Tangible Asset:**
   * Explanation: Real estate is a tangible asset with intrinsic value, and investors can physically inspect and assess their investment.

FIGURE 11-3:
The advantages of direct real estate investing.

When folks dive in to a given topic, the glaring omission can be what negatives they don't see (or plan for). Say that you're unsure about maximizing the tax benefits of real estate. Now you drill down and ask AI about the tax benefits of real estate investing. Use prompts such as the following:

> "Please list the specific tax benefits of real estate in a bullet point style along with an explanation of each item."

Cons of Direct Real Estate Investing:

1. **High Initial Capital Requirement:**
   * Explanation: Purchasing real estate typically requires a significant upfront investment, limiting accessibility for some investors.
2. **Management Responsibilities:**
   * Explanation: Direct investors are responsible for property management, tenant issues, and maintenance, requiring time and effort.
3. **Market Sensitivity:**
   * Explanation: Real estate values are influenced by market conditions, economic factors, and regional trends, leading to potential volatility.
4. **Lack of Liquidity:**
   * Explanation: Selling real estate may take time, and the process can be more complex than selling liquid assets like stocks or bonds.
5. **Risk of Market Downturns:**
   * Explanation: Economic downturns can lead to declines in property values, impacting the overall value of the investment.
6. **Unpredictable Expenses:**
   * Explanation: Unexpected expenses, such as major repairs or property vacancies, can affect the financial performance of the investment.
7. **Limited Diversification:**
   * Explanation: Direct real estate investments are specific to a location and property type, limiting the diversification potential compared to broader investment portfolios.
8. **Legal and Regulatory Challenges:**
   * Explanation: Real estate transactions involve legal complexities, and investors may face challenges related to zoning laws, permits, and other regulatory issues.

It's important for potential real estate investors to carefully consider these factors and conduct thorough research before deciding to invest directly in real estate.

FIGURE 11-4:
Direct real estate investing's disadvantages.

You can also use AI to research the federal tax code to find and summarize relevant tax issues. You can use a prompt such as this:

> "Find the provision in the tax code for allowable depreciation methods."

Then when you find a property, you can feed the property data to AI, and it can calculate the depreciation expense and produce a depreciation schedule for all the years you're holding the property.

The responses in Figures 11-3 and 11-4 are good for starters. Use AI to drill down on each, especially the ones you aren't sure about. By the time you read this, there will likely be AI tools that specialize in the real estate market. Since so much of the real estate market is data-driven, AI is a natural for real estate investors.

TIP

Until you locate your real estate-related AI tool (use the resources in Appendix B), use timely AI-enhanced tools such as Bing Chat and Google Bard. They can help you scan real estate listings, research geographic areas, and crunch the property numbers.

Investing Indirectly in Real Estate

Yes, direct real estate investing isn't for everyone, so why not consider real estate investing through a group as a limited partner? If you want the benefits of real estate investing but without some of the hassles or responsibilities of property management, then this may be a better fit for you.

Let's ask AI about the pros and cons of indirectly investing in real estate:

"What are the pros and cons of investing in real estate limited partnerships? Please answer in bullet point style with an explanation of each line item."

The response is as follows (in text due to its length).

Investing in real estate limited partnerships (RELPs) involves participating in a real estate venture as a limited partner, typically with a general partner who manages the investment. Here are the pros and cons of investing in real estate limited partnerships, presented in bullet point style with explanations:

Pros:

1. Diversification:

Explanation: RELPs provide diversification because they often involve multiple properties or projects, reducing the risk associated with investing in a single property.

2. Professional Management:

Explanation: General partners in RELPs are typically experienced professionals who handle property management, acquisitions, and operations, relieving limited partners of direct management responsibilities.

3. Access to Expertise:

Explanation: Investors can tap into the expertise and industry knowledge of the general partner, potentially benefiting from their real estate experience.

4. Passive Income:

Explanation: Limited partners receive a share of the income generated by the partnership, typically through rental income or property sales, without the need for active involvement.

5. Tax Benefits:

Explanation: RELPs may offer tax advantages, including depreciation deductions, which can reduce taxable income and potentially result in tax savings for investors.

6. Reduced Risk Exposure:

Explanation: Limited partners have limited liability, meaning their financial exposure is generally limited to their initial investment, protecting them from significant losses.

7. Liquidity Options:

Explanation: Some RELPs offer liquidity options, allowing limited partners to sell their ownership interest to other investors or the general partner under certain conditions.

Cons:

1. Limited Control:

Explanation: Limited partners have limited control over the partnership's operations and decisions, as the general partner typically makes major decisions.

2. Illiquidity:

Explanation: RELP investments are typically illiquid, meaning investors may have limited opportunities to sell their ownership stakes or withdraw funds before the investment matures.

3. Potential for Losses:

Explanation: While limited partners have limited liability, they can still incur losses if the partnership underperforms or faces financial difficulties.

4. Fees and Costs:

Explanation: RELPs often involve management fees and profit-sharing arrangements, which can reduce the returns realized by limited partners.

5. Limited Transparency:

Explanation: Investors may have limited visibility into the day-to-day operations and financial performance of the partnership, relying on reports provided by the general partner.

6. Market Dependency:

Explanation: The success of RELP investments is dependent on the performance of the real estate market, which can be cyclical and subject to economic fluctuations.

7. Lock-In Periods:

Explanation: Many RELPs have lock-in periods during which investors cannot withdraw their capital, potentially tying up funds for an extended period.

Investing in real estate limited partnerships can be an effective way to gain exposure to real estate without the full responsibilities of property ownership. However, it's essential for investors to carefully evaluate the partnership structure, the reputation and track record of the general partner, and the specific terms of the investment before committing capital.

RELPs can be a great asset for experienced investors who have substantial portfolios. The income and capital gain potential can be substantial, but expertise and experience are at the forefront. The RELP investor would need to use AI in issues such as market research, real estate regulations, and tax issues.

Small investors, however, are much better off with publicly traded REITs and REIT-related ETFs and mutual funds (covered later in this chapter). In that case, small investors would use AI to research these publicly traded securities and not worry about the more complex and pricier issues that come with RELPs.

TIP

AI can scan documents (including PDFs and the like) as well as analyze and summarize the key points. Check out AI tools such as ChatPDF (www.chatpdf.com) and others found in Appendix B.

All the info in this section about real estate limited partnerships is fine. But my bias is with stocks and exchange-traded funds (ETFs), so I prefer to invest in REITs. What are those, you ask? Keep reading!

Trying Real Estate Investment Trusts

Real estate investment trusts (REITs) are my favorite way to invest in real estate. I like the advantages of real estate but coupled with the transactional ease and convenience of stock investing. We've all heard of horror stories with real estate investing — rotten tenants, burdensome closing costs, and the idea that buying or selling a property could be tough. In a slow market, it could take months to sell a property.

That is what makes a REIT so appealing. You can buy, or sell, with a few clicks on your laptop (or taps on your smartphone). So let's check them out. Here's a sample prompt for asking about REITs:

"What are the pros and cons of publicly traded real estate investment trusts? Please answer in bullet point style with an explanation of each line item."

ChatGPT's response is here in text (*and my comments are in italics*):

Publicly traded Real Estate Investment Trusts (REITs) are investment vehicles that allow individuals to invest in real estate-related assets through publicly traded shares. Here are the pros and cons of investing in publicly traded REITs, presented in bullet point style with explanations:

Pros:

1. Liquidity:

Explanation: REIT shares are traded on stock exchanges, providing investors with liquidity and the ability to buy or sell shares easily.

Comments: Liquidity is a major concern when you're investing directly in real estate, but REITs are just as tradeable and liquid as regular stocks and ETFs.

2. Diversification:

Explanation: REITs typically invest in a diversified portfolio of properties or real estate-related assets, reducing individual property risk.

Comments: A REIT typically has a portfolio of properties usually in various locations, so your fortune is not tied to a single property.

3. Passive Income:

Explanation: REITs are required by law to distribute at least 90% of their taxable income to shareholders in the form of dividends, providing a regular income stream.

Comments: Why work getting rent checks and paying bills? In a REIT, the money comes to you as dividends. Most are quarterly and some pay monthly.

4. Professional Management:

Explanation: REITs are managed by experienced professionals who handle property management, acquisitions, and operations, relieving investors of direct management responsibilities.

Comments: The company's executive management team runs all the operations. No one will call you about fixing a leaky roof.

5. Dividend Yield:

Explanation: REITs often offer attractive dividend yields, making them an appealing choice for income-focused investors.

Comments: As part of their tax-favored status as a REIT, it must disburse at least 90 percent of their net income to shareholders. This typically means higher-than-average dividends.

6. Transparency:

Explanation: Publicly traded REITs are subject to regulatory reporting requirements, providing investors with transparency regarding financial performance and operations.

Comments: Through the REIT's annual report, website, and so on, you see what is happening with performance and company operations.

7. Accessibility:

Explanation: Investing in REITs is accessible to a wide range of investors, including those with limited capital, as shares can be purchased in small increments.

Comments: You don't need to invest huge amounts to invest in a REIT. You can buy as many shares as you like or as you can afford.

8. Portfolio Growth:

Explanation: REITs have the potential for portfolio growth as they acquire additional properties or real estate assets, potentially increasing property values and income.

Comments: Your investment can grow as the REIT expands its property portfolio.

Cons:

1. Market Volatility:

Explanation: REIT prices can be subject to stock market volatility, and their performance may not always correlate with real estate market conditions.

Comments: Although REIT share prices can fluctuate along with the general stock market, REITs tend to rise and fall with factors tied to the real estate market much more so than with stocks.

2. Interest Rate Sensitivity:

Explanation: Rising interest rates can negatively affect REIT prices because higher rates can increase borrowing costs and reduce the relative attractiveness of REIT dividends.

Comments: Rising interest rates tend to be negative not only for REITs but for most real estate investing vehicles.

3. Management Fees:

Explanation: REITs often charge management fees, which can reduce the returns realized by investors.

Comments: The management fees are paid through the company's operations and that will impact aspects of the REIT such as the net income and the dividend payout.

4. Lack of Control:

Explanation: Investors in publicly traded REITs have limited control over the properties and assets in which the REIT invests, as decisions are made by the REIT's management.

Comments: As a REIT investor, you have limited ownership benefits. You do not have a decision-making capacity over company operations or the properties being bought, sold, and managed.

5. Tax Considerations:

Explanation: While REIT dividends are generally tax-advantaged, investors may still have tax implications to consider, such as potential capital gains taxes when selling shares.

Comments: Of course, gains are taxed. The dividends are also taxed at a higher rate than regular stock dividends since they are not qualified dividends, which have the most favorable tax treatment.

6. Market Dependency:

Explanation: The performance of publicly traded REITs is closely tied to the overall stock market, which can be influenced by macroeconomic factors and investor sentiment.

Comments: REIT shares can fluctuate in the ebb-and-flow of daily stock market trading.

7. Management Quality Variability:

Explanation: The quality of management can vary among different REITs, and investors must carefully assess the expertise and track record of the REIT's management team.

Comments: Yes, if you're ever dubious about how the REIT is managed, you can sell shares or add protective measures such as stop-loss orders and/or trailing stops, which are covered in Chapter 5.

8. Risk of Asset Class Concentration:

Explanation: Some REITs may specialize in specific property types (e.g., retail, office, residential), which can expose investors to concentration risk if that sector faces challenges.

Comments: This goes both ways: If that property type is doing well, you will do well; if that property type is doing poorly, so will your REIT investment. This beckons back to what I say earlier in this chapter about understanding the property type.

Investing in publicly traded REITs can be a convenient way to gain exposure to real estate markets while enjoying liquidity and dividend income. However, it's crucial for investors to understand the potential risks and benefits associated with specific REITs and assess how they fit into their overall investment strategy.

Comments: Nice summation!

TIP

Here are some sample prompts for investors regarding REITs:

>> "Which categories and types of REITs are safest for investors? Please list in a bullet point format with explanations for each."

>> "What are the negative aspects of REITs that specialize in Category X and are situated in rural areas?"

>> "Please summarize the following page of XYZ REIT located at [the REIT's web address]."

Examining Real Estate ETFs

So you want to get into real estate, but you're too skittish about direct real estate investing, and even REITs make you wince? No worries! I've got just the thing — just as easy as investing in REITs and perhaps the safest route to real estate investing: REIT ETFs. Here's a sample prompt to get you started:

"What are the pros and cons of real estate–related ETFs? Please answer in bullet point style with an explanation of each line item."

ChatGPT's response is as follows (in text due to its length):

Real estate-related Exchange-Traded Funds (ETFs) are investment funds that provide exposure to real estate assets and related companies. Here are the pros and cons of investing in real estate-related ETFs, presented in bullet point style with explanations:

Pros:

1. Diversification:

Explanation: Real estate-related ETFs typically hold a diversified portfolio of real estate assets, including real estate investment trusts (REITs) and real estate operating companies, reducing individual property risk.

2. Liquidity:

Explanation: ETF shares are traded on stock exchanges, providing investors with liquidity and flexibility to buy or sell shares throughout the trading day.

3. Ease of Access:

Explanation: Investing in real estate through ETFs is accessible to a wide range of investors, including those with limited capital, as shares can be purchased in small increments.

4. Professional Management:

Explanation: ETFs are managed by experienced professionals who make investment decisions and manage the underlying assets, relieving investors of direct management responsibilities.

5. Diversified Exposure:

Explanation: Real estate-related ETFs can provide exposure to various segments of the real estate market, including residential, commercial, industrial, and more.

6. Dividend Income:

Explanation: Many real estate-related ETFs offer dividend income, as they often invest in REITs, which are required by law to distribute a significant portion of their income to shareholders.

7. Transparency:

Explanation: ETFs are subject to regulatory reporting requirements, providing investors with transparency regarding their holdings, financial performance, and operations.

Cons:

1. Market Volatility:

Explanation: Like stocks, ETF prices can be subject to market volatility, which may not always correlate with real estate market conditions.

2. Risk of Tracking Error:

Explanation: ETFs may not perfectly replicate the performance of their benchmark index due to tracking errors or expenses, potentially affecting returns.

3. Management Fees:

Explanation: Investors in ETFs typically incur management fees and expenses, which can reduce the net returns realized by investors.

4. Interest Rate Sensitivity:

Explanation: Real estate-related ETFs can be sensitive to changes in interest rates, which can affect the performance of underlying assets like REITs.

5. Lack of Control:

Explanation: ETF investors have limited control over the composition and management of the ETF's portfolio, as decisions are made by the ETF's management team.

6. Tax Considerations:

Explanation: Tax implications, such as capital gains taxes, may apply when selling ETF shares, depending on individual circumstances and tax regulations.

7. Market Dependency:

Explanation: The performance of real estate-related ETFs is influenced by broader stock market conditions and can be subject to macroeconomic factors and investor sentiment.

8. Lack of Direct Ownership:

Explanation: ETF investors do not directly own the underlying real estate assets; instead, they hold shares in a fund that represents ownership interests in those assets.

Investing in real estate-related ETFs can offer diversification and liquidity, making it a convenient way to gain exposure to the real estate sector. However, investors should carefully assess the specific ETF's tracking error, fees, and underlying holdings to ensure it aligns with their investment objectives and risk tolerance.

TIP

Keep in mind that when you interact with AI, it can understand follow-ups to your prompts much like a conversation. You can continue with prompts such as "Using the above line items, please do a SWOT analysis of XYZ REIT and do so in a table format" or "What are REITs that have the same profile and are in the same category and how do they compare with XYZ REIT?"

For more information and resources on ETFs, check out Chapter 6.

Checking Out Additional Strategies for AI Real Estate Investing Prompts

AI can do so much for you. Here are some productive prompts for the real estate entrepreneur's consideration:

>> "Create an agreement for a landlord and a new tenant and include the following terms _____. Label and number each section."

>> "Provide a checklist of possible repairs necessary for a foreclosed property."

>> "Please create a legal letter for a delinquent tenant and add penalties such as _____."

>> "I will be doing an open house for a property I am selling. Give me a checklist of items I will need to address to ensure it is successful. Do it in bullet point style with an explanation of how and why I should do each item."

When creating prompts for real estate (or actually any topic), keep some points in mind:

>> Be specific — the more specific, the better.

>> Provide sample scenarios with details and numbers involved as part of your question.

>> Give yourself an identity to help you better understand AI's response, such as "answer me as if I am a high school student."

More ideas for prompts are in Chapter 18.

Consulting Real Estate Resources

Put on your AI armor and check out some of the best resources available on real estate investing. Here are some of my favorites:

>> Dummies.com (www.dummies.com) has a wealth of information on real estate investing along with more than half a dozen Dummies guides on various real estate investing topics.

>> To find and analyze properties across the country, check out real estate listing sites such as Zillow (www.zillow.com), Trulia (www.trulia.com), and Realtor (www.realtor.com).

>> For direct real estate investing and limited partnerships, check out the Metro Real Estate Investors Association (www.mreia.com).

>> Peace of Mind Real Estate Investing (www.peaceofmindrealestate.com) is run by one of my favorite real estate educators, David Corsi.

>> National Association of Real Estate Investment Trusts (www.nareit.com) is the leading site of information on REITs.

Chapter **12**

Business and Career Ventures

B usiness and career prospects are obviously connected to the broader finan-cial landscape. Think of the possibilities that AI can help you with in the twin worlds of business and career. Because AI is changing the game, you need to change yours, and this chapter can help. Consider the following:

» Start a business. It can (and should) be a part-time, home-based business to keep the costs and risks low and to add another dimension to your profes-sional profile and your wealth-building capabilities.

» Completely reassess your career/job situation. If the previous point is about your part-time pursuits (at least for now), then this is about your full-time income pursuits. Embrace AI to make yourself as indispensable as possible in your current job, or to make yourself more valuable for the next job.

Understanding the Benefits of Having Your Own Business

The following sections cover a number of reasons why you should consider having a business of your own. Keep reading!

REMEMBER

When you're an employee, you have to look over your digital shoulder to see whether AI is there to undermine you — or worse, replace you. This isn't the case when you're the boss of the enterprise. Your motivation here is how well is AI working for you instead of against you. AI is your first digital employee.

Earning income

Income is the most obvious reason. More income means more possibilities in your life. Sure, you can spend your income, but hopefully you'll save some for a rainy day (your emergency fund) and invest a chunk of it (to accelerate your journey to financial independence).

Enjoying tax benefits

A home business has powerful tax benefits. It has the power to save you thousands of dollars, year after year (see Chapter 16).

Just to whet your tax-saving appetite, a legitimate home business can qualify you to write off a portion of your rent (if you are a renter). If you're a homeowner, a home business gives you the power to write off a portion of your real estate taxes and some property maintenance costs. For both renters and homeowners, you may be able to deduct a portion of utilities and costs such as cleaning and repairs. IRS Publication 587 gives you full details; see www.irs.gov/pub/irs-pdf/p587.pdf.

Having fun

Choose a business in which you enjoy the activity, be it a product or a service. I don't just mean this as the reason you hear cited in motivational and inspirational books and videos. The greater reason is that when you enjoy an activity, you typically get better at it, and you have an easier time in persisting in the activity. Yes, enjoyment is critical to long-term success in your business pursuits.

REMEMBER

Enjoyment is also important for your business to have the financial potential to go from part-time to full-time (if that's a goal). Whenever you heard about that entrepreneur who went from a sideline business in their kitchen or their garage, the entrepreneur's passion is cited as the driving force that turned that fledgling enterprise into a huge, successful enterprise profiled in financial media.

Building wealth with your own retirement account

Yes, you should sock away whatever you can in your 401(k) plan through your current job and your individual retirement account, or IRA (Roth or traditional). But keep in mind that having your own business, even part-time from home, gives you the power to increase the amount you can set aside for your future retirement years. Here are some examples for you (the entrepreneur).

Simplified Employee Pension (SEP) plan

A SEP-IRA is available to anyone running a small business (with or without employees). Contributions are tax-deductible and made by the business owner. The tax-deductible limit for the employer and employee for 2024 is $68,000.

When you're a self-employed person with no employees, it is 25 percent of your net earnings from self-employment, less the following deductions:

>> One-half of your self-employment tax

>> Contributions to your own SEP-IRA

TIP

For more information on the deduction limitations for self-employed individuals, see IRS Publication 560, "Retirement Plans for Small Business," at www.irs.gov/pub/irs-pdf/p560.pdf.

Individual 401(k) plan

An individual 401(k) plan is suited for self-employed individuals or small business owners with no employees (other than a spouse). It allows both employer and employee contributions. The maximum contribution for 2024 is $69,000 (or $76,500 for those aged 50 and older).

TIP

Keep in mind that other rules govern retirement accounts, so discuss them with your tax advisor and, of course, research them with AI. More on taxes is in Chapter 16. For more information on solo 401(k) rules, check out www.irs.gov/retirement-plans/one-participant-401k-plans.

Selling your business for big money

After all the time, effort, and grief you put into your home-based business, the time will come when you cease to run the business. In that event, what better way to end than by receiving a huge amount from selling your business? What better way to boost your nest egg than by getting five or six or seven figures from the sale of your business?

When you create and manage a business, you're creating and managing an asset that potentially has great value. When you're ready to sell your business, check out the following sites where businesses are bought and sold every day:

>> BizBuySell (www.bizbuysell.com/)

>> Flippa (https://flippa.com/)

TIP

If you want to get a great price for your business later, ask AI right now what you need to do to get a good price. Consider a prompt with a question like "How can I get a million dollars for my business five years from now? Tell me what I need to do this year to garner that type of price for my business, which is home-based and is [describe your business]. Please provide a detailed plan." This way, it shouldn't be a mystery in how to sell your business for what it's worth down the road.

Starting a Business

When you're ready to launch your business, AI can help you in every facet — from research to creating necessary business documents. The following sections give you the scoop.

Doing some research

Researching is the big benefit from AI tools, and there is no need to provide lots of text here. Every single question or concern can be turned into a prompt to find answers. Use the AI-enhanced search engines listed in this chapter and in Appendix B.

To get you rolling, here are some prompt examples:

>> "I am launching a web design business from home. Please give me a complete marketing plan with action steps in a bullet point format with explanations and examples of each step."

>> "I am a handyman with expertise in carpentry. Give some 15 specific action steps I can do today to find customers this week."

>> "I am concerned about money. Please give me ten ideas of money-making activities I can start immediately in my area of interest, which is [topic]."

Putting together pieces of a business plan

If you have big plans for your business, a business plan is recommended. Obviously, if you're doing a side gig or a simple part-time activity, a business plan isn't that necessary. But for those who have intentions of ultimately having a large enterprise, a business plan is critical.

A useful exercise for you and AI in terms of your business and/or your competitors is a SWOT analysis, and most business plan templates include some form of this. Find out more about this analysis as well as marketing plans in the following sections. (For plenty of additional help, check out the latest edition of *Business Plans For Dummies* by Paul Tiffany and Steven D. Peterson, published by Wiley.)

A SWOT analysis

A Strengths (S), Weaknesses (W), Opportunities (O), and Threats (T) analysis can be very useful as you strategize to reach your business goals. Here is an example a prompt for ChatGPT:

> "I will be launching a one-person consulting practice in technology for the healthcare industry. Please provide a SWOT analysis and do so in a table format."

A SWOT analysis of your business helps you summarize the major points of strengths opportunities and catches what you may have missed when it comes to potential weaknesses and threats.

A marketing plan

In the world of business, I can boil down any enterprise no matter how large, small, or unusual to two phases:

>> Phase one is the "setup phase." This is the easy one. It means that you set up your enterprise for business. Choose your product or service, register it (proprietorship or incorporate, and so on), and get your "visuals" set up (business card, brochure, website, and so on). This phase was generally easy before AI and it is *much* easier now.

>> But phase two, that is the tough one. Because after you get set up for business, the next step is marketing — in other words, finding and attracting clients and customers.

The setup phase certainly comes first from a functional point of view. But a business is nothing without revenue (coming, of course, from customers). This is where the most important part of the business plan needs to shine: the marketing plan. When consultants and gurus tell you that salesmanship is important, that is correct. In the universe of marketing, salesmanship is the most important galaxy.

Here is a sample prompt I used on ChatGPT to get pointers on a business marketing plan:

> "What are the important elements of an effective marketing plan for a home-based technology consultant?"

The response was extensive, but here are the main elements. (You can ask your AI tool about each one for more details):

>> **Market research:** Understand your target market.

>> **Unique Value Proposition (UVP):** What sets you apart from competitors?

>> **Target audience segmentation:** Segment your audience and customize your approach to each.

>> **Goals and objectives:** Set clear, measurable, and attainable goals.

>> **Budget allocation:** Put together your budget.

>> **Online presence:** Create a blog and/or website.

>> **Content marketing:** Use quality content to attract prospects.

>> **Social media marketing:** Use social media to engage with prospects.

>> **Email marketing:** Develop your email list of prospects/clients.

>> **Networking and partnerships:** Who can you joint venture with?

>> **Online advertising:** Will you advertise online?

>> **Testimonials and case studies:** Showcase your happy clients.

>> **Referral program:** Can you set up your business for referrals?

>> **Tracking and analytics:** Monitor how well your marketing is doing.

>> **Feedback and improvement:** Learn from your customers about improving what you do.

>> **Long-term planning:** Develop a plan to keep your business growing.

TIP

All the preceding responses give you plenty to research. And don't stop there! Here are more ideas for useful prompts when it comes to marketing your new business:

>> "I am starting a drop-ship business on Amazon; please provide a detailed marketing plan in a bullet point, step-by-step approach."

>> "I am launching an online video course at my website. Please provide 20 specific marketing strategies and tactics that are free or low-cost to bring traffic to my course landing page."

>> "I invented a gasoline-powered elephant foot umbrella stand, and I want to market to hotels and motels. Please provide a complete marketing plan that provides specific and detailed step-by-step tactics and strategies."

TIP

A good source of no-cost and low-cost ideas is the extensive marketing course *Zero-Cost Marketing* designed for small businesses that have little or no money for marketing and advertising. Find out more at my site, www.ravingcapitalist. com/home/zero-cost-marketing/.

Funding your business

I'm a fan of everyone starting a business, and we live in a time that doesn't require a lot of money to get started. Many types of businesses can be done from home and with minimal (or no) funding. But if you need some funding, first ask AI. Here's a sample prompt:

"I am starting a business in the [choose industry or field] area, and I may need [$xxx] in funding. Please provide ten specific and creative ways I can obtain that funding."

TIP

Here are a couple of handy websites to consult as well:

>> The Small Business Administration (www.sba.gov) has extensive materials and content for you, and it's free (translation: You paid with your taxes). They have sample business plans, checklists, and business profile documents on many types of businesses. Go there and download what you need. AI can actually help you review their documents and help you analyze the information and answer your questions.

>> The Service Corps of Retired Executives (www.score.org) is a volunteer organization of retired business folks with much experience launching and managing a business so check them. You can usually do a free business consultation either in person or over the phone.

Steering your start-up with the help of AI

Successful businesses need a roadmap to get to a profitable destination. Need help deciphering such a map? Use AI with a prompt such as the following:

> "What can AI do for a person who's starting a business? Please list at least ten specific ways."

Figure 12-1 shows the response from ChatGPT. Just the fact that you have an instant action plan is itself a major good. Whether you need business startup ideas, resources, or a complete lesson in a specific skill (how to write a cold email and the like), you can get rolling in minutes when not so long ago, it took days to do the same groundwork.

What I like is that AI will actually help you do the task. In terms of web design, it can actually build an actual, useable web page instantly (once you feed it the text you want). Need to create a business plan, an analytical spreadsheet, or a press release? Do it without spending a lot (or anything at all) on services. The list in Figure 12-1 is a brief one; I originally asked for 25 specific ways AI can help. Everyone starting a business has strengths and weaknesses, so find what weaknesses/services that AI can help you with.

> **ChatGPT**
>
> Certainly! Here are 10 specific ways in which Artificial Intelligence (AI) can benefit a person starting a home-based business:
>
> * **Automated Customer Interaction:**
>   * Implement AI-powered chatbots to handle customer inquiries, provide information, and facilitate communication on your website.
> * **Social Media Management:**
>   * Utilize AI tools for social media management, including content scheduling, sentiment analysis, and audience engagement analytics.
> * **Personalized Email Marketing:**
>   * Use AI algorithms to analyze customer data and send personalized email campaigns, improving customer engagement and conversion rates.
> * **Virtual Assistance:**
>   * Employ AI-driven virtual assistants to manage administrative tasks, schedule appointments, and handle routine communications.
> * **Financial Tracking and Forecasting:**
>   * Implement AI-based financial tools for tracking expenses, managing budgets, and forecasting financial trends for better financial planning.

FIGURE 12-1: Ways that AI can help you with your new business.

- **E-commerce Recommendations:**
  - Integrate AI-powered recommendation engines for your e-commerce platform to suggest personalized product recommendations to customers.
- **Content Creation and Curation:**
  - Use AI tools to assist in content creation, from generating blog ideas to writing and editing content for your website or social media.
- **Website Optimization:**
  - Apply AI for website optimization, analyzing user behavior, and providing insights to enhance user experience and increase conversions.
- **Inventory Management:**
  - Utilize AI for automated inventory management, ensuring optimal stock levels, reducing costs, and preventing stockouts or overstock situations.
- **Cybersecurity Protection:**
  - Implement AI-driven cybersecurity solutions to protect your business data and customer information from potential threats and cyber attacks.

These AI applications can enhance the efficiency, productivity, and competitiveness of a home-based business. Depending on the nature of your business, selecting the right AI tools can provide valuable support and automation, allowing you to focus on growing your venture.

FIGURE 12-1:
(Continued)

Running Your Business

AI can really make a positive impact for you when it comes to running your business. The basic work functions come down to writing content or to performing clerical, computing, and administrative tasks for you. But you may have other options, as you find out in the following sections.

Getting help with your current software

Many businesses (big and small) still use software such as Excel, Word, Outlook, PowerPoint, Google applications, and other popular widely used software programs and online apps. AI can help you use them with greater ease and efficiency.

TIP

Use prompts such as these:

>> "I use MS Excel, and I have the full names of my customers in column A. How can I parse this data so that I have the customer's first name in Column B and their last name in Column C? Please explain in a step-by-step manner."

>> "I need to create a product description in Microsoft Word that is SEO-optimized for Amazon and that succinctly lays out the benefits and features of [product], which are [A, B, C, and D]."

>> "I will be doing a Zoom meeting and will need to create a PowerPoint presentation. Please take the following text and break it down into ten different panels: [Add your text here]."

Writing a variety of content

One of the immediate benefits of AI is its remarkable ability to produce written content in seconds. Consider the possibilities for your business:

>> Need a well-written post for your blog? How about writing a bio about you for your website?

>> AI can be your digital assistant and respond to generic inquiries. AI tools can now be programmed to serve as a customer service response vehicle and/or being an autoresponder during marketing campaigns.

>> Provide your AI tool with information on your product or service, and it can create advertisements that can be placed in venues such as Google, Facebook, Instagram, and other venues.

>> Press releases are common in the corporate world, and it is like free advertising. There are hundreds of press release distribution sites online (such as www.PRnewswire.com), but the press release must be done a certain way; fortunately, AI knows the way.

>> Create product descriptions like an Amazon pro? Yes, AI can do that for you as well. Virtually any writing assignment needed in the world of business can now be done with an AI tool.

>> Do you need to write an email to a cold prospect? Or write an email that sounds stern to a deadbeat that owes you money? Yes, AI can do that.

All these AI tools can be found through the resources listed in Appendix B.

Generating images

TIP

Need an image for social media or for your blog or website? How about creating a book cover for your new Kindle e-book or an appropriate image for your new course? AI tools like Midjourney (www.midjourney.com), DALL-E 2 (https://openai.com/dall-e-2), or other image-creation tools can be your cost-effective answer. Not too long ago, folks starting a business had to spend plenty on creating website visual images, brand logos, and brochure designs. Today AI can do it in seconds — and keep doing it until you create a visual you're pleased with. You can find more AI tools in Appendix B.

Seeing other ways that AI can help you run your business

The world of responses can be endless, and there isn't enough space for every possibility, but here is a quick list of business functions to get you started. First, here is my prompt:

> "Please provide a list of 25 specific business functions that AI can do for the small business owner. Provide them in a bulleted list and describe each function in full."

ChatGPT's response is shown in Figure 12-2. The tasks that AI can do for you is quite extensive. If you're someone who writes often, the fact that AI can instantly create useable blog posts is great — writer's block is a thing of the past. Services like creating personalized marketing campaigns will come in handy since marketing can be the most daunting tasks for newly minted entrepreneurs.

ChatGPT

Certainly, here is a list of 25 specific business functions that AI can perform for small business owners:

1. **Automated Customer Service:**
   - AI-powered chatbots and virtual assistants can handle routine customer queries, providing instant responses and improving customer satisfaction.
2. **Data Entry and Management:**
   - AI can automate data entry tasks, reducing manual errors and streamlining data management processes for small businesses.
3. **Personalized Marketing Campaigns:**
   - AI algorithms analyze customer data to create personalized marketing campaigns, increasing the effectiveness of targeted advertising efforts.
4. **Financial Forecasting:**
   - AI tools can analyze financial data to provide accurate and timely forecasts, helping small business owners make informed financial decisions.
5. **Inventory Management:**
   - AI systems optimize inventory levels by predicting demand patterns, reducing excess stock, and preventing shortages.
6. **Social Media Management:**
   - AI tools can schedule posts, analyze engagement metrics, and suggest content strategies for small businesses on social media platforms.
7. **Automated Email Marketing:**
   - AI-driven email marketing tools can personalize content, optimize send times, and analyze user behavior for more effective email campaigns.
8. **Fraud Detection:**
   - AI algorithms can detect unusual patterns and identify potential fraud in financial transactions, enhancing security for small businesses.
9. **Market Research and Insights:**
   - AI tools analyze market trends, competitor activities, and consumer behavior to provide valuable insights for strategic decision-making.
10. **Automated Bookkeeping:**
    - AI-powered accounting software automates bookkeeping tasks, including expense categorization, invoice processing, and financial reporting.
11. **Employee Recruitment and HR:**
    - AI assists in candidate screening, resume parsing, and even conducts initial interviews, streamlining the recruitment process for small businesses.
12. **Dynamic Pricing:**
    - AI algorithms adjust pricing based on real-time market conditions, competitor pricing, and demand fluctuations, optimizing revenue for small businesses.
13. **Automated Appointment Scheduling:**
    - AI-driven scheduling tools streamline appointment bookings, cancellations, and reminders, enhancing efficiency for service-oriented small businesses.

FIGURE 12-2:
A number of ways that AI can help you run a business.

14. **Speech Recognition for Transcription:**
    * AI-powered speech recognition tools convert spoken language into text, automating the transcription of meetings, interviews, and other audio content.

15. **Predictive Maintenance:**
    * AI analyzes equipment and machinery data to predict maintenance needs, reducing downtime and extending the lifespan of assets for small businesses.

16. **Expense Management:**
    * AI automates expense tracking, receipt scanning, and reimbursement processes, making financial management more efficient for small business owners.

17. **Natural Language Processing (NLP) for Customer Feedback:**
    * AI with NLP capabilities analyzes customer feedback, reviews, and sentiments, providing valuable insights for improving products and services.

18. **Supply Chain Optimization:**
    * AI optimizes the supply chain by forecasting demand, managing inventory, and improving logistics, ensuring smooth operations for small businesses.

19. **Automated Data Analysis:**
    * AI tools analyze large datasets quickly, extracting meaningful patterns and insights to aid in data-driven decision-making.

20. **Chat-based HR Support:**
    * AI-powered chatbots assist employees with HR-related queries, providing information on policies, benefits, and other HR matters.

21. **Facial Recognition Access Control:**
    * AI-based facial recognition systems enhance security by providing access control to premises, protecting physical assets for small businesses.

22. **Content Creation:**
    * AI-generated content tools assist in creating blog posts, articles, and marketing materials, saving time and resources for small business owners.

23. **IT Security Monitoring:**
    * AI monitors network activities, detects anomalies, and prevents cybersecurity threats, safeguarding small businesses from potential breaches.

24. **Energy Efficiency Management:**
    * AI analyzes energy consumption patterns to optimize usage, reduce costs, and improve the overall energy efficiency of small business operations.

25. **Predictive Analytics for Sales:**
    * AI predicts sales trends, identifies potential leads, and optimizes the sales pipeline, assisting small businesses in achieving higher conversion rates.

These AI-driven functions can significantly benefit small business owners by enhancing efficiency, reducing operational costs, and improving decision-making processes.

FIGURE 12-2:
(Continued)

Using AI to Boost Your Career

Adapt or die. This is what all the AI pundits may be telling every job holder out there. So what will you do? Adapt! There is a reason why I have both business and career pursuits in the same chapter.

If you have a job, whether your job is threatened by AI or not, you should have a business (part-time for now). Running a business makes you a decision-maker and puts you in the role of entrepreneur and (potential) employer. When you have a job where you work for someone else, your income is always dependent on that employer, and you need to be diversified away from the potential downside of that regular job.

Years ago, many labor observers thought that automation and robotics would seriously impact the blue-collar world. Yet fast forward to 2023, and all of a sudden, AI is causing the white-collar world to start sweating bullets.

REMEMBER

One of the primary differences between having a job and being an entrepreneur is that the job holder has to serve one client (the employer) while the entrepreneur has many clients. In the general world of work, you have to satisfy *someone* with the value of your service. Use AI to add value to what you can offer others, and it will ultimately benefit you. The following sections can help you get started.

Discovering the best jobs for your skills and experience

TIP

Before you tackle the job market, it pays to first find out about yourself. Put together a list of your critical skills and experience. Use AI to analyze this. Think about these types of prompts:

>> "I have the following skills of [list your skills] and I have *X* years of experience in the field of [list your field]. What type of job am I most qualified to do?"

>> "What types of jobs are best for workers who have the following skills and credentials: [list your skills]?"

>> "I enjoy doing the following activities and hobbies: [list your hobbies]. What types of jobs are suitable for people who enjoy these activities and hobbies?"

Use your imagination here. You would certainly get an unemotional response, and you could follow up and keep asking for more details and drill down to learn about yourself.

REMEMBER

Getting a job to earn money is a good pursuit, but getting a job you enjoy and are good at is a great pursuit. By the way, the preceding questions are good considerations for those trying to figure out what type of business is a good one to start. Find out more about starting a business with the help of AI earlier in this chapter.

Finding advice for your current job

Here is a question that may be on many employees' minds:

> "What should a person holding a full-time job do if they feel that AI will hurt their employment? Please provide advice in a bullet point style."

Here are the full bullet points provided by ChatGPT (all good considerations):

1. Stay Informed: Continuously educate yourself about AI and its applications in your industry. Understanding AI trends can help you anticipate changes.

2. Skill Development: Acquire new skills that are relevant and in-demand in the AI era, such as data analysis, machine learning, or programming. Consider online courses and certifications.

3. Adaptability: Embrace a growth mindset and be open to change. The ability to adapt and learn new technologies will be crucial.

4. Networking: Build a professional network within your industry and attend conferences or meetups related to AI and automation. Networking can lead to new opportunities.

5. Upskilling at Work: If your employer offers training or upskilling programs related to AI, take advantage of them to enhance your qualifications.

6. Diversify Skills: Develop a diverse skill set that includes both technical and soft skills. Soft skills like problem-solving and communication will remain valuable.

7. Explore New Roles: Investigate how AI can augment your current role rather than replace it. AI can often be a tool to enhance productivity rather than a direct threat.

8. Job Market Research: Keep an eye on the job market and identify emerging roles and industries that align with your skills and interests.

9. Entrepreneurship: Consider entrepreneurship or freelancing if you have a unique skill or business idea that can thrive in the AI-driven economy.

10. Career Resilience: Build career resilience by having a financial safety net, such as savings or investments, to cushion any employment disruptions.

11. Industry Shifts: Assess the direction your industry is taking regarding AI adoption. If it's on the path to significant automation, consider transitioning to a more AI-resistant sector.

12. Consult Career Advisors: Seek guidance from career advisors or mentors who can provide insights into navigating AI-related challenges.

13. Continuous Learning: Commit to lifelong learning. The pace of technological change means that staying current with new developments is essential.

14. Emotional Resilience: Cultivate emotional resilience to cope with uncertainty and job market changes. Support networks and stress management techniques can be beneficial.

15. Government Programs: Explore government-funded retraining programs or subsidies that may be available to help individuals transition to AI-impacted industries.

16. Consider Part-Time Education: If feasible, pursue part-time education while working to gain additional qualifications or credentials in AI-related fields.

17. Monitor Industry Trends: Stay updated on AI's impact within your specific industry. Sometimes, automation may create new roles that require human oversight.

18. Seek Feedback: Request feedback from supervisors and colleagues on how you can adapt your skills and contributions to align with changing job requirements.

19. Financial Planning: Evaluate your financial situation and create a budget that accounts for potential changes in income or employment status.

20. Stay Positive: Maintain a positive outlook and focus on the opportunities that AI can bring, such as increased productivity and innovation, rather than viewing it solely as a threat.

Remember that AI is a tool that can enhance human capabilities, and many roles will continue to require human skills and judgment. By staying proactive and adaptable, you can navigate the evolving job landscape and remain competitive in the AI era.

Not a bad list — a good start for your job-hunting (or career building) pursuits.

Researching new job opportunities

There's an AI for That is an example of a site that actually tracks the "Job Impact" of AI and lets you know (according to their analysis) to what extent AI will have on a given job. You can find it at https://theresanaiforthat.com/job-impact-index/.

At the time of this writing, their analysis indicates that jobs such as communications manager, data collector, and data entry can be replicated by AI up to 90 percent. If that is true — and it likely is — then folks in those jobs would be at risk. If a company had ten data-entry clerks, for example, this "Job Impact Index" suggests that nine of those ten specific positions would be at risk.

The point is obvious: If your work is easily replicated by AI, then start adapting or changing careers before that potential layoff hits you.

On the brighter side, it's critical to see what job opportunities will arise due to the impact of AI. Here is a question I posed to AI (specifically, the AI-enhanced Bing search engine):

> "Where are the AI-related job opportunities in today's labor market? Please answer in bullet point style and describe each one in detail."

Here is Bing's response (at the time of writing):

> Searching for: AI-related job opportunities in today's labor market
>
> Generating answers for you . . .
>
> Certainly! Here are some AI-related job opportunities in today's labor market:
>
> **Medicine:** AI has the potential to revolutionize healthcare by assisting doctors in diagnosing diseases, analyzing medical images, and predicting patient outcomes.
>
> **Law:** AI can help automate legal research, contract analysis, and document review, thereby increasing efficiency and reducing costs.
>
> **Art:** AI is being used to create original artwork, generate music, and even compose poetry.
>
> **Retail:** AI can improve customer experience by providing personalized recommendations and optimizing supply chain management.
>
> **Film:** AI is used in video editing, visual effects, and animation to enhance creativity and streamline production.
>
> **Tech:** AI professionals are needed to develop new algorithms, design intelligent systems, and ensure ethical use of AI technologies.
>
> **Education:** AI can personalize learning experiences, automate administrative tasks, and provide intelligent tutoring systems.

Agriculture: AI can optimize crop yield, monitor soil health, and automate farming processes.

Please note that these are just a few examples of how AI is transforming various industries. The impact of AI on the labor market is vast and evolving rapidly. Exciting opportunities await those interested in exploring the potential of artificial intelligence!

Is there anything else I can assist you with?

Note: Keep in mind that the preceding specific industries mentioned by Bing were hyperlinked so that when you click (or tap) those items you can get more details on that specific industry or job-related issue.

Even in the world of jobs and careers, "supply and demand" come first as a prerequisite for your job-hunting success. If you want to be supplied a job, go where the demand is. Use AI-enhanced search engines like the following to start your job search today:

>> AI-enhanced Microsoft Bing search engine: www.bing.com/chat

>> Google's Bard: www.google.com/bard

>> Phind: (www.phind.com)

>> You.com: (www.you.com)

More AI-enhanced search engines are found in Appendix B.

Creating a winning resume

One of the best uses of AI is to help you with your resume (or bio if it is for your business). It's easier than you think, and it can be done at no charge. Here are some steps to follow:

1. **List your skills and experience in a Word doc. Put them in chronological order and provide details.**

2. **Head over to ChatGPT (for example) or the AI tool of your choice.**

3. **Copy and paste the text from your Word document and put it in the AI tool, and then prompt for ways to improve your resume.**

Here are some ways to do the prompt:

>> "I have been a data-entry clerk for ten years in the automobile manufacturing industry. Please create a resume based on the skills I am listing here: [list of skills]."

>> "Assume that you are an executive recruiter giving me guidance on finding a new job. Based on the resume (or CV) I am providing, please provide a step-by-step action plan on doing an effective job search during the next 30 days."

>> "I am a customer service assistant manager in a hospital, and I would like a promotion to manager. What are the 20 specific steps I need to do in the next 60 days to help me accomplish this?"

REMEMBER

Crafting your prompt is very important for you to get useful, actionable ideas and strategies from ChatGPT and other AI tools. Be specific and provide as much detail as possible. Don't forget to use techniques such as assuming roles (for example, "You are the head of the HR department, and you are advising me. . ."). Don't just ask a question; where appropriate, ask for a type of response (for example, "Provide a step-by-step approach with details"). Head to Chapter 2 for an introduction to AI prompts.

Honing your interviewing skills

TIP

Given that AI can be so interactive, it comes in handy to sharpen your interviewing skills. Here are some prompts to use to gain some interviewing insights and outperform your peers:

>> "I will be interviewed by [company] that is in the [industry]. What questions should I expect? What should I know about them?"

>> "I will be interviewed by [company] that is in the [industry]. What questions should I ask?"

>> "Make believe that you are the interviewer and you are looking at my resume. What questions would you ask me? Here is the text from my resume [resume text]."

>> "I have a gap in my resume between job *A* and job *B*. How can I explain that?"

>> "Here is the link to the LinkedIn profile of my interviewer. What are the important aspects of this person?"

>> "Please help me create a professional email response to my interviewer with a proper thank you."

By now you will think of a hundred more questions, and AI is ready for you. For more on AI tools, check out Appendix B.

4

Smart Investment Tactics

Find out how AI can greatly simplify economic analysis for you.

Get the scoop on financial planning and budgeting ideas with AI.

See how AI makes retirement and estate planning much easier.

Handle tax issues related to investments with AI.

Chapter **13**

Using AI for Economic Analysis

U nderstanding the economy and financial markets may sound too unwieldy to deal with, especially when you hear the mind-numbing jargon that comes with the topic. But you should grasp some of the major points covered in this chapter because the good and bad of the economy's moves will have a huge impact on your financial life — your investments, business, career, retirement, and other life issues depend on how you navigate it.

Fortunately, you've got AI and lots of positive possibilities than can go with it. Imagine if you had learned about what was happening with the economy in 2007 and made some moves that would've avoided the pain of 2008.

Gross Domestic Product (GDP)

REMEMBER

Gross Domestic Product (GDP) is essentially the gross output of goods and services by the nation over a given period or time, typically quarterly and annually. If this number is growing, it's a net positive for the country, and it bodes well for the stock market. If the number is flat or shrinking, it bodes poorly for the country and is not considered a positive for the stock market.

Defining GDP

First, let's get AI's take on this (I used ChatGPT). Here is the question (prompt):

"What is GDP and what are the key points that investors should know about it? Please provide answers in detailed bullet points with an explanation of each."

ChatGPT's response is in Figure 13-1 (drumroll please).

 ChatGPT
Gross Domestic Product (GDP):

GDP is a critical economic indicator that measures the total value of all goods and services produced within a country's borders over a specific time period. It serves as a comprehensive gauge of a nation's economic health and performance.

Key Points for Investors:

1. **Definition and Components:**
   * **Explanation:** GDP is the sum of consumption, investment, government spending, and net exports (exports minus imports). It can be expressed as GDP = C + I + G + (X - M), where C is consumption, I is investment, G is government spending, X is exports, and M is imports.

2. **Three Approaches to Calculating GDP:**
   * **Explanation:** GDP can be calculated using the production approach (sum of value-added), income approach (sum of incomes earned), and expenditure approach (sum of expenditures).

3. **GDP Growth Rate:**
   * **Explanation:** The percentage change in GDP from one period to another indicates economic growth or contraction. Positive growth rates are generally favorable for investors as they suggest a growing economy, while negative growth rates may signal economic challenges.

4. **Leading Indicator of Economic Health:**
   * **Explanation:** GDP is considered a leading indicator of a country's economic health. Investors often use GDP data to assess the overall direction of an economy and make informed decisions about investment strategies.

5. **Impact on Financial Markets:**
   * **Explanation:** GDP data releases can influence financial markets. Higher-than-expected GDP growth can lead to positive investor sentiment, driving stock markets higher. Conversely, lower-than-expected growth may lead to market declines.

FIGURE 13-1:
Explaining GDP.

---

6. **Sectoral Analysis:**
   * **Explanation:** Investors should consider the sectoral composition of GDP. A growing economy may not benefit all sectors equally. Analyzing which sectors are driving GDP growth can guide investment decisions, as certain sectors may outperform others.

7. **Inflation and GDP:**
   * **Explanation:** Inflation is a key factor influencing GDP. Investors should consider real GDP (adjusted for inflation) to understand actual economic growth. Inflationary pressures can erode the real purchasing power of consumers and impact investment returns.

8. **Employment Implications:**
   * **Explanation:** GDP growth is closely linked to employment trends. Robust economic growth tends to lead to job creation, which can positively impact consumer spending and corporate profitability.

9. **International Comparisons:**
   * **Explanation:** Investors often compare GDP growth rates across countries to identify investment opportunities. Countries with strong and stable economic growth may attract foreign investment, while slowing growth rates could raise concerns for investors.

10. **Recession Indicators:**
    * **Explanation:** A decline in GDP for two consecutive quarters is often considered a technical recession. Investors should be aware of recessionary signals, as they can impact various asset classes and investment strategies.

Understanding GDP and its implications is crucial for investors as it provides a broad overview of a country's economic performance, helping them make informed decisions about asset allocation, risk management, and overall investment strategies.

▢ ♡ ♀ ↻

FIGURE 13-1:
(Continued)

The breakdown of GDP in Figure 13-1 is a good one. The primary points to keep in mind is that GDP is the overarching aggregate of what an economy produces and that it is a leading economic indicator. This means that when the economy is expanding today, it bodes well (more growth and potential prosperity) for tomorrow. Given that, GDP is a generally positive harbinger for the stock market. Why? When the economy grows, businesses tend to grow and become more profitable. If profitability grows, the value of the enterprise grows, which tends to have a positive effect on the stock of that particular enterprise (if it is a public company).

Delving into the details

When you have a grasp of the "big picture" on GDP, you can get more specific with investment ideas so you can drill down and narrow your search for appropriate strategies. Here's another prompt for example:

> "List five specific investments that do well when GDP is rising and explain why for each one."

Figure 13-2 gives you the scoop from ChatGPT. As the GDP expands, those things dependent on a growing GDP (such as businesses) tend to do well. In this regard, the stock of companies that are public tend to do well. This is why stocks in general are listed as a specific investment that will do well. Figure 13-2 also points out a subset of stocks called "cyclical stocks," which is a reference to the stocks of companies that do well when GDP is growing such as travel, hospitality, and restaurant companies. When consumers do well and the economy is growing, they tend to spend more on discretionary items such as eating out, entertainment, and so forth.

Then we do the obvious next prompt, because what goes up must come down.

> "List five specific investments that do well when GDP is declining and explain why for each one."

In Figure 13-3, ChatGPT answers my prompt. GDP doesn't rise all the time; that is part of the general ebb and flow of the overall economy. When GDP is down and/or shrinking (recessionary), consumers and businesses behave differently, so investors need to notice and adjust their investing strategies accordingly. When the economy is nearing or in a recession, general spending turns downward. Because consumers pull back their spending in general and consider buying only necessities, sectors such as utilities and consumer staples (considered defensive sectors) tend to hold their value. Given that, investors reduce their exposure from "wants" (consumer discretionary) and shift to investments that benefit from continued spending in "needs" (such as utilities and consumer staples).

Oh sure, I could've tormented this AI tool and asked for 47 investment tactics and ideas, but then I would have driven my editors nuts. In your case, go to town! Ask for ten or more great investment ideas given that particular economic scenario, and you'll have plenty to discuss with your financial advisor. But it also makes for a good checklist to match up with your portfolio choices. Additionally, the choices that AI brings to your attention can be used for your particular style.

ChatGPT

When GDP is rising, it generally indicates a growing and healthy economy. Certain investments tend to perform well in such environments due to increased consumer spending, corporate profits, and overall economic activity. Here are five specific investments that often do well when GDP is rising, along with explanations for each:

1. **Equities/Stocks:**
   * **Explanation:** Rising GDP is associated with increased corporate profits and business expansion. As companies grow and generate higher earnings, stock prices tend to rise. Investors often find equities attractive during periods of economic expansion, as companies benefit from increased consumer demand and improved business conditions.

2. **Cyclical Stocks:**
   * **Explanation:** Cyclical stocks are tied closely to economic cycles. Industries such as manufacturing, technology, and consumer discretionary are examples of sectors that tend to perform well during economic expansions. As GDP rises, consumers and businesses are more likely to spend on discretionary items, boosting the earnings of cyclical companies.

3. **Real Estate:**
   * **Explanation:** A growing economy often leads to increased demand for real estate. As businesses expand, they may require more office space, and consumers may seek new homes or commercial properties. Real estate investments, including real estate investment trusts (REITs), can benefit from rising property values and rental income during periods of economic growth.

4. **Commodities:**
   * **Explanation:** Commodities, such as industrial metals and energy, are positively correlated with economic activity. When GDP is rising, there is usually an uptick in demand for raw materials and energy to support increased production and construction. Investing in commodities or related industries can provide a hedge against inflation and benefit from higher demand during economic expansions.

5. **Financial Stocks:**
   * **Explanation:** Financial institutions, Including banks and insurance companies, often thrive in expanding economies. As GDP rises, interest rates may also increase, allowing financial institutions to earn higher profits on lending activities. Additionally, a growing economy typically leads to increased demand for financial services, further benefiting the financial sector.

It's important to note that while these investments often perform well during periods of economic expansion, they also come with risks, and market conditions can vary. Diversification, thorough research, and consideration of individual investment goals and risk tolerance are essential when making investment decisions. Additionally, economic conditions can change, and investors should stay informed about macroeconomic indicators and trends that may impact their investment portfolios.

FIGURE 13-2: Investments to consider when GDP is rising.

ChatGPT

When GDP is declining, it often signals economic challenges such as a recession or economic contraction. During these periods, investors may seek investments that can provide relative stability or even outperform in the face of economic headwinds. Here are five specific investments that tend to perform well when GDP is declining, along with explanations for each:

1. **Government Bonds (Treasury Bonds):**
   * **Explanation:** During economic downturns, central banks often implement monetary policies to stimulate the economy. This may include lowering interest rates. As a result, the prices of existing government bonds rise, and yields fall. Investors flock to government bonds seeking safety and stable returns during periods of economic uncertainty.

2. **Gold and Precious Metals:**
   * **Explanation:** Precious metals, particularly gold, are often viewed as safe-haven assets. When GDP is declining, and there's economic uncertainty, investors may turn to gold as a store of value. Gold tends to perform well during times of financial instability, serving as a hedge against inflation and currency devaluation.

3. **Utilities Stocks:**
   * **Explanation:** Utilities are considered defensive stocks because the demand for essential services like electricity, water, and gas tends to remain relatively stable even during economic downturns. Companies in the utilities sector often have regulated pricing structures, providing a degree of income stability for investors.

4. **Consumer Staples Stocks:**
   * **Explanation:** Companies producing consumer staples, such as food, beverages, and household products, tend to see consistent demand regardless of economic conditions. People still need to purchase everyday essentials even during a recession. As a result, consumer staples stocks are considered defensive investments that can provide more stable returns during economic downturns.

5. **Healthcare Stocks:**
   * **Explanation:** The healthcare sector is often less sensitive to economic cycles. Regardless of economic conditions, people require medical services, pharmaceuticals, and healthcare products. Healthcare companies, including pharmaceutical and biotech firms, may exhibit resilience during economic downturns, making them attractive to investors seeking defensive positions.

It's crucial to note that while these investments may be relatively more resilient during economic declines, they are not entirely immune to market fluctuations, and individual performance can vary. Diversification across different asset classes and regular reassessment of investment strategies based on evolving economic conditions are essential components of a well-rounded investment approach. Additionally, investors should stay informed about macroeconomic indicators and consider seeking advice from financial professionals when making investment decisions.

FIGURE 13-3:
Investments to consider when GDP is declining.

TIP

Vary your prompt. Instead of just asking about good investment ideas during general economic growth (a rising GDP), get more focused and personal with a prompt like this:

"I am 55 years old, still employed, and I am seven years away from my retirement target date. The GDP is growing nicely, but I am risk averse. Please provide a list of ten conservative income investing strategies and list them in order of safety."

REMEMBER

The bottom line is that your strategies should generally be bullish and growth-oriented during times of GDP increases while your strategies should be bearish and more cautious/defensive when the GDP is declining.

The Labor Market

When the economy is growing, this bodes well for jobs since a growing economy means expanding job opportunities, which is a very good thing for both the economy and the financial markets. Let's get some answers about the labor market as it relates to investing from ChatGPT. Check out this prompt:

"What types of investment strategies tend to do well when the labor market is strong? Secondly, what investment strategies should be considered when the labor market is weak and there is high unemployment? Please provide the answer in a bullet point style along with an explanation for each point.

The first part of ChatGPT's response about a strong labor market is in Figure 13-4. Seasoned investors and portfolio managers who are forward-thinking ask themselves, "What investments will benefit from this type of labor market?" Labor markets are strongly correlated to the housing sector. When the labor market is robust, the housing sector benefits, so housing-related investments tend to do well.

Strong labor markets are also bullish for stocks in general since more working people means more spending which, in turn, means better results for those businesses that profit from this, and their stock tends to go up in due course.

Figure 13-5 has more information from ChatGPT about investments in a weak labor market. Again, here is where folks start learning about cause and effect with interrelated areas. Weak labor markets tend to occur when the economy is stagnant and declining. Lower economic growth ultimately means fewer jobs. A weak economy and a weak jobs market means much less spending on "wants" but continued spending on "needs."

ChatGPT

Investment Strategies for a Strong Labor Market:

1. **Equity Investments:**
   - **Explanation:** A robust job market often correlates with increased consumer spending and corporate profitability. Equity investments, especially in sectors sensitive to consumer behavior (e.g., technology, consumer discretionary), may benefit from strong employment levels.

2. **Cyclical Stocks:**
   - **Explanation:** Industries such as manufacturing, construction, and technology, which are sensitive to economic cycles, tend to perform well when the labor market is strong. Consumer confidence and spending are typically higher, driving earnings for companies in cyclical sectors.

3. **Real Estate:**
   - **Explanation:** A strong labor market supports housing demand as people feel more confident about making home purchases. Real estate investments, including residential and commercial properties, may experience increased demand and potentially appreciate in value.

4. **Consumer Discretionary Stocks:**
   - **Explanation:** With more people employed and earning stable incomes, consumer discretionary spending tends to rise. Companies in this sector, which offer non-essential goods and services, may see increased sales and higher stock prices during periods of strong employment.

5. **Small-Cap Stocks:**
   - **Explanation:** Small-cap stocks often benefit from a strong labor market as these companies are more domestically focused. With increased consumer spending and economic optimism, small-cap stocks may outperform their larger counterparts.

FIGURE 13-4:
Investments for a strong labor market.

WARNING

The ChatGPT responses in Figures 13-4 and 13-5 were real-time answers at the time of writing, and I think that generally the responses are good and the information appropriate for most investors, but AI is changing rapidly. The response you get from ChatGPT in your time will see a significantly different response. Additionally, different AI tools may generate very different responses.

Because more specialized AI tools are getting developed virtually every day, look to reviews of various tools and stick to AI tools that specialize in financial subject matter since a more suitable array of specialists will have given their input regarding useful responses.

TIP

Check out Appendix A for resources that review AI tools and educate users. Then find those AI tools in Appendix B. Just to take this a step further, the general investment-related resources in Appendix C will very likely test and review many finance-related AI tools.

Investment Strategies for a Weak Labor Market and High Unemployment:

1. **Government Bonds:**
   - **Explanation:** In times of economic uncertainty and high unemployment, investors often seek safety in government bonds. The fixed-income nature of bonds provides a reliable income stream, and government bonds are considered lower-risk assets.

2. **Defensive Stocks:**
   - **Explanation:** Defensive stocks, such as those in the utilities and healthcare sectors, may be more resilient during economic downturns. These sectors offer essential services that people continue to use even in challenging economic conditions.

3. **Dividend Stocks:**
   - **Explanation:** Companies with a history of stable dividends may be attractive to investors during times of high unemployment. Dividend payments can provide a consistent income stream, and dividend stocks are often perceived as more stable investments.

4. **Gold and Precious Metals:**
   - **Explanation:** Precious metals like gold are considered safe-haven assets. During economic uncertainty and high unemployment, investors may turn to gold as a store of value and a hedge against inflation and currency devaluation.

5. **Quality Bonds and Defensive Funds:**
   - **Explanation:** Quality bonds with strong credit ratings and defensive mutual funds can provide stability in a weak labor market. These investments may focus on sectors less affected by economic downturns and prioritize capital preservation.

It's important to note that these strategies are generalizations, and individual circumstances may vary. Market conditions, economic indicators, and geopolitical factors should be considered when crafting an investment strategy. Diversification and periodic reassessment of investment goals and risk tolerance are crucial components of a well-rounded investment approach in any economic environment. Additionally, seeking advice from financial professionals can help tailor strategies to individual needs and goals.

FIGURE 13-5: Investments for a weak labor market.

Income Taxes

Whatever taxes you personally pay (see Chapter 16), keep in mind that national tax policy does indeed have an impact on your investing and financial success. In this case, I focus on income taxes levied on productive activity. I distinguish income tax from taxes that are levied on consumption, such as sales taxes or value added taxes (VAT). Taxes do indeed impact activity, and you can use AI to help you understand how taxes

>> Affect the economy and the financial markets

>> Hurt or help industries, which affect any related company or fund (ETF or mutual fund) you are investing in

>> Affect your investing success (such as capital gains taxes)

>> Affect your ability to produce income

>> Affect your long-term goals such as retirement planning, your estate, and so forth

High taxes — especially income taxes — do have a tangible (negative) effect on general economic health. People (especially financial and economic pundits) need to understand the correlation. Some of the most infamous downturns in the economy (both in the United States and across the globe) were preceded by higher costs, leaving consumers and businesses with less money to spend on their personal priorities. Check out Chapter 16 for ideas and resources (and AI prompts) on tax strategies, and many of the investing resources listed in Appendix C also cover taxes.

This is where using ChatGPT to look at history can come into play to help you with your overall strategies. In the past hundred years or so, we have learned that economies tend to do well during periods of low or falling tax rates. The reverse also tended to be true: High or rising tax rates tended to have a negative effect on overall economic growth.

TECHNICAL STUFF

When the Kennedy tax cuts were enacted in the early 1960s and the Reagan tax cuts took hold in 1981, both events ignited strong economic growth and rising stock markets. Conversely, when taxes were raised during the early 1930s and the early 1940s, this negatively impacted both the economy (the Great Depression) and the financial markets.

Interest Rates

REMEMBER

Interest rates have a major impact on both the economy and the financial markets:

>> Rising interest rates can increase the cost of borrowing, make large purchases more difficult, and have a negative impact on both the stock market and on some types of bonds (such as fixed-interest rate, long-term bonds).

>> When interest rates are lowered, this in turn has a positive impact on the economy and the financial markets.

Given how powerful an effect interest rates can have, it behooves investors to use AI to find out the effects to make better investing decisions. Here is a prompt to consider:

"What should investors know about interest rates? Please provide answers in detailed bullet points with explanations for each item."

I won't provide that answer here — that is your homework. The answer I received listed 15 items. Among them are "Rising interest rates have an adverse effect on stocks and fixed-interest rate debt instruments."

Let's switch to some targeted prompts about investment strategies and interest rates. For example:

"What are five investing strategies an investor should consider during a period of rising interest rates?"

Figure 13-6 from ChatGPT shows some vehicles that can benefit from rising interest rates. Short-term debt vehicles (such as money market accounts) and adjustable-rate vehicles (such as EE savings bonds) are suitable. Ask AI for an extensive list of investments and funds that reflect these types of vehicles.

Consider a prompt like the following to ask about declining rates:

"What are five investing strategies an investor should consider during a period of falling interest rates?"

Figure 13-7 is from ChatGPT. When interest rates are declining, you should think of the beneficiaries. As consumers seek alternatives to vehicles that benefit from declining interest rates, they tend to shift money to stocks (since lower interest rates mean declining costs on borrowed funds by companies) in general. Also, dividend stocks tend to do well since dividends tend to become an attractive alternative to vehicles that produce lower interest income.

TIP

All these items in Figures 13-6 and 13-7 are valid ideas, and now you need to either discuss them with your spouse or financial advisor, or drill down with AI to get more details (or, even better, all of the above).

ChatGPT

When interest rates are rising, investors often need to adjust their strategies to navigate the changing economic landscape. Here are five investing strategies that investors may consider during a period of rising interest rates, along with explanations for each:

1. **Shift Toward Short-Term Bonds and Cash:**
   - **Explanation:** Rising interest rates can lead to a decline in the value of existing long-term bonds as their yields become less attractive compared to newly issued bonds with higher rates. Investors may shift toward short-term bonds and cash to reduce interest rate risk and have the flexibility to reinvest at higher rates as market conditions change.

2. **Focus on Dividend Growth Stocks:**
   - **Explanation:** Companies with a history of consistent dividend growth may be attractive during periods of rising interest rates. These stocks often have strong fundamentals and the ability to generate stable cash flows, making them resilient in changing economic conditions. Dividend growth stocks can provide an income stream that may outpace inflation.

3. **Consider Inflation-Linked Securities:**
   - **Explanation:** Inflation-protected securities, such as Treasury Inflation-Protected Securities (TIPS), can be a hedge against rising interest rates and inflation. These securities adjust their principal and interest payments based on changes in the Consumer Price Index (CPI), providing investors with protection against the eroding effects of inflation.

4. **Invest in Floating Rate Securities:**
   - **Explanation:** Floating rate securities, such as bank loans or floating-rate bonds, have interest that adjust periodically based on changes in benchmark rates. These investments can be appealing during rising interest rate environments as they provide a degree of protection against interest rate risk.

5. **Consider Defensive Sectors and Quality Stocks:**
   - **Explanation:** Defensive sectors, such as utilities and healthcare, and quality stocks with strong fundamentals may be more resilient during periods of rising interest rates. These sectors often have stable cash flows and may be less sensitive to interest rate movements compared to more cyclical sectors. Quality stocks with a history of consistent performance may provide stability in changing market conditions.

It's important to note that the impact of rising interest rates can vary across asset classes, and individual investors should tailor their strategies based on their financial goals, risk tolerance, and time horizon. Diversification remains a fundamental principle in navigating changing market conditions, and seeking advice from financial professionals can help align investment strategies with specific circumstances. Additionally, staying informed about economic indicators and central bank policies is crucial for making well-informed investment decisions.

FIGURE 13-6:
Investments for rising interest rates.

ChatGPT

During a period of falling interest rates, investors often need to adapt their strategies to take advantage of the changing economic environment. Here are five investing strategies that investors may consider during a period of falling interest rates, along with explanations for each:

1. **Extend Duration in Bond Portfolios:**
   - **Explanation:** Falling interest rates generally lead to higher bond prices. Investors may consider extending the duration of their bond portfolios to capture capital appreciation as bond yields decline. Longer-term bonds tend to experience larger price increases in response to falling rates.

2. **Invest in High-Quality Dividend Stocks:**
   - **Explanation:** As interest rates decline, the relative attractiveness of dividend-paying stocks increases. Investors may look for high-quality stocks with a history of stable dividends. These stocks can offer an income stream that may be more attractive compared to fixed-income investments in a low-interest-rate environment.

3. **Explore Real Estate Investment Trusts (REITs):**
   - **Explanation:** Falling interest rates can be beneficial for real estate investments. Lower borrowing costs and higher property valuations may support the performance of REITs. Investors seeking income and potential capital appreciation may consider adding REITs to their portfolios during periods of declining interest rates.

4. **Consider Growth Stocks:**
   - **Explanation:** Growth stocks, especially those in technology and innovation sectors, may perform well during periods of falling interest rates. Lower interest rates can reduce the discount rate applied to future earnings, potentially leading to higher valuations for companies expected to deliver strong growth.

5. **Diversify Across Asset Classes:**
   - **Explanation:** In a low-interest-rate environment, diversification becomes crucial as traditional fixed-income investments may offer lower yields. Investors may consider allocating capital to a diversified mix of asset classes, including equities, real assets (such as commodities), and alternative investments to enhance portfolio resilience and potential returns.

It's essential to note that while these strategies are considerations during periods of falling interest rates, investors should carefully assess their individual financial goals, risk tolerance, and investment horizon before making decisions. Additionally, staying informed about economic indicators, central bank policies, and global market conditions is crucial for adapting investment strategies to evolving circumstances. Seeking advice from financial professionals can provide personalized insights and guidance based on an investor's specific situation.

FIGURE 13-7: Investments for falling interest rates.

Leading Economic Indicators (LEI)

When we invest, we always have an eye for the future, and we scan the economic, social, and financial landscape for clues and indicators so that we can stay a step ahead of trends, good or bad. Although there are many worthy indicators to cover (too many to include here anyway), I can at least spotlight one of the most watched (and considered a reliable harbinger for the economy at large) — the index of Leading Economic Indicators (LEI).

What's LEI, you wonder? Let's ask ChatGPT about this:

"What is the index of Leading Economic Indicators?"

Figure 13-8 from ChatGPT shows LEI as one of the most watched and most prominent indicators for investors. Perhaps it's too obvious — investors want to move their money today so they can benefit from potential economic conditions that may occur tomorrow. The LEI is an efficient summary and one that every investor should get to know very well.

 ChatGPT

The Index of Leading Economic Indicators (LEI) is a composite economic indicator designed to provide insights into the future direction of the economy. Compiled by The Conference Board, a non-profit research organization, the LEI aggregates various individual indicators to create a single comprehensive measure. The purpose of the LEI is to help forecast changes in economic activity, allowing businesses, policymakers, and investors to make more informed decisions.

The LEI consists of several components, including but not limited to:

1. **Average weekly hours worked by manufacturing employees.**
2. **Initial claims for unemployment insurance.**
3. **New orders for consumer goods and materials.**
4. **Stock prices.**
5. **Building permits for new private housing.**

These components are chosen based on their historical ability to precede and predict overall economic trends. When the LEI rises, it suggests that economic conditions are likely to improve in the coming months. Conversely, a decline in the LEI may indicate a potential economic slowdown.

Investors pay close attention to the LEI as it provides valuable signals about the future health of the economy. However, it's important to note that no single indicator is foolproof, and a combination of economic indicators should be considered for a comprehensive analysis of economic conditions.

FIGURE 13-8: Details about LEI.

REMEMBER

The bottom line is that a rising LEI is a good and generally reliable omen of positive times for the economy, and, by extension, it bodes well for the stock market. Of course, the opposite is a bad omen. A declining LEI warns that a recession or economic slowdown is near.

Inflation

The first time I asked ChatGPT "What is inflation?" out of curiosity, the response made my eyes bug out as it said, "It is a period of generally rising prices of goods and services." As a long-time teacher and educator, that response made me bristle. I got better answers as I pushed it with more pointed prompts such as "Please tell me the difference between monetary inflation and price inflation," and I was able to coax some decent responses out of it. I can't blame ChatGPT, or any AI tool for that matter. This is an example of "garbage in, garbage out."

REMEMBER

Let's talk inflation reality. Price inflation is an effect, and monetary inflation is the cause. So part one of inflation is the simple overproduction of a given currency. When you produce (either by printing or by digital production) trillions of dollars, you have inflation. The next step is, where do those dollars go? This now becomes an extension of supply and demand, which directs where those excess dollars flow. If those dollars flow into the consumer goods and services area, then we have consumer price inflation. This is the kind most folks talk about when the coffee table conversation goes into the "prices are just too darn high" scuttlebutt.

Just keep in mind: The question is where is the money flowing? When that money flows into the stock market (or real estate, or precious metals, or other assets) then we have asset inflation! And no, no one complains about asset inflation. If folks see this in their 401(k) plans, they won't complain since asset inflation is viewed as a positive.

In recent years, for reasons I detail in my online videos, monetary inflation has headed toward consumer goods (food, energy, and so on), and it's a problem since it squeezes the consumer's budget and has a negative impact across may economic areas. What's an investor to do?

That's right: Ask ChatGPT for tactics and strategies in the inflationary environment. Here are some prompts for the inflation-minded:

>> "What investments perform well during inflation?"

>> "What income strategies are most effective in meeting or exceeding the rate of inflation?"

>> "What cost-cutting strategies can a consumer employ during inflationary times?

TIP

Historically, hard assets (such as real estate and precious metals) and commodities tend to do well during inflationary times. Find out more in Chapter 9. For cost-cutting ideas for consumers, check out Chapter 14.

The Federal Reserve

The Federal Reserve (www.federalreserve.gov) is the United States' central bank. Their ultimate mission is to manage the money supply (U.S. dollars in circulation). They play a critical role in both the economy and the financial markets since it has massive — and I mean *massive* — influence in not only America's national economic affairs but also in the global economy and financial landscape as well. For investors, the "Fed" is both a mega-player to watch for and a resource to help them in their decision making.

The role of the "Fed"

Here are the major tasks the Fed undertakes in its day-to-day activities:

>> Managing the money supply

>> Managing the key interest rates

>> Buying federal government debt

>> Setting overall policy for the banking system

Your mission as an AI user? Start using your AI tool of choice to inquire about the Fed's actions and how they impact the investing climate in general and your portfolio in particular. Here are some prompts to start you off:

>> "Please provide a time line juxtaposing Federal Reserve interest rate movements and the movement of the S&P 500 from 1990 to 2023."

>> "Examine the most recent actions and statements from the Federal Reserve. Provide insights into how these decisions may influence stock market trends and investor sentiment."

>> "Examine the impacts of recent Federal Reserve decisions. Provide a report on how specific sectors such as technology, banking, or healthcare may be influenced. What are the potential risks and opportunities?"

TIP

When using an AI tool, make sure it can access real-time news, views, and data. Use chatbots such as Bing Chat (Microsoft's AI-enhanced search engine), Google Bard, or the specialized finance-driven AI tools available (see Appendix B for the most prominent ones). ChatGPT unfortunately doesn't have real-time market information and data past January 2022 (at the time of writing).

Here's a sample prompt:

> "What are the five most important points that investors should know about the Federal Reserve?"

Figure 13-9 has the response from ChatGPT. Take each item individually and ask AI about how each point will affect the type of investments you hold in your portfolio. You can ask, "Which monetary policy tools will have a greater effect on growth stocks over the long term and why? Please provide a detailed explanation."

 ChatGPT

The Federal Reserve, often referred to as the Fed, plays a central role in the U.S. economy and financial markets. Here are five essential points that investors should know about the Federal Reserve:

1. **Mandate and Objectives:**
   - **Explanation:** The Federal Reserve's primary objectives, as mandated by Congress, are to promote maximum sustainable employment, stable prices, and moderate long-term interest rates. This dual mandate underscores the Fed's commitment to fostering a healthy labor market and controlling inflation.

2. **Monetary Policy Tools:**
   - **Explanation:** The Fed influences the economy through its control over monetary policy. Its primary tools include open market operations (buying and selling government securities), the federal funds rate (the interest rate at which banks lend to each other overnight), and reserve requirements. By adjusting these tools, the Fed seeks to achieve its monetary policy goals.

3. **Interest Rate Decisions:**
   - **Explanation:** The Federal Open Market Committee (FOMC) is responsible for setting the federal funds rate. Changes in this key interest rate have a profound impact on various financial instruments, including bonds, mortgages, and lending rates. Investors closely monitor FOMC meetings and statements for insights into future interest rate movements.

FIGURE 13-9:
The scoop on the Federal Reserve.

FIGURE 13-9:
(Continued)

The "Fed" as an investor resource

Few sources have more economic and financial data than the Fed. Before AI, much of it was too cumbersome and unwieldy; many investors wouldn't bother wading into it due to how voluminous and clunky it could be. Fortunately, in recent years the Fed has gotten much better at providing data, and AI is a powerful tool to use (it came just in time!).

TIP

When you get a chance, go see FRED at `https://fred.stlouisfed.org/`. FRED stands for Federal Reserve Economic Data, and the site has plenty of great news and information. AI tools can actually scan online documents and posts (such as the ones at the Fed's website) and explain and summarize for you. Check out the finance-related AI tools in both Appendixes B and C for more details.

The Political Landscape

Keep in mind that politics (in terms of the impact of overall laws and regulations) have a powerful (negative or positive) effect on the economy. In other words, who you vote for will have a material impact on the economy directly and on you and your financial issues indirectly (and directly, too!). Here is where you need to use your AI tools to discern the good and bad of a given set of policies so you can vote accordingly.

REMEMBER

Don't vote for someone due to their personality or political party; vote according to the aggregate net effect of what policies they will push. Don't ask AI "which candidate is better, A or B, for the economy?" Ask "What are the top three economic policies of candidate X and what are the pros and cons of each?" Follow up with "What has candidate Z done for the [specific] industry?"

Here are some questions to ask yourself and AI:

>> How will this particular law affect a given company, its industry, or its sector?

>> What laws will directly affect my stock investment adversely?

>> Will any laws affect the company's industry and/or sector?

>> Will any current or prospective laws affect the company's sources of revenue?

>> Will any current or prospective laws affect the company's expenses or supplies?

>> Am I staying informed about political and economic issues that may possibly have a negative impact on my investment?

>> Will such things as excessive regulations, price controls, or new taxes have a negative impact on my stock's industry?

Regardless of the merits (or demerits) of the political situation, investors must view it through the lens of economic causes and effects, which in turn leads to their decisions on which companies (and their stocks) are impacted positively or negatively.

Chapter **14**

Financial Planning and Other Money Matters

lthough this book's focus is on AI's use and impact on investing, investing is really just a portion of the larger world of financial planning. Investing comes together with the other components of your financial world for you to achieve all the financial goals necessary for a good life.

Financial planning is the universe, and investing is just a primary galaxy, so to speak. If you focus on investing success but have flaws or weaknesses in other aspects of your financial situation, then you risk falling short of your ultimate goals.

What good is successful investing if you have significant problems with your career, burdensome debt, or overspending habits? In this chapter, you take a com-prehensive snapshot of your finances and budget with the help of AI.

TIP

I realize that financial planning and its associated topics can easily be an entire book (and you can be sure to find great books at www.dummies.com). But I hope that you see that virtually every aspect of your financial and business worlds can be impacted for the better when you harness AI.

Walking through the Steps of Financial Planning

Confused about where to start with financial planning? What better way to begin than to ask AI? Here's a sample prompt:

> "What is the complete financial planning process? Please provide the answer in bullet point style with a comprehensive explanation of each item and in the person's chronological order of their life."

ChatGPT's response is in the following text (my added comments are in *italics*):

> The financial planning process is a structured approach to managing one's finances throughout their life. It typically consists of several stages, from setting financial goals to retirement planning.
>
> Here's a chronological breakdown of the complete financial planning process with explanations for each stage:
>
> **Stage 1: Setting Financial Goals (Early Adulthood)**
>
> **1. Determine Financial Goals:** Identify short-term and long-term financial objectives, such as buying a home, paying off student loans, or saving for retirement.
>
> *Comments: Whatever your activity is, what is the result you want? The studies over the years have shown that college graduates, for example, frequently miss their retirement funding targets. Recent studies show that approximately half of Americans have less than $1,000 in savings and/or are a paycheck away from financial difficulty. Teaching financial literacy such as determining financial goals (and sticking to them!) should be part of young adults' learning during high school and college years so there are more happy financial endings. Use AI to set goals, your action plan, and so forth.*
>
> **2. Establish a Budget:** Create a budget to track income, expenses, and savings goals. This helps you allocate resources to achieve your goals.
>
> *Comments: If you can't manage your finances (inflow and outflow of your funds), then you will have difficulty managing and growing your investments. You don't need AI for that conclusion. More about budgeting appears later in this chapter.*
>
> **Stage 2: Building Financial Foundation (Early Adulthood)**
>
> **3. Emergency Fund:** Build an emergency fund to cover unexpected expenses, typically 3–6 months' worth of living expenses.

REMEMBER

Comments: Before you start investing, address this issue. Having an emergency fund is not only a financial good; it's a psychological good. If, for example, you have $10,000 in a savings account, you will have less stress over your day-to-day finances, which can result in better financial decisions. Who will have a better time avoiding a panicky or hasty financial decision — the person with a solid emergency fund who is regularly paying their daily obligations or the person with no savings who is a paycheck away from difficulty? Use AI to learn tactics and strategies to increase your savings and establish an adequate emergency fund for your particular situation.

4. Debt Management: Manage and reduce high-interest debts, like credit card balances and student loans.

WARNING

Comments: At the time of writing, debt in all categories (consumer, corporate, government, and so on) is at or near all-time highs. Whether interest rates continue to rise or not, the debt load is unsustainable. Consumers should make every effort to pare this back before a financial crisis unfolds. Use AI to learn strategies and tactics to manage and ultimately reduce your overall debt (and other liabilities).

5. Insurance: Acquire appropriate insurance coverage, including health, auto, home, and life insurance, to protect against unexpected events.

Comments: Too often, investors and consumers don't prioritize insurance. Insurance is there to keep large, unforeseen expenses from blowing up your finances. Examples include the death of the main breadwinner or the disability of a significant job holder in your household. Use AI to analyze your insurance needs and then speak with an insurance pro.

Stage 3: Wealth Accumulation (Mid-Adulthood)

6. Investing: Develop an investment strategy based on risk tolerance and financial goals. Consider assets like stocks, bonds, real estate, and retirement accounts.

Comments: Gee, should I really spend time commenting here? Review the table of contents; chapters and resources address all of these investing topics!

7. Retirement Planning: Contribute to retirement accounts, such as 401(k)s and IRAs, to ensure a comfortable retirement. Consider employer matches.

Comments: This topic is covered in Chapter 15 and general investing resources are in Appendix C. Obviously the more you can set aside and keep managing for growth, the better you will be at the retirement finish line. Once there, you will focus on income generation.

8. Tax Planning: Optimize your tax situation by taking advantage of deductions, credits, and tax-efficient investments.

Comments: In the world of managing cash flow in which money flows in (income and gains) and money flows out (outgo such as debt and expenses), taxes are a major expense. The more you can reduce it, the more funds you can devote to your current and future financial needs. Find out more in Chapter 16.

Stage 4: Major Life Events (Various Life Stages)

9. Marriage and Family: Adjust financial plans for significant life changes, such as getting married, having children, or sending kids to college.

Comments: Your finances are ultimately there to support your important social goals. Strong finances tend to help bolster your marital bliss and to better your children and other dependents. Use AI to gain insights and learn strategies to support this area. Major life events such as weddings, education (covered later in this chapter), and funerals tend to be expensive, so plan accordingly and long before they become issues.

10. Estate Planning: Create a will, assign beneficiaries, and set up powers of attorney and healthcare directives to manage your assets and healthcare decisions.

Comments: Estate planning is a necessity, and it can be a complicated one. Use AI to create checklists, understand wills and trusts, and so on. More on this topic is in Chapter 15.

Stage 5: Midlife Adjustments (Midlife)

11. Education Funding: Save for your children's education expenses by utilizing tax-advantaged accounts like 529 plans.

Comments: Yes, this is a biggie. First, decide whether a traditional college route is the right path. In recent years, the overall return on investment has greatly diminished. More and more folks are seeking college alternatives so they can decrease the massive cost while still enhancing job prospects. I discuss college planning later in this chapter.

12. Debt Reduction: Focus on paying off remaining debts and becoming more debt-free as retirement approaches.

Comments: See #4 earlier in this list for my thoughts on debt management.

Stage 6: Preparing for Retirement (Late Adulthood)

13. Social Security and Pension: Plan for the utilization of Social Security benefits and any employer pensions to supplement retirement income.

Comments: I usually tell my retirement planning students and clients to plan your retirement as if Social Security is not happening. Although I am sure that Social Security will be there for you, I am not 100 percent certain. But if you achieve financial independence without it, then getting it is gravy! Use AI to help you understand your Social Security benefits, how to file, and soon.

14. Healthcare Costs: Consider healthcare costs in retirement and investigate Medicare and supplemental insurance options.

Comments: For retirees, would-be and current, health is both a major physical concern and a financial concern. Use AI to help you figure out health issues, Medicare, and so forth.

15. Long-Term Care: Plan for potential long-term care expenses by exploring insurance options or savings strategies.

Comments: Same issue as item #14. Explore long-term care and see whether it is a viable consideration for you. Use AI, but it's best to confer with a human specialist.

Stage 7: Retirement (Late Adulthood)

16. Asset Allocation: Adjust your investment portfolio to prioritize income and preservation of capital over growth.

Comments: Great investing issue! Specialized AI (such as robo-advisors covered in Chapter 7 and the rest of this book) will help here. The main focus here at this stage of life is safety of principal through conservative, dividend-paying stocks, treasury bonds, bank CDs, and so forth.

17. Withdrawal Strategy: Develop a systematic withdrawal plan for retirement accounts to ensure your savings last through retirement.

Comments: Here the issue highlighted is recommended minimum distributions (RMD) among others. You have grown and accrued assets all your working life for a purpose, and that has arrived. Start enjoying your money.

18. Estate Distribution: Review and update estate plans to ensure a smooth transfer of assets to heirs or charitable organizations.

Comments: This is part of your estate planning strategies. Check out Chapter 15 for more on this.

Stage 8: Legacy Planning (Late Adulthood)

19. Charitable Giving: Plan for charitable contributions and develop strategies for giving back to the community.

Comments: For those folks who have more than is needed for the tail end of their life, charitable giving becomes a consideration to help reduce what could become a taxable estate.

20. Legacy and Estate Preservation: Explore options to minimize estate taxes and preserve wealth for future generations.

Comments: With whatever is left at the end of your life, you should have the decision to give as much of it as possible to whom you want to give it to (family, friends, charities, and so on).

The financial planning process is dynamic, and individuals may revisit these stages as their life circumstances change. Working with a certified financial planner can provide valuable guidance and ensure that financial goals are aligned with the most current strategies and investment options.

Comments: Nice summation! Given that I was a CFP during my career, that was a nice plug!

TIP

OK, pilgrim, start your AI engines and get cracking on financial planning. Here are some prompts to consider:

>> "What are the legal forms of ownership? Provide an explanation and an example of each." (This is especially crucial in estate planning, which is covered in Chapter 15.)

>> "How do I file for Social Security? Please provide a step-by-step approach and then provide ten ways I can boost my benefits."

>> "What are ten ways to easily add extra income to my situation in the near future using only my laptop and/or my smartphone? Provide an explanation of each along with resources online that can help me."

Getting a Handle on Budgeting

Budgeting is all about managing financial inflow and outflow. When you budget, you know where the money is coming from, and you know where it's going — every penny (or close enough).

REMEMBER

The goal for having a budget is simple:

>> Keep increasing your inflow and keep decreasing your outflow.

>> Then save and invest the difference. Then it's rinse and repeat until you meet your financial goals.

If your financial goals include financial independence and a comfortable lifestyle, then you know what needs to be done.

Let's ask AI about inflow. Check out the following prompt:

"Please give me five specific strategies to increase the amount of money I bring into my financial situation for the next 12 months."

ChatGPT's response is in Figure 14-1. Although I specialized in financial planning and investing education for nearly four decades, I was always an advocate for anyone (everyone!) to have a home-based business in their spare time. Fast-forward to today's world, and the variety of ways to earn extra income is greater than ever. Check out Chapter 12 for further ideas on business and career pursuits.

TIP

By the way, a good way to start is by listing/selling your unwanted stuff on venues such as eBay and Amazon (and dozens of other venues). Yes, ask AI lots of questions about home business ideas, part-time gigs, and so forth.

 ChatGPT

Certainly! Here are five specific strategies to increase the amount of money you bring into your financial situation over the next 12 months:

1. **1. Diversify Income Streams:**
   * Explore opportunities to diversify your sources of income. This could involve taking on a side job, freelancing, consulting, or starting a small business. By diversifying, you reduce reliance on a single income stream and create multiple avenues for earning money.

2. **2. Enhance Skills and Marketable Qualifications:**
   * Invest in developing or enhancing skills that are in demand in the job market. This might involve taking courses, obtaining certifications, or acquiring new qualifications. Increasing your expertise can make you more valuable in your current job or open doors to higher-paying opportunities.

3. **3. Negotiate a Raise or Promotion:**
   * Evaluate your performance and contributions in your current job. If you believe you've added significant value, consider negotiating a raise or promotion. Prepare a case outlining your achievements, responsibilities, and the impact you've had on the organization. Be ready to discuss how you can contribute even more in the future.

4. **4. Create Passive Income Streams:**
   * Explore opportunities to generate passive income. This could involve investing in dividend-paying stocks, real estate, or creating and selling digital products. Passive income streams can provide a steady flow of money with less active involvement over time.

5. **5. Cut Unnecessary Expenses:**
   * Review your monthly expenses and identify areas where you can cut unnecessary costs. This might involve renegotiating bills, canceling subscription services you don't use, or finding more cost-effective alternatives for daily expenses. The money saved can be redirected towards increasing your overall financial situation.

Remember to approach these strategies with careful planning and consideration of your personal circumstances. Building additional income or cutting expenses requires effort and discipline. Combining multiple strategies can have a compounding effect, contributing to a more significant positive impact on your financial situation over the next 12 months.

FIGURE 14-1:
Increasing
your inflow.

And then you can use AI to get ideas for the outflow. Here's a sample prompt:

"Please give me five specific strategies to decrease the amount of money that is flowing out of my financial situation for the next 12 months."

ChatGPT's response is in Figure 14-2. Reducing your "outflow" should be easier than increasing your "inflow." Too many folks are buying stuff that is simply not needed. Ask yourself whether a given purchase will add psychological or material value to your situation in the coming months. My neighbor, for example, bought an RV. They were likely better off renting it as they needed it — and saving thousands of dollars. In addition, the RV is a depreciating asset that will lose value over time. What are you considering buying now that is better off delayed or done a cheaper way?

 ChatGPT

Certainly! Here are five specific strategies to decrease the amount of money flowing out of your financial situation over the next 12 months:

1. **1. Create a Detailed Budget:**
   * **Strategy:** Develop a comprehensive budget that outlines your monthly income and all your expenses. Categorize expenses into fixed (e.g., rent, utilities) and variable (e.g., dining out, entertainment). Analyze the budget to identify areas where you can cut costs.

2. **2. Cut Unnecessary Expenses:**
   * **Strategy:** Review your spending habits and identify non-essential expenses that can be reduced or eliminated. This might include subscription services, dining out, impulse purchases, or unused gym memberships. Consider negotiating bills or finding more cost-effective alternatives.

3. **3. Refinance or Consolidate Debt:**
   * **Strategy:** If you have outstanding loans or credit card debt, explore options for refinancing or consolidating. Lowering interest rates or combining multiple debts into one can reduce monthly payments and overall interest costs.

4. **4. Negotiate Bills and Services:**
   * **Strategy:** Contact service providers, such as internet, cable, or insurance companies, and negotiate better rates. Many providers are willing to offer discounts or promotions to retain customers. Shop around for better deals and consider switching providers if it results in cost savings.

5. **5. Build an Emergency Fund:**
   * **Strategy:** Establish or strengthen an emergency fund to cover unexpected expenses, reducing the need to rely on credit cards or loans. Having a financial buffer can prevent additional debt and interest payments.

FIGURE 14-2: Decreasing your outflow.

Spotlighting College Expenses

The major expenses we typically deal with are usually milestones in our life: weddings, births (and raising children), college funding, and funerals. AI can certainly give you lots of research, ideas, and so on about all of those. In this section I focus on one of those — college.

Among that list of major expenses, college is likely #1 given that it's easy to end up spending six-figures on a four-year college education. But as you read this, the college world is facing tectonic shifts, and consumers (parents!) are spending more and more money for less and less educational value.

Obviously if you're opting for a traditional four-year degree for your child, I wish you success. But before you take this expensive plunge, consider the alternatives since there may be greater satisfaction there for your child (and a lot less cost for you). Here's an example prompt that's food for thought:

> "Please give me ten practical alternatives to an expensive four-year traditional college degree. Please provide a good rationale for each choice."

ChatGPT's response is in Figure 14-3. I cover this as a recent phenomenon has shown that college debt surpassed the $1 trillion mark during 2022–2023 and an extraordinary number of college graduates have taken on jobs that didn't require a college education. I speak for those who personally know many college graduates with huge college debt balances who are working as cashiers and office clerks.

TIP

Keep in mind that any huge cost you undertake (college, buying a house, and so on) should be done through the lens of "return on investment" (ROI). Whatever money you put in, you should have reasonable expectation of gaining benefit (financial or otherwise) that is ultimately greater in its totality than the total amount that was invested. Consider using AI to construct a spreadsheet to do the financial pros and cons, cost comparisons, and so forth to make an informed decision. Consider plotting that same spreadsheet with the choices/ideas in Figure 14-3.

Of course, there are still some subjects where a traditional four-college route is still the best way to go. Examples include engineering and medical careers. Fortunately, the well of college money is still deep and more students than ever can qualify. Here is a sample prompt on this to get you started:

> "List seven sources of grants and scholarships to help fund a traditional four-year college education for a student in liberal arts who comes from a middle-income family. Also, include a description and the relevant URL or website."

If a four-year traditional college can help you gain a lucrative job coupled with career satisfaction, then AI's help has been worth it.

Certainly! Pursuing alternatives to a traditional 4-year college degree can be a practical and cost-effective way to gain valuable skills and credentials. Here are 10 alternatives, along with their rationales:

1. **Community College or Two-Year Associate's Degree:**
   * Rationale: Community colleges offer affordable tuition and provide a solid foundation for various careers or as a stepping stone to a 4-year degree.

2. **Trade or Technical School:**
   * Rationale: Technical and vocational schools focus on specific trades, such as plumbing, electrician, or medical assisting, and provide hands-on training for high-demand jobs.

3. **Apprenticeships:**
   * Rationale: Apprenticeships combine on-the-job training with classroom instruction and are an excellent way to earn while you learn in fields like construction, healthcare, and information technology.

4. **Online Courses and Certifications:**
   * Rationale: Many accredited institutions and platforms offer online courses and certifications in various subjects, allowing you to gain knowledge and skills at your own pace and often at a lower cost than traditional college.

5. **Bootcamps and Coding Schools:**
   * Rationale: Coding bootcamps provide intensive training in web development, software engineering, and data science, preparing you for high-demand tech jobs in a shorter time frame.

6. **Entrepreneurship and Business Start-up:**
   * Rationale: Starting your own business or pursuing entrepreneurial ventures can provide valuable experience and, with success, potentially lead to financial independence without a degree.

7. **Military Service:**
   * Rationale: Joining the military can offer valuable training, education benefits, and a structured career path in various fields, from aviation to healthcare.

8. **Online Freelancing or Gig Work:**
   * Rationale: Platforms like Upwork and Freelancer allow you to offer your skills and services to clients, creating income opportunities in writing, design, programming, and more.

FIGURE 14-3:
Alternatives to four-year college degrees.

9. **Nonprofit and Volunteer Work:**
   - Rationale: Volunteering and nonprofit work can provide valuable experience and networking opportunities in social services, community development, and other fields.
10. **Apprenticeships:**

   - Rationale: Apprenticeships combine on-the-job training with classroom instruction and are an excellent way to earn while you learn in fields like construction, healthcare, and information technology.

   Each of these alternatives offers a different path to gaining skills, experience, and credentials without the high cost of a traditional 4-year college degree. Your choice should align with your career goals and personal interests while considering the financial aspects and time commitment.

FIGURE 14-3:
(Continued)

Chapter 15

Retirement and Estate Planning

A
lthough retirement and estate planning should be on every adult's radar screen, it is most "top of mind" for those folks past 50 (give or take a decade). Between the two, estate planning is the more complicated and daunting for many of us. Fortunately, AI is a powerful and welcome tool that makes both pursuits much less daunting.

Digging into Retirement Planning

Whether you're planning your retirement when you're 20 years old, 40, 55, or beyond, part one of the plan is quite simple: Spend less than you earn, invest/save the difference, rinse and repeat. Part two of your approach is this: Figure out your income needs at the age you are hoping/planning to retire so you can accrue enough assets to generate that needed income. The following sections can help you get started.

REMEMBER

Be sure to consult a professional as you plan your retirement.

Your starting point: A personal balance sheet

To get rolling with your retirement planning, assessing what you currently own (assets) and owe (liabilities) is obviously an essential first step. Here's a sample prompt for AI:

> "To retire I will need a personal balance sheet. Please create an extensive personal balance sheet complete with each line item as a bullet point coupled with an explanation for each line item."

ChatGPT's response is in the following text:

> Creating a personal balance sheet is an essential step in understanding your financial health and planning for retirement. A personal balance sheet summarizes your assets, liabilities, and net worth at a specific point in time. Here's an extensive personal balance sheet with each line item as a bullet point, along with an explanation for each:
>
> **Assets:**
>
> **1. Cash and Cash Equivalents:**
>
> **Explanation:** This includes money in checking accounts, savings accounts, and any other easily accessible cash.
>
> **2. Investment Accounts:**
>
> **Explanation:** The value of your investment portfolios, including stocks, bonds, mutual funds, and brokerage accounts.
>
> **3. Retirement Accounts (e.g., 401(k), IRA):**
>
> **Explanation:** The total value of your retirement savings, which can include employer-sponsored plans and individual retirement accounts.
>
> **4. Real Estate:**
>
> **Explanation:** The estimated value of your primary residence and any other real estate properties you own.
>
> **5. Vehicles:**
>
> **Explanation:** The value of your cars, motorcycles, boats, or other vehicles you own.
>
> **6. Personal Property:**
>
> **Explanation:** The value of valuable personal possessions such as jewelry, art, antiques, and collectibles.

7. Business Ownership:

Explanation: If you own a business, the value of your ownership stake should be included here.

8. Cash Value of Life Insurance:

Explanation: If you have life insurance policies with a cash value component, include the current cash value.

9. Other Investments:

Explanation: Any other investments not mentioned above, such as real estate investment trusts (REITs) or certificates of deposit (CDs).

10. Other Assets:

Explanation: Include any miscellaneous assets like loans owed to you, prepaid expenses, or any significant assets not covered in the categories above.

Liabilities:

11. Mortgage(s):

Explanation: The outstanding balance on your mortgage(s) for your primary residence and other properties.

12. Home Equity Loans or Lines of Credit:

Explanation: Any outstanding balances on home equity loans or lines of credit secured by your home.

13. Auto Loans:

Explanation: The amount you owe on car loans or leases.

14. Credit Card Debt:

Explanation: The total balance on all your credit cards.

15. Student Loans:

Explanation: Outstanding student loan balances, if applicable.

16. Personal Loans:

Explanation: Any unsecured personal loans or debts owed to friends or family.

17. Other Loans:

Explanation: Include any other outstanding loans, such as business loans or medical debts.

18. Taxes Payable:

Explanation: Outstanding income taxes or property taxes due but not yet paid.

19. Other Liabilities:

Explanation: Include any miscellaneous liabilities not covered above.

Net Worth:

20. Net Worth (Assets – Liabilities):

Explanation: Calculate your net worth by subtracting your total liabilities from your total assets. This represents your true financial position.

A personal balance sheet provides a snapshot of your financial situation, helping you assess your progress toward retirement goals and make informed financial decisions. Regularly update your balance sheet to track changes in your wealth over time and make adjustments to your retirement plan as needed.

REMEMBER

For most folks, doing a "financial inventory" is the first and most essential step for retirement planning. All your assets (as much as possible, anyway) should be on the path to growth, and you should be reducing your liabilities. Ideally when retirement time comes, your assets should be positioned to generate income (dividends, interest, and so on) needed for a comfortable retirement.

The "5–10 approach" and a reality check

In my retirement planning seminars and workshops, I reference something I refer to as the "5–10" approach. It refers to an assumption of "5 percent income and 10 percent growth." Whenever you're doing retirement planning, you can't avoid the fact that since you're planning for the future (and typically many years into the future), you have to make assumptions because you have no idea what the distant future looks like until you get there.

Given that, assume that you can reasonably expect to generate an income from future assets of 5 percent (when you complete reconstructing your portfolio for optimal income generation at that time). Also assume that you could (on average) achieve 10 percent growth in your assets between today and when you're ready to shift to income mode later on at retirement time.

For example, say you will need at retirement time $25,000 of investment income (perhaps as a supplement to your future Social Security annual income). If $25,000 is 5 percent as income, then in that case you would need at least $500,000 in investable assets to generate that amount ($25,000 is 5 percent of $500,000). That way you could have income without needing to dip into principal (in other words, start cashing in some of that $500,000 amount).

Since you'll need $500,000 at that time, you'll need a financial calculator (or AI) to figure out how to get from where you are currently (your net worth from the personal balance sheet covered earlier in this chapter) to where you need (or want) to be.

So here's the first prompt I used:

"I have $150,000 in investments and I want to grow it to $500,000. If it is growing annually at an average rate of 10 percent, how long will it take in years?"

After a long explanation and layout of the formula and calculation, ChatGPT ended its response with the following:

So, it will take approximately 20.14 years for your $150,000 investment to grow to $500,000 at an annual growth rate of 10 percent. Since you can't have a fraction of a year in reality, you'd likely need to wait for 21 years to reach your goal.

The interesting thing is that when I asked that same exact question to Bing's AI-enhanced Bing Chat, it gave the answer in Figure 15-1.

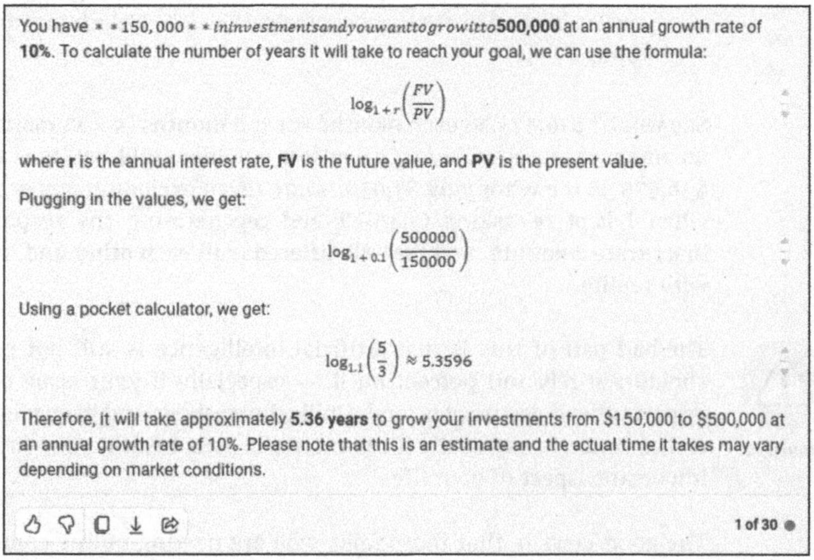

You have * * 150,000 * * *ininvestmentsandyouwanttogrowitto*500,000 at an annual growth rate of **10%**. To calculate the number of years it will take to reach your goal, we can use the formula:

$$\log_{1+r}\left(\frac{FV}{PV}\right)$$

where **r** is the annual interest rate, **FV** is the future value, and **PV** is the present value.

Plugging in the values, we get:

$$\log_{1+0.1}\left(\frac{500000}{150000}\right)$$

Using a pocket calculator, we get:

$$\log_{1.1}\left(\frac{5}{3}\right) \approx 5.3596$$

Therefore, it will take approximately **5.36 years** to grow your investments from $150,000 to $500,000 at an annual growth rate of 10%. Please note that this is an estimate and the actual time it takes may vary depending on market conditions.

1 of 30 ●

FIGURE 15-1:
One of several answers from AI on reaching an investment goal.

Hmmm. While ChatGPT estimated "21 years" (rounded up from 20.14 years), Bing estimated 5.36 years. Interesting — both AI estimates were off.

Then I went to a reliable (non-AI) online financial calculator (found at www.calculator.net; I used the investment calculator), and I got the answer of 12.632 years. My conclusion is that the actual answer is in the neighborhood of 12 to 14 years given my experience with financial projections.

REMEMBER

Artificial intelligence (in spite of the name) is *not* artificial perfection! For sensitive or important calculations or issues, consult more than one source — and add a competent, experienced human to the mix, too.

But here's where folks need to be really careful in terms of AI reliability. I took the preceding example a step further and added (what I thought) was a simple additional step. Here's the revised prompt:

> "I am starting today with an investment amount of $150,000, and I want it to reach $500,000 in 9 years. Assuming an annual growth rate of 10 percent during that period of time, how much should my regular monthly contribution be?"

After a long explanation and layout of the formula and calculation, ChatGPT's response caused my jaw to drop:

> So, to reach $500,000 in 9 years with an average annual growth rate of 10 percent, you would need to invest approximately $36,575.38 each month during that time frame.

Say what?! $36,575.38 each month? For 108 months (9 × 12 months)? Wow! That's an amazing inaccuracy! Any calculator would've told you that 108 months times $36,575.38 is a whopping $3,950,141.04 (even excluding any growth at all!). Even when I kept re-asking ChatGPT and regenerating the response, I got wildly inaccurate amounts, and they all differed with each other and, more importantly, with reality.

WARNING

The bad part of this is that artificial intelligence is still not perfected, and you should not rely 100 percent on it — especially if your issue or concern is very important and accuracy is vital. Unlike horseshoes and grenades, accuracy will be a vital concern, especially if the matter is your health, your finances, or another important aspect of your life.

The good news is that those folks who are posting online content about how AI will take over the world, take a breath. AI first needs to get the math correct (among other things).

TIP

Meanwhile, do your research with multiple sources, human as well as AI. For starters, you may want to consider my free retirement planning video titled "Rescue Your Retirement" (found at www.ravingcapitalist.com/rescue-your-retirement/). The investing resources listed in Appendix C also cover retirement planning topics and issues.

A helpful checklist

With your personal balance sheet done, now you can roll up your sleeves and get rolling with planning. Consider a prompt like this:

"Please create a comprehensive checklist of documents and steps for retirement planning. Do it in a checklist approach complete with an explanation of each item."

ChatGPT's response is in the following text:

Retirement planning is essential to ensure financial security and a comfortable lifestyle during your retirement years. Here's a comprehensive checklist for retirement planning, complete with explanations for each item:

1. Set Retirement Goals:

Explanation: Determine your retirement age, lifestyle expectations, and financial goals. Understanding what you want will guide your planning.

2. Calculate Retirement Expenses:

Explanation: Estimate your future expenses, including housing, healthcare, daily living costs, travel, and entertainment. Be realistic and account for inflation.

3. Assess Current Financial Situation:

Explanation: Review your current assets, debts, income, and expenses to understand your financial position.

4. Create a Retirement Budget:

Explanation: Develop a budget that aligns with your retirement goals. This will help you track your spending and ensure you don't outlive your savings.

5. Determine Retirement Income Sources:

Explanation: Identify potential sources of retirement income, such as Social Security, pensions, IRAs, 401(k)s, annuities, and investment accounts.

6. Maximize Employer Retirement Contributions:

Explanation: Contribute the maximum allowable amount to employer-sponsored retirement plans like a 401(k) and take advantage of any employer matching contributions.

7. Open and Fund an IRA:

Explanation: Consider opening an Individual Retirement Account (IRA) to supplement your employer-sponsored retirement plan. Contribute regularly to benefit from tax advantages.

8. Diversify Your Investment Portfolio:

Explanation: Spread your investments across different asset classes to manage risk and potentially increase returns. Consult a financial advisor for guidance.

9. Establish an Emergency Fund:

Explanation: Set aside three to six months' worth of living expenses in a liquid, easily accessible account to cover unexpected expenses during retirement.

10. Pay Off High-Interest Debts:

Explanation: Prioritize paying off high-interest debts, such as credit cards and personal loans, to reduce financial stress in retirement.

11. Review Social Security Benefits:

Explanation: Understand your Social Security benefits, including when you can start receiving them and how your age at retirement affects the amount you receive.

12. Consider Healthcare Costs:

Explanation: Plan for healthcare expenses, including insurance premiums, deductibles, and potential long-term care needs. Explore Medicare and Medigap options.

13. Create a Withdrawal Strategy:

Explanation: Develop a plan for withdrawing money from your retirement accounts to minimize taxes and make your savings last throughout retirement.

14. Evaluate Long-Term Care Insurance:

Explanation: Consider purchasing long-term care insurance to protect your assets in case you require extended care in a nursing home or at home.

15. Update Legal Documents:

Explanation: Review and update important legal documents, such as your will, power of attorney, and healthcare proxy, to ensure they reflect your wishes.

16. Assess Life Insurance Needs:

Explanation: Determine whether you still need life insurance in retirement. It can be a valuable asset or a source of income for beneficiaries.

17. Plan for Estate Distribution:

Explanation: Outline your wishes for the distribution of your assets after your passing and consider minimizing estate taxes through estate planning strategies.

18. Explore Part-Time Work or Hobbies:

Explanation: Think about how you'd like to spend your time in retirement, whether it's through part-time work, volunteering, or pursuing hobbies and interests.

19. Review and Adjust Your Plan Regularly:

Explanation: Periodically revisit your retirement plan, especially as you get closer to retirement, to make necessary adjustments based on changing circumstances and goals.

20. Seek Professional Advice:

Explanation: Consult with a financial advisor, accountant, or retirement specialist to ensure your retirement plan is on track and aligned with your objectives.

Retirement planning is an ongoing process, and early preparation is key to achieving a secure and fulfilling retirement. Regularly monitoring and adjusting your plan as needed will help you stay on course to meet your retirement goals.

The preceding response is generally good. But let's make AI work a little harder. Keep reading!

Even more AI retirement planning prompts

TIP

Sometimes what retirees need (current and future) are more than answers; they need to ask good questions to uncover solutions, including some they may not have considered. AI tools like ChatGPT are not only good for answers; they can help with questions, too. Consider the following prompt:

"Please provide a list of prompts for ChatGPT that a retiree would need to know. Give each one as a question or request and provide an accompanying explanation as to why that is a good prompt."

ChatGPT responded as follows:

Certainly, here is a list of prompts/questions that a retiree might find useful when interacting with ChatGPT. Each prompt is followed by an explanation of why it's a good question or request:

1. "How can I maximize my retirement income?"

Explanation: This prompt seeks advice on optimizing retirement income sources, including investments, Social Security, and pensions, to maintain financial security.

2. "What are the best investment options for retirees?"

Explanation: This question helps retirees explore safe and income-generating investment options suitable for their retirement portfolio.

3. "Can you explain the tax implications of my retirement withdrawals?"

Explanation: Understanding the tax consequences of retirement account withdrawals is crucial for financial planning. This request seeks clarification on this topic.

4. "What are some effective strategies for managing healthcare costs in retirement?"

Explanation: Retirees often face rising healthcare expenses. This question seeks advice on managing and budgeting for healthcare in retirement.

5. "How can I create a retirement budget that ensures I don't outlive my savings?"

Explanation: Planning a realistic budget is vital for maintaining financial stability throughout retirement. This prompt seeks guidance on creating such a budget.

6. "Tell me about long-term care insurance options and considerations for retirees."

Explanation: Long-term care insurance can be a critical component of retirement planning. This question seeks information on available options and factors to consider.

7. "What are the advantages and disadvantages of downsizing or relocating in retirement?"

Explanation: Deciding whether to downsize or relocate is a significant retirement decision. This question explores the pros and cons of these options.

8. "How can I ensure my estate is properly planned and distributed to my heirs?"

Explanation: Estate planning is essential for retirees. This prompt seeks advice on wills, trusts, and strategies to minimize estate taxes.

9. "What are some creative ways to stay mentally and physically active during retirement?"

Explanation: Staying active and engaged in retirement is essential for overall well-being. This question explores activities and strategies for doing so.

10. "Tell me about the best practices for managing my time and setting goals in retirement."

Explanation: Retirement often comes with newfound free time. This prompt seeks guidance on time management and goal setting to maintain purpose and fulfillment.

11. "Can you explain the basics of required minimum distributions (RMDs) from retirement accounts?"

Explanation: Understanding RMDs is crucial to avoid penalties and manage retirement account withdrawals effectively. This question seeks clarification on this topic.

12. "What are some strategies for leaving a financial legacy or making charitable contributions in retirement?"

Explanation: This prompt explores options for retirees who wish to leave a legacy or make charitable contributions as part of their financial plan.

13. "How can I protect myself from financial scams and fraud in retirement?"

Explanation: Retirees can be vulnerable to financial scams. This question seeks advice on protecting one's finances and identity.

14. "What are some best practices for maintaining a healthy work-life balance in retirement?"

Explanation: Achieving a satisfying work-life balance in retirement is essential. This question seeks strategies to help retirees manage this balance effectively.

15. "Can you provide tips on effective communication with family members about financial and estate matters?"

Explanation: Open communication with family members about finances and estate planning is crucial. This request seeks advice on how to approach these discussions.

These prompts cover a range of important topics for retirees, helping them navigate various aspects of retirement planning and lifestyle.

REMEMBER

In terms of a clearly laid-out action plan, AI is shining bright. The earlier experience in this chapter regarding an overall calculation (refer to Figure 15-1) was off — something you would think that AI should be strong on. I am sure that by the time you read this, the calculating power of AI will be refined to provide better results (at least I hope!), but in the meanwhile, folks planning for retirement should be using multiple tools and services (both AI and non-AI) for a more accurate picture of their future prospects.

Thinking about Estate Planning

Your retirement planning was a success! You'll be able to cover your retirement living expenses, and you'll have more than you need (sweet!). But now the issue is deciding what to do about your remaining assets (your estate). Now you need to do estate planning (ugh).

Defining "estate planning"

First, let's define it. Whaddya say, AI?

> "What is estate planning, and why should I do it? Explain it as if I am a high school student."

ChatGPT's response is in Figure 15-2. I don't know about you, but I consider the language of estate planning right up there with Aramaic and Martian. Understanding the terms and concepts is the first battle, and AI is very useful in this regard. I like the feature where I can specify a way to communicate to me because success in a pursuit begins with basic understanding.

With estate planning, the bulk of the work is assembling and recording all the assets (financial, real property, personal effects, and so on) and deciding on the ownership status of each item (I own this, we own that, and so forth). That's most of the physical work of assembling the estate — and AI can help at each juncture.

TIP

In the preceding exchange with ChatGPT, I asked for an answer to be at the "high school student" level. In a prior exchange, my requested level was an "eighth-grade student," so I chuckled when it started off with "Estate planning is like making a plan for your stuff. . ." The point here is to remind you that the style and grade level of ChatGPT's response is within your control.

Beginning the estate planning process

REMEMBER

Keep in mind that estate planning is, of course, done with an experienced attorney. I don't suggest you go it alone even if you do use AI. But you should consider using it to make the process as simple and as painless as possible. Here's a prompt to start you off:

> "Please create a comprehensive checklist of documents and steps for estate planning. Do it in a checklist approach complete with an explanation of each item."

ChatGPT's response is in the following text due to length.

> Estate planning is a crucial process that involves organizing your financial and personal affairs to ensure that your assets are distributed according to your wishes after your passing. It also involves making arrangements for your healthcare and decision-making in case you become incapacitated. Below is a comprehensive checklist for estate planning, along with explanations for each item:

ChatGPT

Estate planning is a crucial process that involves making decisions about how your assets and affairs will be managed, distributed, and cared for after your death or in the event of incapacity. Here are several compelling reasons why you should consider estate planning:

1. **Asset Distribution:** Estate planning allows you to specify how your assets will be distributed among your heirs, beneficiaries, or charitable organizations. Without a plan, state laws may determine the distribution, which might not align with your wishes.

2. **Probate Avoidance:** Proper estate planning can help minimize or avoid probate, a legal process that validates a will and oversees the distribution of assets. Probate can be time-consuming, expensive, and public, but certain estate planning strategies can help streamline this process.

3. **Minor Children's Guardianship:** If you have minor children, estate planning allows you to designate guardians who will take care of them in the event of your death. This ensures that your children are placed under the care of individuals you trust.

4. **Incapacity Planning:** Estate planning includes documents such as a durable power of attorney and healthcare directives, which designate someone to make financial and medical decisions on your behalf if you become incapacitated.

5. **Tax Planning:** Estate planning enables you to minimize potential estate taxes, ensuring that more of your assets go to your chosen beneficiaries rather than to taxes. This is particularly important for individuals with larger estates.

6. **Business Succession Planning:** If you own a business, estate planning can facilitate a smooth transition of ownership to your chosen successors, ensuring the continuity of the business.

7. **Medical Preferences:** Through advance healthcare directives or living wills, estate planning allows you to express your medical treatment preferences in case you are unable to communicate them yourself.

8. **Family Harmony:** Having a clear and comprehensive estate plan can help prevent disputes among family members and reduce the likelihood of conflicts regarding asset distribution or other important decisions.

9. **Charitable Giving:** Estate planning provides an opportunity to include charitable giving as part of your legacy. You can specify how you want to support charitable organizations and causes that are meaningful to you.

10. **Peace of Mind:** Knowing that you have a well-thought-out estate plan in place can provide peace of mind. It allows you to have control over your affairs and ensures that your wishes are carried out according to your intentions.

FIGURE 15-2:
AI's explanation
of estate
planning.

11. **Asset Protection:** Certain estate planning tools can be used to protect your assets from creditors, lawsuits, or other potential threats. This can be especially important for individuals with significant wealth.
12. **Family Business Protection:** For families with businesses, estate planning can help protect the business by establishing plans for succession and providing liquidity for tax obligations.
13. **Avoiding Intestacy Laws:** If you pass away without a will or estate plan, the laws of your state will determine how your assets are distributed, which may not align with your preferences.

In summary, estate planning is a proactive and responsible way to manage your financial and personal affairs, ensuring that your wishes are honored and that your loved ones are taken care of. It provides peace of mind and helps create a legacy that reflects your values and priorities.

FIGURE 15-2: (Continued)

1. Create or Update Your Will:

Explanation: A will is a legal document that outlines how your assets should be distributed upon your death. It can also appoint guardians for minor children and an executor to manage your estate.

2. Establish a Trust:

Explanation: Trusts allow you to transfer assets to beneficiaries with specific conditions or instructions. They can help avoid probate, provide for minors or individuals with special needs, and manage assets over time.

3. Choose an Executor or Trustee:

Explanation: Appoint a responsible person to carry out your wishes as outlined in your will or trust. This person will be responsible for managing your estate and distributing assets.

4. Designate Beneficiaries:

Explanation: Ensure that your retirement accounts, life insurance policies, and other financial assets have designated beneficiaries. These assets pass directly to beneficiaries and bypass the probate process.

5. Create a Durable Power of Attorney (POA):

Explanation: Appoint someone to manage your financial affairs if you become incapacitated. A durable POA remains valid even if you are unable to make decisions.

6. Establish a Healthcare Power of Attorney:

Explanation: Designate someone to make medical decisions on your behalf if you are unable to do so. Discuss your healthcare preferences with your chosen agent.

7. Draft a Living Will or Advance Healthcare Directive:

Explanation: Outline your preferences for medical treatment, end-of-life care, and organ donation in case you are unable to communicate your wishes.

8. Organize Important Documents:

Explanation: Gather and store essential documents, including birth certificates, marriage certificates, deeds, titles, financial statements, and insurance policies in a secure location. Ensure your executor or trustee knows where to find them.

9. Create a Digital Estate Plan:

Explanation: Document your digital assets, such as email accounts, social media profiles, and online financial accounts. Specify how you want them managed or closed after your passing.

10. Review and Update Beneficiary Designations:

Explanation: Periodically review and update beneficiary designations on your retirement accounts, life insurance policies, and other assets to reflect changes in your life.

11. Minimize Estate Taxes:

Explanation: Explore strategies to minimize estate taxes, such as gifting assets, establishing trusts, or taking advantage of the estate tax exemption.

12. Plan for Business Succession:

Explanation: If you own a business, create a succession plan that outlines how it will be managed or transferred to family members or partners.

13. Consider Long-Term Care and Medicaid Planning:

Explanation: If applicable, plan for long-term care needs and consider Medicaid planning strategies to protect your assets.

14. Consult an Estate Planning Attorney:

Explanation: Seek professional legal advice to ensure that your estate plan complies with state and federal laws and is tailored to your specific needs and goals.

15. Communicate Your Wishes:

Explanation: Discuss your estate plan and your intentions with your family members, beneficiaries, and the individuals you've chosen to fulfill key roles to avoid confusion and conflicts.

16. Periodically Review and Update Your Estate Plan:

Explanation: Life circumstances change, so regularly review and update your estate plan to ensure it reflects your current wishes and financial situation.

17. Consider Life Insurance:

Explanation: Evaluate whether life insurance can help provide for your loved ones or cover outstanding debts and funeral expenses.

18. Plan for Funeral and Burial Arrangements:

Explanation: Document your preferences for your funeral and burial or cremation arrangements and ensure your loved ones are aware of them.

19. Secure Your Digital Assets:

Explanation: Create a list of your digital accounts, passwords, and access instructions for your executor or trustee.

20. Preserve Family Heirlooms and Sentimental Items:

Explanation: Specify how you want sentimental items and family heirlooms to be distributed among your heirs.

Estate planning is a complex process that should be done with careful consideration and the guidance of professionals like attorneys and financial advisors. It's crucial to keep your estate plan up to date to reflect your evolving circumstances and ensure that your wishes are carried out as intended.

Yes, estate planning can be complicated and involved. Fortunately, tools such as AI are there to help you in the process. By the time you read this, there will likely be an AI tool specialized in estate planning and you'll most likely find it in the resources listed in Appendix B.

REMEMBER

As with retirement planning, use AI to drill down on each topic and discuss them with your advisor (hopefully, an experienced estate planning attorney). For more information on estate planning, check out the investing resources in Appendix C.

IN THIS CHAPTER

» **Understanding how investments are taxed differently**

» **Giving a piece of your gains to the IRS**

» **Investigating tax deductions for investors**

» **Getting a handle on retirement accounts**

» **Trying AI strategies and other tax resources**

Chapter **16**

Tax Considerations

Y ou're making big profits with your AI strategies — aren't you looking smart! Unfortunately, the taxman cometh for his share, as he always does. In this chapter, I focus on general tax rules that all investors should know about, along with some AI tools and resources to help with taxes.

REMEMBER

Throughout this chapter I refer to the Internal Revenue Service (IRS), tax laws, and IRS publications; visit www.irs.gov. That site has every tax form and tax publication available for easy download. Some of the topics are now in e-book form for easy viewing on your smartphone or laptop. Here are a couple of additional resources from the IRS:

» In the event you need some questions answered by a live IRS customer service person, you can give them a shout at 800-TAX-1040 (800-829-1040). If you need hard copies of forms and publications (for the current tax year or a prior year), you can call the IRS publications department at 800-TAX-FORM (800-829-3676).

» An easy place to go to see the tax reform changes is to go to the IRS's site www.taxchanges.us. Currently it shows you the tax changes from the most recent major tax legislation (circa 2018) but expect updates in the near future as more tax changes (both big and small) become reality.

REMEMBER

At the time of writing, the information in this chapter was considered accurate, but it's always best to double-check with your tax advisor (and triple-check with AI) since tax laws can (and do) frequently change or get modified. Usually the laws change annually, but occasionally they can change mid-year if there are outstanding situations.

Reviewing the Tax Treatment of Different Investments

Different types of investments require different tax treatments. The following sections break down what you need to know.

Understanding ordinary income and capital gains

Profit you make from your stock investments can be taxed in one of two ways, depending on the type of profit:

>> **Ordinary income:** Your profit can be taxed at the same rate as wages or interest — at your full, regular tax rate. If your tax bracket is 28 percent, for example, that's the rate at which your ordinary income investment profit is taxed. Two types of investment profits get taxed as ordinary income (check out IRS Publication 550, "Investment Income and Expenses," for more information; visit www.irs.gov/pub/irs-pdf/p550.pdf):

- **Dividends:** When you receive dividends (either in cash or stock), they're taxed as ordinary income. This is true even if those dividends are used to reinvest in stock through a dividend reinvestment plan (whether through the stock brokerage account or through a formal dividend reinvestment plan).

  If, however, the dividends occur in a tax-sheltered retirement account, such as an IRA or 401(k) plan, then they're exempt from taxes for as long as they stay inside the retirement account. (Retirement plans are covered later in this chapter.)

  REMEMBER

  Keep in mind that dividends can be either "ordinary" or "qualified" and both are taxed differently. Ordinary dividends are taxed as ordinary income at the highest tax rate. Qualified dividends are taxed at a greatly reduced tax rate, and fortunately, the dividends of most stocks and exchange-traded funds (ETFs) are qualified (whew!).

- **Interest:** Most interest income such as interest paid by corporate bonds, treasury bonds, and regular bank accounts is considered ordinary income and taxed at the higher ordinary income tax rate. Keep in mind that interest from municipal bonds can be tax-free, but check with your tax advisor about this.

» **Capital gains:** Outside of income, investors invest for appreciation (an investment goes up in value) as they hold investments, and when they realize this appreciation, it is a capital gain (and a realized loss is a capital loss). Here are the two types of capital gains:

  - **Short-term capital gains:** If you sell stock for a gain and you've owned the stock for one year (or less), the gain is considered ordinary income, which is the highest tax rate for individuals. To calculate the time, you use the *trade date* (or *date of execution* as reported on the trade advice from your brokerage firm). This is the date on which you executed the order, not the settlement date. Keep in mind that if these gains occur inside a tax-sheltered plan, such as a 401(k) or an IRA, no capital gains tax is triggered.

  - **Long-term capital gains:** These are usually taxed at a much better (lower!) rate for you than ordinary income or short-term gains. Yes, the tax laws reward patient investors. For just waiting one more measly day (after the year since the purchase), you get to keep a bigger chunk of your gain; yes, it's worth it.

  Capital gains and losses are covered in greater detail in IRS publication 550, "Investment Income and Expenses." See www.irs.gov/pub/irs-pdf/p550.pdf.

Determining your best timing

A capital gains tax may be a coercive event (so much for "voluntary" taxation), but the good news is that you have control regarding the timing and circumstance of the purchase or sale transaction. You can delay the sale so that you can lower your capital gains tax (from short-term to long-term). You can even time it to take advantage of different tax calendar years.

TIP

Everyone meets with their tax person during the tax season, of course, to prepare and submit the tax return for the prior tax year, but forward-looking investors also meet with their tax person in November or so to discuss which stocks should be sold before the year's end and which stocks should be delayed to the subsequent year (or decide to not sell a stock at all). A common strategy is to sell "losing stocks" in a given year to help minimize or remove potential capital gains taxes. And if a stock with large unrealized gains needs to be sold, then sometimes it makes sense to defer the stock sale until the new year to postpone that potential gain to a future tax year.

TIP

When you buy stock, record the date of purchase and the *cost basis* (the purchase price of the stock plus any ancillary charges, such as commissions). This information is very important come tax time should you decide to sell your stock. The date of purchase (also known as the *date of execution*) helps establish the *holding period* (how long you own the stocks), which determines whether your gains are considered short-term or long-term.

Fortunately most stock brokerage websites let you easily download a spreadsheet of your positions, and you can separate and view those positions with realized gains/losses and those with unrealized gains/losses so that you can optimize net gains and losses with both your financial advisor and your tax person.

Looking at a capital gains example

Table 16-1 gives you an ultra-simple visual about a simple difference financially between the short-term capital gains tax (ordinary income tax) and the long-term capital gains tax (a lower rate and therefore more favorable).

TABLE 16-1   **Short-Term versus Long-Term Capital Gains Tax**

Simple Scenario Example	Short-Term Capital Gains Scenario	Long-Term Capital Gains Scenario
Gain	Short-term gain of $10,000	Long-term gain of $10,000
Tax category	Ordinary income	Long-term capital gains
Tax rate	28%	15%
Tax amount	$2,800	$1,500
Tax savings	Nothing . . . ugh!	Save $1,300 on taxes ($2,800 less $1,500)

This example is only simple in that you need to see the savings. Of course the typical tax scenario is more complex, and you'll get into the nitty-gritty with your tax person, but this example helps with clarity (it's nice to see the potential tax savings!).

Say you bought 100 shares of Fake Genius AI Inc. (symbol: FGAI) at $10 per share, and you pay a stock brokerage commission of $5. Your cost basis would be $1,005 (100 shares times $10 plus $5 commission). If you sold that FGAI stock at $40 per share (and then pay a $6 commission), then the total sale amount would be $3,994 (or 100 shares times $40 per share less the $6 commission). The realized capital gain would be $2,989 (sale proceeds of $3,994 less the original cost basis of $1,005). But the timing here is important:

>> If this sale occurs a year — either exactly or less than a year — after the purchase date, then it is a short-term capital gain.

>> If this sale occurs a year *and* a day — or longer — after the purchase date, then it's a long-term capital gain, taxed at a lower rate. (See the next section for more details.)

WARNING

Those sneaky folks in Washington, D.C., are always looking for new ways to get a growing piece of your money so don't be passive about it. In early 2022, there were rumblings among the politicians about finding a way to tax "unrealized gains," which is shocking. Imagine paying taxes on a gain that you didn't realize . . . ugh! As I write this, it hasn't become a formal piece of legislation but keep watching. The point here is to keep yourself informed (some tax resources are listed at the end of this chapter) and to please communicate to your representatives how you feel about tax increases (don't be shy!).

Minimizing capital gains taxes

REMEMBER

Long-term capital gains are taxed at a more favorable rate than ordinary income. To qualify for long-term capital gains treatment, you must hold the investment for at least a year and a day (yes, that specific).

Building on the example in the previous section, assume you have stock in Fake Genius AI Inc. (symbol FGAI). As a short-term transaction at the 28 percent tax rate, the tax would be $837 (28 percent of $2,989).

However, if that gain was long-term, what would the tax be? That gain of $2,489 would be taxed at the more favorable long-term capital gains tax rate of 15 percent or a tax of $448 (a tax savings amount of $389, which is the difference).

REMEMBER

Capital gains taxes *can* be lower than the tax on ordinary income, but they aren't higher. If, for example, you're in the 15 percent tax bracket for ordinary income and you have a long-term capital gain that would normally bump you up to the 28 percent tax bracket, the gain is taxed at your lower rate of 15 percent instead of a higher capital gains rate. Check with your tax advisor on a regular basis because this rule could change due to new tax laws.

REMEMBER

Don't sell a particular stock or ETF just because it qualifies for long-term capital gains treatment, even if the sale eases your tax burden. If the investment is doing well and meets your long-term investing criteria, hold on to it. Plus if it is a dividend-paying stock, then it may be serving your passive income needs. Lastly, that dividend may very well be a qualified dividend, which means lower taxes on it.

Cutting taxes with capital losses

REMEMBER

It's always good to have stock investing gains — but at least losses can have a consolation prize — lowering your taxes. A capital loss means that you realized a loss on a given investment. The loss amount is generally deductible on your tax return, and you can claim a loss on either long-term or short-term stock holdings. This loss can go against your other income and lower your overall tax.

Say you bought Natural Stupidity Co (NSC) common stock for a total purchase of $5,000 and you sold it later for $700. This means you realized a capital loss of $4,300 ($5,000 purchase price less the $700 sale price). Your tax-deductible loss would be the same, $4,300.

REMEMBER

The one string attached to deducting investment losses on your tax return is that the most you can report in a single year is a net loss of $3,000. On the bright side, though, any excess loss isn't really lost — you can carry it forward to the next year.

Let's use the example of NSC. If it's the only loss ($4,300 loss), then you can deduct only $3,000 of it, and the remaining $1,300 would be carried over to a subsequent year.

And note that any loss you realize can go against any gains that you realize since that $3,000 loss limit is a net amount after you calculate all your gains and losses. Before you can deduct losses, you must first use them to offset any capital gains. If, for example, you realize long-term capital gains of $7,500 in Stock A and long-term capital losses of $6,000 in Stock B, then you have a net long-term capital gain of $1,500 ($7,500 gain less the offset of $6,000 loss). Whenever possible, see whether losses in your portfolio can be realized to offset any capital gains to reduce potential tax. IRS Publication 550 includes information for investors on capital gains and losses; visit www.irs.gov/pub/irs-pdf/p550.pdf.

REMEMBER

Here's your optimum strategy: Where possible, keep losses on a short-term basis and push your gains into long-term capital gains status. If a transaction can't be tax-free, at the very least try to defer the tax to keep your money working for you.

Evaluating gain and loss scenarios

Of course, any investor can come up with hundreds of possible gain and loss scenarios. For example, you may wonder what happens if you sell part of your holdings now as a short-term capital loss and the remainder later as a long-term capital gain. You must look at each sale of stock (or potential sale) methodically to calculate the gain or loss you would realize from it.

Fortunately, tracking sales and expenses is easier than ever before since every brokerage site gives you the ability to download transactions to either a spreadsheet format or a data format that can easily be imported and used in financial and/or tax software.

REMEMBER

Figuring out your gain or loss isn't that complicated. Here are some general rules to help you wade through the morass. If you add up all your gains and losses and

>> **The net result is a short-term gain:** It's taxed at your highest tax bracket (as ordinary income).

>> **The net result is a long-term gain:** It's taxed at 15 percent if you're in the 28 percent tax bracket or higher. Check with your tax advisor on changes here that may affect your taxes.

>> **The net result is a loss of $3,000 or less:** It's fully deductible against other income. If you're married filing separately, your deduction limit is $1,500.

>> **The net result is a loss that exceeds $3,000:** You can only deduct up to $3,000 in that year; the remainder goes forward to future years.

Sharing with the IRS

Of course, you don't want to pay more taxes than you have to, but as the old cliché goes, "Don't let the tax tail wag the investment dog." You should buy or sell a stock because it makes economic sense first and consider the tax implications as secondary issues. After all, taxes consume a relatively small portion of your gain. As long as you experience a *net gain* (gain after all transaction costs, including taxes, brokerage fees, and other related fees), consider yourself a successful investor — even if you have to give away some of your gain to taxes.

In the following sections, I describe the tax forms you need to fill out, as well as some important rules to follow.

TIP

Try to make tax planning second nature in your day-to-day activities. No, you don't have to immerse yourself with a dumpster full of forms and paperwork. I simply mean that when you make a taxable transaction, keep the receipt and maintain good records. When you make a large purchase or sale, pause for a moment and ask yourself whether this transaction will have positive or negative tax consequences.

Tax forms

Investors report their investment-related activities on their individual tax returns (Form 1040). Here are the reports that you'll likely receive from brokers and other investment sources:

>> **Brokerage and bank statements:** Monthly statements that you receive.

>> **Trade confirmations:** Documents to confirm that you bought or sold stock.

>> **1099-DIV:** Reporting dividends paid to you.

>> **1099-INT:** Reporting interest paid to you.

>> **1099-B:** Reporting gross proceeds submitted to you from the sale of investments, such as stocks and mutual funds.

>> **K-1:** If you're invested in ETFs, you'll likely receive this for any distributions.

REMEMBER

The IRS schedules and forms that most stock investors need to be aware of and/or attach to their Form 1040 include the following:

>> **Schedule A:** To report investment interest and investment-related expenses

>> **Schedule B:** To report interest and dividends

>> **Form 8949 and Schedule D:** To report capital gains and losses

>> **Form 4952:** Investment Interest Expense Deduction

You can download these forms from the website (www.irs.gov). For more information on what records and documentation investors should hang on to, check out IRS Publication 552, "Recordkeeping for Individuals." You can find the latest version of this publication online at www.irs.gov/pub/irs-pdf/p552.pdf.

The wash-sale rule

This section is for those of you who are thinking of getting "imaginative" with your stock buying and selling tax strategies. You may get the idea of "Hmmm. Maybe I should sell those stocks that have unrealized losses in December and gain those capital losses, and then buy the stock back in January." Would that work?

REMEMBER

Not really. The IRS zapped that crafty idea with something called the wash-sale rule. This rule states that if you sell a stock for a loss and buy it back within 30 days, the loss isn't valid because you didn't make any substantial investment change. The wash-sale rule applies only to losses. The way around the rule is simple: Wait at least 31 days before you buy that identical stock back again.

REMEMBER

Some people try to get around the wash-sale rule by doubling up on their stock position with the intention of selling half. Therefore, the IRS makes the 30-day rule cover both sides of the sale date. That way, an investor can't buy the identical stock within 30 days just before the sale and then realize a short-term loss for tax purposes.

Looking at Tax Deductions for Investors

As you oversee and manage your portfolio, you may incur expenses along the way. Some expenses can be tax-deductible, and some won't be — even some that you would think would logically be deductible. Keep in mind that logic and tax law are not always in sync.

The most common place where you would take investment-related expenses legitimately would be on Schedule A, which is an attachment to Form 1040 (which is frequently referred to as the "long form").

REMEMBER

For 2024, the standard deduction for individuals increased so you may not need to (or be able to) itemize. Table 16-2 lists the standard deductions for 2024.

TABLE 16-2 ## Standard Tax Deductions

Type of 1040 Filer	Then Your 2024 Standard Deduction Is
Married filing jointly or qualifying widow(er)	$29,200
Head of household	$21,900
Single or married filing separately	$14,600

TIP

The data in Table 16-2 was extracted from Form 1040-ES, which is used for estimating taxes and related data for those forward thinkers who want to plan their taxes (always a good thing to do!) by checking the upcoming year (in this case 2024), but you should make it a habit and always check out and estimate your potential tax liability for a subsequent year.

TIP

If you're reading this in 2024, then you should check out the 1040-ES for subsequent years so that you can stay a step ahead of your tax liability and be able to strategize with your tax person about how to lower it.

The following sections go into more detail on different types of tax deductions.

Investment interest

If you pay interest such as "margin interest" in your stock brokerage account due to borrowing to acquire a taxable investment (such as common stock or ETFs), then that interest is categorized as "investment interest" and can be fully tax-deductible in the "interest" category of Schedule A (but only up to the amount of your net taxable income).

WARNING

Be careful because not all interest is deductible. Consumer interest (such as what you may pay on balances on your credit card) are not deductible. Also, the use of funds will matter regarding the deductibility of the interest.

For example, if you borrow money from your broker (via a margin loan that is secured by your securities portfolio) and use those funds for investment purposes (such as acquiring other taxable stock), then the interest is deductible as investment interest. However, if these borrowed funds are used to make a consumer purchase (such as furniture for your home or a vacation), then the use is characterized as a consumer loan, which means that the interest is considered consumer interest and, therefore, not deductible.

REMEMBER

Again, tax rules can change from time to time, so keep checking with IRS publications and other tax resources (covered later in this chapter), and check with your tax person.

Foreign taxes on investments

In recent years many U.S. investors have been able to purchase shares of foreign securities (such as European or Asian stocks) in their brokerage accounts. Typically there may be taxes charged by those governments (such as on dividends).

These foreign taxes are usually deductible and reported on Schedule A.

Miscellaneous expenses (on Schedule A)

For individual taxpayers, reporting and deducting investment-related expenses are usually done on Schedule A (an attachment to your Form 1040).

Even more specifically, they are reported on the section on Schedule A referred to as "miscellaneous expenses."

>> Any tax-related expense such as tax software, tax preparation fees, tax courses, and so on.

>> Legal fees in investment-related issues such as stockholders' lawsuits.

>> Bank safe deposit box fees for holding taxable securities.

>> Travel expenses to advisors regarding investments.

>> Service charges for collecting and distributing income from taxable dividends and interest.

>> Expenses for accounting/bookkeeping.

>> If you use a computer 50 percent or more of the time to help you manage your expenses, you may be able to partially deduct the computer's purchase price as an expense.

>> Depreciation can be a deduction for business owners who have assets and/or equipment used in business activity. Investors may or may not be able to claim it as a deduction and should consult with their tax advisor.

REMEMBER

On Schedule A, you can deduct only that portion of your miscellaneous expenses that exceeds 2 percent of your adjusted gross income. For more information on deducting miscellaneous expenses, check out IRS Publication 529, "Miscellaneous Deductions." You can find it online www.irs.gov/pub/irs-pdf/p529.pdf.

The donation of securities

Many folks have a favored charity, and many typically donate cash. Some who are feeling particularly generous may feel the impulse to cash out a stock (or other security such as a bond or ETF) and donate the proceeds. It's a noble idea, but you may want to rethink how you do it.

WARNING

Say you have stock worth $10,000, and it was stock you purchased long ago for, say, $2,000. If you sell the stock, receive the $10,000 in cash, and give it to charity, you would feel good, but you would likely owe taxes on that $8,000 realized gain after all is said and done. Not a good way to do this. Here's a better way: Simply donate the $10,000 worth of stock directly without selling it. Simply transfer the stock to the charity of your choice. You'll get the full benefit of the $10,000 as a tax deduction but without the tax pain. Cool, right?

For more details on this type of transaction, check out IRS Publication 526, "Charitable Contributions," and discuss the pros and cons of this with your tax person. You can find the publication online at www.irs.gov/pub/irs-pdf/p526.pdf.

Nondeductible items

WARNING

In case you were tempted to deduct some nondeductible items, let's make it obvious here what you can't deduct:

>> Financial planning events

>> Investment seminars

>> Any travel expenses to a stockholders' meeting

>> Home office expenses (as you manage your portfolio)

For more details on investment income and expenses, check out the IRS publications listed later in this chapter.

Getting Tax Benefits with Retirement Accounts

Long-term investing is best done in retirement accounts that offer tax benefits so you can maximize your long-term success. The following sections cover the most obvious tax-advantaged accounts.

IRAs

Individual Retirement Accounts (IRAs) are accounts you can open with a financial institution, such as a bank or a mutual fund company. An IRA is available to almost anyone who has earned income, and it allows you to set aside and invest money to help fund your retirement. Opening an IRA is easy, and virtually any bank or mutual fund can guide you through the process. Two basic types of IRAs are traditional and Roth.

Traditional IRAs

The traditional IRA (also called the *deductible IRA*) was first popularized in the early 1980s. In a traditional IRA, the contribution limits for 2023 are $6,500 for those under age 50 and $7,500 for those 50 and older. For 2024, the contribution limits are $7,000 for those under age 50 and $8,000 for those age 50 or older. Some restrictions may apply.

The money can then grow in the IRA account without being encumbered by current taxes because the money isn't taxed until you take it out. Because IRAs are designed for retirement purposes, you can start taking money out of your IRA in the year you turn 59½. (Hmm. I guess that means if you want your cash at age 58⅞, then you are out of luck?)

The withdrawals at that point are taxed as ordinary income. Fortunately (or hopefully?!), you may be in a lower tax bracket during your retirement years so the tax shouldn't be as burdensome.

REMEMBER

Keep in mind that you'll likely be required to start taking distributions (RMDs or Required Minimum Distributions) when you reach age 72 (a bummer for those of you that prefer a later time like 73⅔).

WARNING

If you take out money from an IRA too early, the amount is included in your taxable income, and you may be zapped with a 10 percent penalty. You can avoid the penalty if you have a good reason. The IRS provides a list of reasons in Publication 590-B, "Distributions from Individual Retirement Arrangements (IRAs)." Check it out online at www.irs.gov/pub/irs-pdf/p590b.pdf.

Keep in mind that to contribute money into an IRA, it must be earned income (such as from a job or net business income) and that the amount you're contributing is equal or less than your earned income.

For more details, check out IRS Publication 590-A, "Contributions to Individual Retirement Arrangements (IRAs)." Visit www.irs.gov/pub/irs-pdf/p590a.pdf.

Roth IRAs

The Roth IRA is a great retirement plan that I wish had existed a long time ago. Here are some ways to distinguish the Roth IRA from the traditional IRA:

» The Roth IRA provides no tax deduction for contributions.

» Money in the Roth IRA grows tax-free and can be withdrawn tax-free in the year that you turn 59½.

» The Roth IRA is subject to early distribution penalties (although there are exceptions). Distributions have to be qualified to be penalty- and tax-free; in other words, make sure that any distribution is within the guidelines set by the IRS (see Publication 590-B at www.irs.gov/pub/irs-pdf/p590b.pdf).

The maximum contribution per year for Roth IRAs is the same as for traditional IRAs. You can open a self-directed account with a broker as well. See IRS Publication 590-A (www.irs.gov/pub/irs-pdf/p590a.pdf) for details on qualifying.

401(k) plans

For employees, the 401(k) plan is the holy grail of retirement accounts (or is that the 800-pound gorilla?). Generally this account is managed by financial institutions (utilizing a menu of mutual funds), but there are self-directed plans, too (especially if you own and run a business).

Even if your particular 401(k) is conventional and you have no role in its management, I still mention these in the scope of this book because you do have input ability in terms of mutual fund selection. Perhaps not today, but in due course, you may have greater latitude in choosing funds. As AI investing gains prominence, more and more 401(k) administrators will likely add these choices to the mix so . . . stay tuned!

For 2023, employees can contribute up to $22,500. Those employees who are age 50 or over can be eligible for an additional "catch-up" contribution of $7,500.

At the time of this writing, the limits for 2024 rise to $23,000 with $7,500 catch-up respectively.

Checking Out AI Tax Tactics and Strategies

The bottom line is if artificial intelligence can make you money, then using it to save on taxes is a no-brainer (I couldn't resist).

Later in this chapter I note some AI tools for tax purposes. But let's cover some AI strategies you can do with tools such as ChatGPT (see Chapter 2 for more details):

>> Ask ChatGPT to produce a detailed checklist of tax documents (1099s, statements, and so on) you'll need so you can be more organized.

>> For any of your activities, request that ChatGPT provide an extensive list of tax deductions for that activity and where (tax form) those deductions reported.

>> Ask all your tax questions and be specific and detailed.

>> Ask questions such as "What are common tax deductions for investors/job hunters/freelancers, etc."

>> Provide details on two different tax scenarios that you may face and ask for a comparison on pros and cons.

>> Ask it to summarize lengthy public posts at either the IRS or other public tax information sites. Chapter 2 can help with this. For other ideas on prompting, check out Chapter 18.

WARNING

As I write this, the free version of ChatGPT (version 3.5) only has information updates as of January 2022. In other words, don't bother asking it about tax law changes in 2023 or 2024. You will have better luck with the premium (paid) version, which is version 4.0 (as of the time of writing). Lastly (and perhaps most advisedly), check out the tax-specific AI tools listed later in this chapter.

REMEMBER

AI tools can help you summarize and explain tax documents found at the IRS site. If there is a tax issue or point that sounds complicated, you can ask ChatGPT, for example, to "explain this to me as if I were a seventh grader" and then describe your issue or question. More pointers are in Chapter 2.

Tapping into Tax Resources

Seriously, the tax stuff earlier wasn't that bad, right? But just because this tax chapter ended, it doesn't mean that tax fun has ended. Here are more resources to keep your tax savings rolling. As you can see, the IRS has ramped up their assistance to entrepreneurs big and small, so take a look. Or have AI help you take a look (more on this later in the chapter).

IRS publications

Just to round out this chapter, here are the main IRS publications you (and or your tax person) should be aware of and which can be found at www.irs.gov:

>> Estimated taxes info for 2023 (Form 1040-ES; www.irs.gov/pub/irs-pdf/f1040es.pdf)

>> Personal tax guide for 1040 filers (Publication 17; www.irs.gov/pub/irs-pdf/p17.pdf)

>> Retirement plans tax info (Publication 560; www.irs.gov/pub/irs-pdf/p560.pdf)

>> Investment income and expenses (Publication 550; www.irs.gov/pub/irs-pdf/p550.pdf)

And for those of you who are thinking of doing a business with your newfound AI tools and strategies, then also consider getting

>> Starting a Business and Keeping Records (Publication 583; www.irs.gov/pub/irs-pdf/p583.pdf)

» Tax Guide for Small Business (IRS Publication 334; www.irs.gov/pub/irs-pdf/p334.pdf)

» Business Use of Your Home (Publication 587; www.irs.gov/pub/irs-pdf/p587.pdf)

AI tax tools

Keep in mind that this is not a comprehensive list as more programs and apps will likely get added soon. In the meanwhile, check out the following programs and get the full details at the site provided:

» TaxGPT (www.taxgpt.com/)

» ZeroTax AI (www.zerotax.ai)

» TaxLy (www.taxly.ai)

» FlyFin (www.flyfin.tax)

» Keeper (www.keepertax.com)

» AiTax (www.aitax.com)

» WellyBox (www.wellybox.com)

TIP

Check out Appendix A for a list of AI database sites that are updated daily with new AI tools. I'm sure more have been added since I finished this paragraph. Also, Appendix A also lists sources that review AI tools and lets you know how good (or not so good) they are.

Tax sites

Congratulations! You made it to the end of a chapter on taxes in one piece, but your journey to tax savings has only just begun. Here are some places to visit for help on keeping your tax bill as low as possible:

» Tax Foundation (www.taxfoundation.org)

» Tax Mama (www.taxmama.com)

» CPA Journal (www.cpajournal.com)

» National Taxpayers Union (www.ntu.org)

» Americans for Tax Reform (www.atr.org)

Tax software

Here is where I'm grateful for technology. Tax software can keep us from leaping off into the nearest ravine. Here are three major popular tax software sites to help you with your daunting tax preparation issues:

>> Turbo Tax (www.intuit.com)

>> TaxCut (www.hrblock.com)

>> Tax Act (www.taxact.com)

Tax resources from yours truly

After all that, you didn't think I would leave you hanging, right? Here are some resources straight from me:

>> "How to Make Any Expense Tax-Deductible" (online tax course): An extensive yet easy step-by-step course that talks about tax concepts and strategies without getting complicated. Find out more at www.ravingcapitalist.com/home/how-to-make-any-expense-tax-deductible/.

>> "How to Take the Home Office Tax Deduction": This is a mini-course that focuses on the home office deduction and how to take it properly. Done right, this tax deduction could be worth thousands all by itself. Find out more at www.ravingcapitalist.com/home/home-office-tax-kit/.

5

The Part of Tens

Discover ten cautions before you jump into the world of AI investing.

Check out ten prompting strategies you can use with ChatGPT.

Turn to ten AI tools and resources for beginners.

Read about ten strategies that can complement your AI investing pursuits.

Chapter **17**

Ten Cautions about Artificial Intelligence

"**D**anger, Will Robinson!" was the urgent alarm from the robot (named "Robot," by the way) in a classic TV show on space travel some decades ago . . . and I feel the impulse here to talk about AI's dangers in the digital age. AI, like any new innovation or ground-breaking development, has plenty of great potential but also has issues and potential problems that should make you more cautious. In this chapter, I dive right in.

Inaccuracy and Errors

Yes, I get it — AI is "super intelligent" and the stuff of science fiction movies, but let's keep the science and do what we can about the "fiction." With all of its advancement, AI is still the perfect real-world example of "garbage in, garbage out." If you give it questions like "What is the square root of 1,012?" you will likely get the correct answer — but it can provide inaccurate answers depending on the topic. I have asked it questions from history, politics, and economics (that I already knew the answer) and got an inaccurate spin.

The bottom line is that you should use several sources (AI and otherwise) if the answer is vital to your major investing concern. If you come across an obvious inaccuracy, be sure to tell the source so that this particular AI tool is more accurate going forward.

REMEMBER

On complex and/or controversial topics, including investing, check several sources (human as well as AI) before you make your judgement or decision.

REMEMBER

A good example about inaccuracy is the issue of "hallucination" in the world of AI (no, I'm not kidding you). Those who have used generative AI tools such as ChatGPT and Bing Chat have reported that these AI tools have invented answers that sound realistic but were, in fact, totally wrong. This was identified by the folks at Bedrock AI (www.bedrock-ai.com/post/why-you-shouldn-t-trust-generative-ai-to-do-stock-research).

Bias

Yes, bias is a concern. If you use AI to find information and/or neutral facts on a given topic, the more controversial the topic is, the more likely you will get a slanted view.

I was born in a communist country, and I know this wretched system better than most. Communism (as an engine of economic decisions) destroys economies, and it destroyed my former country. When I asked the AI tool ChatGPT "Did communism destroy Yugoslavia?" it responded with "No . . . Yugoslavia was destroyed by financial mismanagement, etc." and it rattled off a set of bad economic policies. It didn't realize that it provided a list of symptoms of . . . communism. In other words, it accurately listed the problems of communism but didn't blame communism. It's as if I asked it if John Wilkes Booth killed Abraham Lincoln, and it responded "No, Lincoln was killed by a bullet shot from a gun that was fired by an actor that fits the description of some guy whose last name is Booth."

I am sure that you'll find your own examples of bias.

REMEMBER

If the information is sensitive and/or very important to you or for an important purpose, double-check what result you get from AI. If possible, check with several different sources. When it comes to investing, review the resources in this book's appendixes for further guidance.

Fraud

You KNOW that there is someone out there — *right now* — trying to figure out how to use AI to defraud you of your money. Count on it. AI is being used in telephone scams, email scams, and so forth. AI has an amazing ability to replicate the human voice and mimic interaction, so you as the consumer have to be on guard.

Right now lawmakers at all levels of government are grappling with appropriate levels of regulations to protect consumers, investors, and others from abuse that will inevitably arise from AI-related fraud.

REMEMBER

In the same way you've guarded yourself from human fraud, do the same with AI-related fraud. Don't provide sensitive account information, passcodes, and so on.

TIP

Stay in touch with regulations and ongoing developments in the AI space with resources that are listed in Appendix A.

Job Displacement

Adapt or die. You've heard that before (but not from Blockbuster Video or Enron). Artificial intelligence will likely replace many functions that we have taken for granted or that have been undertaken by other humans, but we need to be vigilant for our own sake and those dependent on us.

By now you've probably seen some well-publicized reports that a zillion people will lose their jobs because of AI; meanwhile I saw another report that AI had created 800,000 jobs during 2021–2022. What is the deal?

When the automobile came widely onto the public market during the 1910–1930 period, the reports of potential unemployment in the horse and buggy industry and related industries were indeed correct, but of course, then employment opportunities emerged in the manufacture, marketing, and maintenance of automobiles. For the nimble worker, how quickly did they make that switch to avoid career pain?

How quickly will you embrace AI so that your career doesn't go the way of the horse and buggy worker? Do your research and find out what AI tools and resources will help you. I am of the mind that the more self-sufficient and independent you are, the better off you will be (especially financially).

I've always been an advocate for people to start a part-time home business as a form of diversification from their job. If you're 100 percent financially reliant on a single, full-time job, then that could easily become a huge problem if something goes wrong with that job. Having a second source of income should be a no-brainer.

TIP

Learn AI as soon as possible to make yourself indispensable at your job, and in your spare time, start a home-based business with the help and power that AI can give you. For more details on career and business ideas, check out Chapter 12.

Overreliance on Technology

The same way a good cook always checks the stove or other cooking gadget to make sure the meal comes out great every time, so should you with AI. Just because a piece of information is AI generated, that doesn't mean it's perfect or that your oversight is not required.

If AI generates a report at your work, for example, read it and maybe discuss it with a trusted associate before it goes to your client or to your boss. Until AI goes through more vetting and refinement, double-checking the work (especially critical work for you) is highly recommended. If you're using AI for tax matters, get a second opinion or a review from a human tax specialist.

Information versus Wisdom

REMEMBER

We're drowning in a sea of information and data, but we're parched for wisdom and discernment. Never forget that AI is a tool that can be awesome and powerful with tasks at hand but that judgment and discernment are still in the human realm. Natural intelligence and wisdom are the best navigators in the world — guideposts no matter how sophisticated artificial intelligence gets in its role as your servant.

Use of the Right AI Tool

In the beginning, there was AI. And then there was ChatGPT. But then hundreds and probably soon thousands of AI tools and apps were born. In the same way we've learned that hammers and screwdrivers were different tools meant for different uses, we'll soon (and very likely right now) learn that there are different tools in this new and dynamic realm.

If I ask ChatGPT a financial or economic question and then ask the same question of a robo-advisor or financial AI tool, will I get the same answer?

Likely not. Each will be reliant on different inputs from different databases overseen by different human professionals.

Use the appropriate AI tool for your specific purposes. Check out the various tools, apps, and information sources listed in this book's appendixes so that you can gain the most useful responses (text or otherwise) for your given issues and needs.

Your Input versus AI Output

You read earlier in this chapter (and also earlier in this book) about "garbage in, garbage out," and that point was made in regards to that army of folks who created the world of AI. But now I ask that question of you: Are you using AI the right way so that you get the optimal results for your purposes?

You can describe what you want to ten different people and ask each one to get an answer from their given AI tool, and I'm reasonably certain that you'll get ten different results. Perhaps not markedly different, but materially different — enough to make a significant difference in the result. If one person asked the same exact question to ChatGPT 3.5 as the next person asked to ChatGPT 4.0, you'll get a material difference.

Learn to be a proficient user or "prompt engineer" so that your results are as relevant and useful as possible to your goals and aspirations. Check out the resources in Appendix A.

Faulty Predictions

Because of issues addressed earlier in this chapter (such as inaccuracy or bias), AI could issue forecasts or predictions that will, in turn, also be inaccurate. If forecasts and predictions are important to your pursuits (business or financial, for example), then it will be important for you to ensure that predictions issued from AI tools and/or apps are as realistic as possible.

Keep in mind that "predictions" or "forecasts" are different for various occupations and disciplines. Asking AI about forecasts on social trends or financial, economic, or business purposes are varied, so make sure you're using the right AI tool for the right purpose, goal, or category.

Privacy

Be careful out there. With AI, you get the benefit of it scanning the big, wide world of data. But keep in mind that when you get involved, you become part of the big wide world of data. In other words, what you do as an AI user can certainly mean that you'll be tracked, monitored, and subject to discovery by someone or some agency in the near or distant future.

In the late 1990s, I was very wary of email, and I mean *very* wary of email. Given my origin (coming from a society that . . . ahem . . . "monitored" their citizenry as often as possible), I was always careful about what and how I communicated in an email. I remember asking myself, "Will I be embarrassed if someone or some organization reads this back to me five years from now? How will it make me feel?"

REMEMBER

Be very mindful of rules and regulations that protect your privacy, and communicate with your representatives to formulate laws to protect yourself and others from abuses of your privacy. Lastly, be a healthy self-monitor of what and how you communicate, including in AI tools, so that you aren't harmed or embarrassed down the road.

Chapter **18**

Ten or So Types of Prompts You Can Use for AI Investing

he AI prompts in this chapter were designed with the investor in mind. There are questions and requests for your consideration as good starting points. Of course, you're encouraged to be as creative and as imaginative as possible. Unless otherwise indicated, these prompts can be used on ChatGPT (and similar AI chat tools).

TIP

Keep in mind that the following prompts are merely starters for your AI investing adventures and are not meant to be a comprehensive list. I've seen tutorials and videos in which they take prompting to new levels of awesome usefulness! But no worries; those sources are in Appendix A.

Simple Questions

Perhaps the first prompt should be the simplest ones to get you rolling. Ask about the definitions of investments like these:

- » "What is a common stock?"

- » "What is a closed-end fund?"

- » "What is a covered call option?"

The great thing about AI is that no matter how simple or simplistic the question, you'll get a serious response.

Other good simple questions to ask would be about financial jargon or acronyms such as "What is a SPAC?" (If you're curious, SPAC stands for special purpose acquisition company.) I'm up on my financial jargon and acronyms, but I could have really found this valuable when I communicated with my kids when they were teens.

Another simple question to ask is about the appropriateness of specific investing or speculative vehicles, such as "For whom would a cryptocurrency be appropriate?" or "Is a double short inverse exchange-traded fund appropriate for a retiree worried about a market crash?"

When you're ready, you can go on to the next level of complexity. Keep reading.

Complex Questions

Now you can take the simple questions in the preceding section and take your prompt further. For example:

- » Instead of "What is a common stock?" you can ask, "What is a common stock, and what should I know about how to invest in it as a beginner?"

- » Instead of "What is a closed-end fund?" you can ask, "What is a closed-end fund, and when is it good for a risk-adverse 65-year-old male?"

- » Instead of "What is a covered call option?" you can ask, "What is a covered call option, and how can I safely do one as a retiree during a recession?"

TIP

Most tools such as ChatGPT give you the ability to essentially have a dialogue so that you can ask a follow-up question, and it will remember the context from the prior prompt. You can also ask it to regenerate a response or to clarify further.

Personal Scenarios with Goals in Mind

Give ChatGPT a scenario with a goal in mind. I actually tried the following:

> "I am dirt poor with no assets, and I make $17,000 per year as a mattress tester. How can I create a million-dollar net worth within ten years?"

Keep in mind that this isn't my personal situation (don't send me any sympathy cards). But think of your situation or describe an issue in your life with a goal in mind and give it a shot (as often as you like). You can even provide a detailed account of your issue or situation along with your concerns, and AI can give you a detailed response along with what it generates to be suitable recommendations.

Formulas

Keep in mind that ChatGPT and other AI tools can do everything from designing a complicated formula in your spreadsheet program to actually doing the programming for a web page (HTML or other programming language).

You can even have ChatGPT explain a formula to you such as "How does the dividend payout ratio work?" Or you can describe your issue and have ChatGPT create a formula for it.

You can even have ChatGPT solve the missing variable in a formula you're creating for your situation. For example:

> "I will be retiring in 20 years, and I want to have a nest egg worth $2.5 million dollars. How much would I need to save each month if the average growth rate during that timeframe is 8 percent?"

Lists

TIP

In the world of money, you don't want to miss a step. Creating a list of items or creating a checklist for things you don't want to miss in a given process is very useful. Here are some ideas:

>> Getting ready for tax season? Have AI create your checklist of documents.

>> Worried about a stock in your portfolio? Have a list of reasons created for why you should consider selling it.

>> Attracted to a stock or other investment and not sure about it? Create a list of pros and cons along to discuss with your advisor or spouse.

>> Getting ready to do estate planning? Create a checklist of documents and why they are needed.

>> Starting a business? Create a checklist of every step you'll need to address to get started successfully.

Second Opinions

We always hear in the medical world that getting a second opinion is a good thing. Getting a second in the financial world is a good thing, too. When your financial advisor tells you that "this is the best approach" for you, get a second opinion with your AI tool.

Your prompt would be something like this:

"I am an investor in situation A [be detailed here] and a financial advisor told me to do Strategy B so that I can [reach my goal] or [overcome a financial issue or problem]. Please provide a list of reasons why it may not be a good strategy for me."

Now don't use this strategy to stir up a conflict with your advisor, but certainly bring up those points to discuss all the possibilities so that you're clearer about an optimal approach.

Pros and Cons

Describe a particular investing/financial strategy, approach, idea, or vehicle (or asset or type of investment), and you can ask for an extensive list of pros and cons or advantages/disadvantages given to you in a format of your choosing, such as a bulleted or numbered list or in table format.

Figure 18-1 shows an example in which I asked ChatGPT for a list of pros and cons for bank savings accounts versus money market funds, set up in a table format.

You

Please give me a detailed list of pros and cons of bank savings accounts versus a money market fund and give it to me in a table format.

 ChatGPT

Certainly! Below is a detailed list of pros and cons for bank savings accounts and money market funds presented in a table format:

Criteria	Bank Savings Account	Money Market Fund
Interest Rates	*Pros:* Typically offer some interest.	*Pros:* Generally offer higher yields compared to savings accounts.
	Cons: Lower interest rates compared to money market funds.	*Cons:* Yields may vary and are subject to market conditions.
Liquidity	*Pros:* Easily accessible, allows quick withdrawals.	*Pros:* Offers liquidity, allowing easy access to funds.
	Cons: Limited monthly withdrawals, withdrawal restrictions.	*Cons:* Redemption restrictions may apply, limiting immediate access.
Risk	*Pros:* Low-risk, deposits are insured by government agencies.	*Pros:* Generally low-risk, investments are in short-term, highly liquid securities.
	Cons: Minimal risk, but no guarantee against inflation.	*Cons:* Slight risk, not completely immune to market fluctuations.
Initial Deposit	*Pros:* Usually low or no minimum initial deposit.	*Pros:* Minimum investment amounts may vary but can be relatively low.
	Cons: Higher interest rates for larger deposits may apply.	*Cons:* Some funds may require a higher initial investment.
Account Fees	*Pros:* May have minimal fees or none at all.	*Pros:* Generally low fees, some funds may have no transaction fees.
	Cons: Monthly maintenance fees may apply in some cases.	*Cons:* Expense ratios and fees may reduce overall returns.
Insurance Protection	*Pros:* Deposits are usually insured up to a certain limit.	*Pros:* No insurance, but considered relatively safe investments.
	Cons: Limited insurance coverage, may vary by country.	*Cons:* No government-backed insurance for potential losses.

FIGURE 18-1:
Pros and cons of investment accounts in a table format from ChatGPT.

Flexibility of Use	*Pros:* Can be linked to other accounts for easy transfers.	*Pros:* Flexibility to buy and sell shares, often with check-writing abilities.
	Cons: Limited in terms of investment options.	*Cons:* Limited to specific types of securities within the fund.
Tax Implications	*Pros:* Interest earned is usually subject to taxation.	*Pros:* Tax-efficient, with potential advantages for certain investors.
	Cons: Interest income may be subject to higher tax rates.	*Cons:* Capital gains distributions are taxable in non-retirement accounts.

It's important to note that individual preferences, financial goals, and risk tolerance may vary. The comparison provided above is a general overview, and specific products from different institutions may have variations. Always consider consulting with a financial advisor to make decisions tailored to your personal financial situation.

👍 👎 🗨 ↺

FIGURE 18-1:
(Continued)

Comparisons of Performance

Through tools such as Google's Bard or Microsoft's Bing Chat, you can ask to compare the performance of a given stock, fund, or other vehicle versus some other standard such as the S&P 500 index, a given sector, or another stock or vehicle. Then create a visual or text chart to see their comparative performance over a given period of time, such as last year or the most recent quarter.

For example:

> "Please provide a side-by-side comparison as a chart of the performance of the S&P 500 index versus the spot price of gold during the calendar year of 2023."

You can also see how well an investment performed against the Consumer Price Index (CPI) or the growth of Gross Domestic Product (GDP).

TIP

Of course, the best AI tools for this task are the investment research tools listed in Appendix B and/or robo-advisors covered in Chapter 7.

Prompts in Different Languages

Don't forget that tools like ChatGPT are fluent in languages besides English. You can have it summarize a Spanish-language document in English for you. Or you can have it translate or summarize an English document in a different language.

TIP

To find the best AI tool for a language given your particular needs, check out the AI directories in Appendix B.

Prompts at a Basic Level

Role playing may not sound very financial, but the name of the game is about learning and understanding. As adults we have certainly come across issues or topics that can be too technical or academic to grasp immediately. Sometimes you may understand something but may have difficulty putting it into words to make it understandable to someone else. How do you make something as clear as possible, especially if it's a serious matter that means a great deal financially, physically, or legally or is otherwise impactful?

In this case, you can have AI (such as ChatGPT or a similar tool) explain it to you at a different level. You can use prompts such as these:

>> "Explain to me concept A as if I were a fifth grader."

>> "In a casual, non-technical manner/style, please explain it."

>> "Tell me step-by-step as if you were a high school tutor."

You can even use this style to explain a detailed or legalistic document.

Document Analysis

Very often as an investor you'll come across an extensive document (many pages long) regarding a particular investment. Perhaps it's a 10K report from the U.S. Securities and Exchange Commission, a prospectus from a mutual fund company, or a detailed stock or fund research report. It may be text or in a PDF. You don't have the time or the inclination to read ("Can't I wait for the movie?!"). What should you do?

AI tools such as Copy.ai and/or ChatPDF (see Chapter 2 and Appendix B for these sites and more) can help. You can use these tools either online or on your hard drive, but you can do a prompt such as "Please review [document PDF] and give me a summary of all the important points," and you will get that in seconds.

Perhaps that document is an extensive online web page. Depending on the type of AI tool you use, you can either cut and paste the full text into the AI tool and then request a useful response, or you can cut and paste the URL for that document, and it will perform the complete task.

Chapter **19**

Ten Tools and Resources That AI Beginners Should Consider

rtificial intelligence is an epic and monumental element affecting almost every area of your financial and working life (and is changing by the minute!). With so much to view and consider, it's easy to freeze up and do nothing. What should you do first?

No worries. I distilled all that vast info into a simple list of ten places to go to or tools to use as you get familiarized with this new, AI-pervasive investing land-scape. The nexus here is that to be on this particular list of ten, it had to have value for my readers on the overlapping subjects of AI and money.

OpenAI.com

ChatGPT (https://chat.openai.com/auth/login) is the first tool to consider; it was created by the folks at OpenAI (https://openai.com/). Get the free edition (starting off without paying is always good). The screen is simple; the interface is easy; and the price is right. The only work you do (at least initially) is ask questions and make requests. It's like being a kid again!

For newcomers to the AI world, I like the obvious point that you can ask ChatGPT about . . . ChatGPT. You can ask AI . . . about AI. No expensive, impatient tutors to deal with. The great thing is that your primary challenge is how to ask your questions (prompts) and/or how to make your requests about various facets of investing.

TIP

This book is your "information genie," so dive in starting with Chapter 2, which is all about ChatGPT. And when you are ready, you can move on to

>> The plus version if you like ($20/month). Compare the free and premium versions at https://openai.com/chatgpt.

>> AI tools and databases (listed in Appendix B) for plug-ins that can make your ChatGPT experience better and more productive.

Investopedia

Yes, Investopedia (www.investopedia.com) is a non-AI site, but it's a good example of a site with a body of knowledge that is useful both before and after you get familiar and proficient with AI.

TIP

This book looks at AI as a tool, and the real goal of this book is to provide information about investing and other financial tasks that will help you change your overall prosperity for the better. Sites like Investopedia have been teaching about and building knowledge about the very results that AI aficionados are seeking. To turbo-charge your usage of AI, use Investopedia for the following:

>> Confirm the results that AI tools such as ChatGPT are getting.

>> Find terms, concepts, and investment vehicles where you can use AI to "drill down" and learn more.

>> Find extensive posts and reports where you can use AI to review, critique, and ask about important points.

>> Ask AI about what you read at Investopedia and how it relates to your specific needs or scenarios.

ToolsAI.net

This site (https://toolsai.net) is a popular site well-stocked with AI tools in its searchable database. It's well categorized, and the number of AI tools seem to be growing daily. Find a tool for almost any AI need. More tools like this are found in Appendix B.

YouTube AI Channels

For a fast education, few things beat a YouTube video (www.youtube.com) by some authority on a given topic. (Yes, I do videos, so I'm a little biased.) If you want to hit the ground running on AI, start with some 20-minute videos on what it is, how to use it, and so on. Its rival Rumble (www.rumble.com) also has a growing slate of AI video offerings.

Appendix A has a list of some great AI channels, and I'm certain many more insightful videos and educational channels are on the way.

LinkedIn

LinkedIn (www.linkedin.com) is my favorite social media platform for professionals. No matter how comfortable or familiar you get with AI, stick to humans you know and trust for a variety of reasons, including getting productive with AI. Most professional groups are grappling with AI and learning the good, the bad, and the ugly as it relates to their specific work.

Whatever profession or financial interest you have, find and get involved in those LinkedIn groups because you'll learn how real-world folks are either struggling or succeeding with AI. Doing a search for "AI" coupled with the name of your specialty or professional category is good for starters. At a minimum, find relevant professional groups and drill down from there for professionals, newsletters, and posts that specialize in AI for a given profession.

AI Productivity Tools

Some AI tools are designed to make you more productive. An AI tool I've used for more than a year is Otter (www.otter.ai). It can hear me talk, and it will transcribe and turn my voice into text. I can also upload an audio file and in minutes have a remarkably accurate transcript of it. I can also use it to take detailed notes of a virtual meeting.

Consider any AI-based productivity tool or app that fits your needs. If you do lots of writing, consider Grammarly. If you do web design, find one of the many that can create a web page for you in minutes versus the old days when it took hours (or in my case, days). Go to Appendix B and find your AI-based "soul mate."

Bedrock AI

TIP

In the world of investing, you come across lots of daunting documents. Whether it is a lengthy 10K report from the U.S. Securities and Exchange Commission (SEC) or the 47-page PDF mutual fund research report, AI tools like Bedrock AI (https://www.bedrock-ai.com/) make it easier and more efficient to sift through all that data and information to get what you need in order to make an informed decision with your money.

Find out more about AI tools like this in Appendix B.

Your Brokerage Site's Robo-Advisor

Get familiar with the robo-advisor at your brokerage site. Or find a robo-advisor you like that you can use with your account, no matter the brokerage firm. You know that every brokerage firm and their website will be knee-deep in AI mania, so find out now how their specific AI technology will be a positive boost to your personal prosperity.

Find out more about robo-advisors in Chapter 7.

Udemy and Other Online Courses

Udemy (www.udemy.com) is a huge online educational site with millions of students and thousands of courses. Udemy has expensive advanced courses as well as free and low-cost courses. I am both an instructor at Udemy (investing, business and tax courses) and a student.

They have a burgeoning menu of AI-related courses, and both the technical aspects (good video and audio quality) and the educational value (folks very proficient in their specialties) of these courses are high, so find an AI course that fits your needs.

Keep in mind that there are also excellent AI-related courses on sites such as Coursera (www.coursera.com), Teachable (www.teachable.com), Skillshare (www.skillshare.com), and Money Clips U (www.moneyclipsU.com).

Discord and Other Groups

It's always good to commiserate or get boosted by a group of like-minded folks on a given concern or topic; just don't let the name fool you. Discord (www.discord.com) runs a large community of forums and specialty interest/user groups on a variety of topics. For those who want to communicate with others about ChatGPT, for example, you can go to https://discord.com/invite/openai. Just sign up for a free account, log in, and start exploring different groups.

Keep in mind that maybe your ideal community of fellow AI-minded kindred spirits aren't on Discord. No worries! Plenty of groups are springing up on platforms such as Facebook (www.facebook.com) and Meetup (www.meetup.com). More support group ideas are in found in Appendix A.

Chapter **20**

Ten Strategies to Complement Your AI Investing Pursuits

lthough AI is certainly promising and its pervasiveness is only beginning, investors must make important considerations in areas not dominated by AI. AI does have its drawbacks and risks, and we'll find out about its unintended consequences in the coming months and years.

In this chapter, the emphasis is on investment diversification to add safety to your financial situation. Yes, AI will be able to help you in the following ten items; just keep in mind that an overdependence or overexposure to a single vehicle or theme can backfire. Here are some ideas, cautionary tales, and strategies to consider as you forge ahead.

Focusing on Fundamentals

As you read this, more and more AI startups are coming out of the starting gates. Some will do fabulously well. Some will thrive, and others will just survive. But many will lose money or just go out of business. I cover small-cap stocks and initial public offerings (IPOs) in Chapter 5, so review that chapter before you chase the next great stock opportunity.

REMEMBER

Given how fragile small-cap stocks can be (along with even smaller stocks referred to as micro-cap and "penny stocks"), the focus on fundamentals (such as a company's net profits, sales, and so on) is especially important. Don't just rely on using AI to investigate a company; do the old-fashioned work in researching a company's fundamentals. Find out more about fundamentals in Chapter 8.

Investing in Utilities

Even after the decades-long national push toward renewable energy such as wind power, solar power, and so on, oil and gas are still at a whopping 80 percent of U.S. national energy needs (at the time of writing). It was at about 82 percent roughly a decade ago. Hydrocarbons (the technical name for "fossil fuels") are still dominant in the realm of energy usage and consumption, and will likely continue to dominate for the foreseeable future.

TIP

Consider adding some exposure in your portfolio to utilities, which many consider to be a safe harbor sector, especially during uncertain or negative economic times. A safe way to diversify your portfolio is through utilities and energy-related exchange-traded funds (ETFs) and mutual funds; see Chapter 6 and Appendix C for more information.

Investing in Consumer Staples

REMEMBER

As I write this book, the economy is flashing signs of slowing down. In good times and (especially) bad, I emphasize in my live and online investing seminars, as well as books such as this, that investors should be acutely aware of stocks that cater to "needs" (versus those that cater to "wants"). I refer to it as "human need" investing, and those companies that actively pursue this typically weather the economic storms very well. For you, it boils down to a simple question: "What will people keep buying no matter how bad the economy is?" You can bet that the lion's share of that answer is "food, water, energy. . ."

Given that, investors should consider consumer staples, which include food, water, beverages, energy, and so forth. A nice feature of these stocks is that they tend to pay higher than average dividends as well. (I discuss dividends later in this chapter.)

A convenient way to include consumer staples in your portfolio is through consumer staples sector ETFs and/or mutual funds. Yes, AI is great, but food and water trump it during a downturn or a crisis. ETFs and mutual funds are covered in Chapter 6, and some ETF resources are listed in Appendix C.

Investing in Healthcare

Healthcare stocks and ETFs deserve a place (no matter the percentage) in most investment portfolios. It's a necessary part of modern civilization, and everyone needs health, or at least a way to deal with poor health or illness. This sector is both a good diversification away from the technology sector, and paradoxically, it's also a good beneficiary of it.

In recent decades, healthcare has become very data-dependent, and AI has made it more manageable and has helped the bottom line (profitability) of healthcare-oriented companies. Healthcare is covered in Chapters 4 and 6.

Considering Dividends

AI stocks (both large-cap and small-cap) and AI-related ETFs and mutual funds will have either a small dividend or no dividend at all. For those investors at or near retirement, this may be an issue. Most folks are looking to this group of stocks for purposes of appreciation (capital gains). However, conservative investors shouldn't ignore dividends.

Dividends have great advantages; for example, over the years dividend payouts tend to meet or exceed the inflation rate, which means they can be a great part of a retirement plan. Dividend investment resources are included in Appendix C.

Limiting Your Losses

There goes your AI stock (or ETF); its stock price is skyrocketing. You're doing fine and feeling good over your stock selection. Maybe it was a large-cap stock that has doubled or tripled since you acquired it not too long ago. Or even better, that small-cap stock you recently bought has been on fire and has soared a gazillion percent, and those dollar signs in your eyes have only gotten bigger. What could go wrong?

You and I have seen it too often. At least once a decade (and usually more), the market has a painful correction or crash — or worse, an extended bear market. Watching your stock drop 20 percent or more can be very stressful. We saw stocks drop by more than 30 percent (and more) during the 2020 pandemic/lockdown gyrations. In 2008, the market was pummeled with a 50 percent drop; many volatile or weak stocks fell by even more. This is where we say that an ounce of prevention is worth a pound of cure.

REMEMBER

When your investments (AI or otherwise) are doing well and you start to see the economic storm clouds start to be reported in the financial media, don't wait for the rain to buy that umbrella. Take some protective steps while your portfolio is still doing well. Here are some considerations to discuss with those helping you with your investments:

>> Stop-loss orders

>> Trailing stops

>> Protective puts

>> Covered call writing

Each of these are hedging approaches designed to help you limit the downside. Your homework is to ask AI to give you detailed descriptions and examples of each of the preceding strategies. Using AI isn't just about increasing the good in your financial life; it's also about decreasing the bad (learning how to limit losses).

You can also find out more about these strategies with ChatGPT (see Chapter 2) and with the resources listed in Appendix C. Lastly, I have done entire chapters on these loss-limiting strategies in the latest edition of *Stock Investing For Dummies* (Wiley).

Choosing the Right Savings Bonds

You've heard over the years (decades in fact) that bonds are a good diversification away from stocks. That's been traditionally true. However, many categories of bonds are at risk due to the dangers of rising interest rates and inflation (both are concerns as I write this). If the economy does inevitably slow down, which in turn can be problematic for stocks in general (and growth stocks like AI-related stocks in particular), then diversifying with the *right type* of bond will be beneficial.

Enter stage right . . . the U.S. savings bond. U.S. savings bonds are highly rated and easy to buy, and you can start with as little as $25 (sweet!). The two types to research are

>> EE bonds, which are issued by the U.S. Treasury and whose interest rate is pegged to treasury notes

>> I bonds, which are also issued by the U.S. Treasury and whose interest rate is pegged to the official rate of inflation (the Consumer Price Index)

TIP

For more information and to buy them, head over to the U.S. Treasury's site on U.S. Savings Bonds at www.savingsbonds.gov.

Diversifying with Hard Assets

AI is digital. Nothing wrong with that! But here is true diversification: non-digital assets. More specifically, a corner of the non-digital world called "hard assets." Most folks are familiar with hard assets such as real estate and collectibles, and here the consideration is physical precious metals such as gold and silver.

As digital gets more pervasive, whether we're talking AI or digital versions of paper assets (such as stocks, bonds, cryptocurrencies, and so on) or the pending issuance of Central Bank Digital Currencies (CBDCs), these areas have their own unique hazards. And yes, ask ChatGPT and other AI research tools about those hazards. The more you research, the more you realize what the wealthy have known for millennia: Be diversified in your wealth and consider a small portion in gold and/or silver.

Physical gold and silver have unique benefits that make them a good diversification away from both paper and/or digital assets. Paper and digital assets have counter-party risk. In other words, their value is tied to the success and integrity of the counter party.

AI stock (as with any other stock) is only as good as the performance of the underlying company. If the company isn't performing well (profit, sales, debt levels, and so forth), then it risks bankruptcy just as much as any other company, AI or not. For investors, it always comes back to fundamentals (see Chapter 8 for details).

For more information on precious metals and other hard assets, check out Chapter 9.

Personal Preparedness

Do you have cash on hand? I mean actual cash? What would you do in the event of a blackout that could last days? What about necessities on hand?

As I write this, our society is electrifying to a great extent. Electric vehicles and AI use plenty of electricity and are very prominent examples. But the federal government is aiming to reduce our "carbon footprint," which means an unprecedented push to reduce our dependence on many modern conveniences that are driven by hydrocarbons (natural gas, oil, and so on). However, during this process, the national infrastructure is not equipped (yet) to cover the massive new burdens on it. Places as diverse as California and Germany have felt the pain of these outages. More outages are likely given today's top-down (government-mandated) initiatives.

Given that, what prudent preparedness should you undertake? What is especially reliant on electricity in your life that should make you consider a backup plan or Plan B? For more details, check out www.ready.gov. In the meanwhile, consider prompting AI with questions like "What should investors do to prepare for emergencies such as power outages?"

Keeping a Paper Trail

Managing your financial life means lots of data, statements, reports, and much more. But the world keeps lurching toward total digital dependency. That means you may be faced with one of more of the following risks:

>> What happens to your digital documents when the lights go out?

>> What happens when you can't access your data or documents when the internet is down?

>> What happens to your digital data/documents when your computer (laptop or otherwise) doesn't function properly? Or doesn't function at all?

>> Are your data and documents safe from hacking and other computer crimes?

TIP

Plenty of scenarios could put you at risk with your data and documents if they are 100 percent digital, so the prudent person makes sure that vital documents are safeguarded with digital and paper redundancy. Yes, ask your AI tool about suggestions here (and you may want to print out the answers). Meanwhile, you can also do the following:

>> Get an external backup drive and routinely back up your critical data.

>> Scan and save all your important documents as PDFs and keep them in multiple locations (a flash drive in a safe, for example).

>> Consider the value of other technologies such as backup services to a cloud and virtual privacy networks (VPNs).

Appendixes

Find a wealth of educational and informational AI resources.

Check out an extensive list of AI tools and apps.

Discover general investing and financial resources.

Appendix **A**

AI Resources

I really — and I mean *really* — want you to keep on top of the fast-changing world of AI. In this book I try to stick to ideas, information, and strategies that are as timeless as possible — or at least good for a long time. But the tools, information, and related data and events in the AI area change more quickly than anything I've ever seen before.

This appendix focuses on AI guidance and education from sources that I feel will still be at it and hopefully flourishing so that you can take advantage of the cutting-edge details coming out. Appendix B focuses on actual AI tools that can be useful for you immediately. Appendix C focuses on general investing resources.

Beginners' Tutorials and Courses on AI

Society at large needs to catch up with AI so everyone knows the good, the bad, and the ugly. No worries — there are plenty of ways beginners can start. These places have free or low-cost educational programs to get you up to speed:

» ChatGPT (https://openai.com/chatgpt): Learn about AI . . . from AI? Sure! The free version offers lots of education and information, and the natural language format means you can ask all of your AI-related questions (and truly much more). See Chapter 2 for more details on this platform.

>> *For Dummies* (www.dummies.com): The official Dummies site has plenty on AI including posts and checklists.

>> Raving Capitalist (www.ravingcapitalist.com): This is my educational site with many courses for beginners on investing, personal finance, and business. The page on AI education and resources is at www.ravingcapitalist.com/AI.

>> Stack Skills (www.stackskills.com): This site offers many low-cost courses and apps on a variety of technical and business topics. They have added some great video courses on AI, and they usually run specials of 80 percent off or better.

>> Tech Crunch (www.techcrunch.com): Lots of posts, news, and guidance here with plenty of courses and how-to on AI.

>> Tech Republic (www.techrepublic.com): More of the same as Tech Crunch and plenty of tech courses.

>> Udemy (www.udemy.com) and Coursera (www.coursera.com) literally have millions of students and thousands of courses. Check them out — by now there are plenty of free and low-cost AI-related courses.

AI YouTube Channels

Sometimes a quick explanatory video is all you need to have your "aha!" moment with understanding something complex. Yes, you'll find plenty of videos, but a good way to address the issue is to go straight to the sources that have proven knowledge and guidance on the topic. Here are a batch of YouTube channels that will scratch the AI knowledge itch:

>> AI Scholar: www.youtube.com/@theAIscholar

>> AI Uncovered: www.youtube.com/@AI.Uncovered

>> Howtoai: www.youtube.com/@howtoai

>> Matt Wolfe: www.youtube.com/@mreflow

>> The Artificial Analyst: www.youtube.com/@TheArtificialAnalyst

>> Tim Harris Video www.youtube.com/@TimHarrisVideo

Books on AI

By now there are likely dozens of books on AI, but I do have my favorites. The following books (available as e-books too) give beginners the lowdown on AI in an understandable manner that readers can absorb and put into action quickly:

» *Artificial Intelligence For Dummies,* 2nd Edition, by John Paul Mueller and Luca Massaron (Wiley): Possibly the most ironic title in *For Dummies* publishing history, it is great at explaining AI.

» *ChatGPT For Dummies* by Pam Baker (Wiley): An excellent explanation and guide on ChatGPT (I got myself a copy!).

» *ChatGPT for Finance* (PDF) by Nicholas Boucher (https://nicolasboucher. online/): For analyzing the numbers for a given public company with AI, this book has excellent guidance.

» *The Ultimate Directory of AI Tools and Resources* by Adam Mladjenovic and Paul Mladjenovic (Prosperity Network): An extensive listing of AI-related tools and resources (from a source I trust).

AI News and Views

These sites offer ongoing news and views which is certainly important for you in the fast-paced AI world.

» AI Magazine: www.aimagazine.com

» AI News: www.artificialintelligence-news.com/

» Forbes AI: www.forbes.com/ai/

» LifeWire: www.lifewire.com/

» Science Daily's AI page: www.sciencedaily.com/news/computers_math/ artificial_intelligence/

» VentureBeat: https://venturebeat.com/

» Wired: www.wired.com/tag/artificial-intelligence/

» Writesonic: www.writesonic.com

AI E-Zines

An e-zine is simply a newsletter delivered via email (like most newsletters these days). E-zine is from older days and it is (was) a combination of "electronic magazine." Here are e-zines that specialize in AI:

>> **AI Tools Report** (https://aitoolreport.com): I've gotten to know their work and they do a great job of reporting not only news and views but also about new AI tools and developments.

>> **The Neuron Daily** (https://www.theneurondaily.com/): This e-zine is also good at AI reporting and it's currently free.

>> **ToolsPedia Weekly** (https://toolspedia.beehiiv.com/subscribe): Sign up for free alerts on AI tools and news.

AI Resource Compilations

Here are several sources that do a good job on compiling AI-related sites and resources:

>> **Bedrock AI:** Bedrock AI (www.bedrock-ai.com) has some great AI resources for investors who really want to "drill down." Check out their AI-related resources for investors here: www.bedrock-ai.com/learn/categories/investing-tools-resources.

>> **Best of the Web's artificial intelligence directory:** Best of the Web has been an aggregator of sites by subject/topic categories for many years, and they have a good site for AI sites at https://botw.org/computers-and-artificial-intelligence/.

>> **Feedspot:** This site (www.feedspot.com) is an excellent aggregator. If you want an extensive list of investing sites, career sites, and so on, their compilations are very useful. Here, for example, is their page specifically for YouTube channels on AI: https://videos.feedspot.com/ai_youtube_channels/.

>> **There's an AI for That:** A great title and a great resource at https://theresanaiforthat.com/. If you have a function in mind, head over here and do a search, and you'll likely find what you need.

User Groups about AI and ChatGPT

As quickly as AI has grown, the interest is growing just as quickly. Here are some of the largest and most active groups on AI and/or ChatGPT that you can join to increase your knowledge and abilities:

» **AIForumHub:** https://aiforumhub.com/

This very active forum has regular posts and discussions for both experts and beginners.

» **Discord groups:** This site has probably the first active users' group on ChatGPT, and its posts and discussions cover all major issues and concerns tied to the popular AI tool.

- Discord's ChatGPT user group: https://discord.com/servers/ chatgpt-1092173065967911002

- Discord's OpenAI forum: https://discord.com/invite/openai

» **Facebook:** www.facebook.com

For the AI aficionado, plenty of groups on Facebook will get you informed and engaged. Here are three large active groups (among many):

- ChatGPT Ideas, Tips & Tricks: www.facebook.com/ groups/1208729370067516/

- ChatGPT Experts: www.facebook.com/groups/gptexperts/

- ChatGPT & OpenAI: www.facebook.com/groups/698593531630485/

» **LinkedIn:** www.linkedin.com

I add LinkedIn here not because it is AI-centric (it's not) but because if you are a professional and financial success–minded in any way, you'll need to check out LinkedIn and find (and get active in) those groups tied to your professional and investment pursuits. These groups will definitely (sooner or later) cover AI as it impacts them and their interests.

» **Meetup:** www.meetup.com

Meetup is well-known for helping folks organize face-to-face groups and live events, so check them out. If you search for "AI," you'll find many events and groups in your local area.

>> **Reddit:** www.reddit.com

This is a very active community, and you should seek out those groups (sub-reddits) that cover your interests not only in AI but also in investing, careers, and so on. As of this writing, the following are the most active AI-related sub-reddits:

- www.reddit.com/r/ChatGPT/
- www.reddit.com/r/ChatGPTPromptGenius/
- www.reddit.com/r/ArtificialInteligence/

Appendix **B**

AI Tools

A ppendix A focuses on resources that provide guidance and help you learn about the world of AI. Those resources are perfect even if you can't spell AI. As they say, you must learn to walk before you run.

In this appendix, the focus is on actual tools and apps (software applications) that you can use for a variety of purposes. Find the ones most relevant to you and your needs.

Investing AI Tools

For investing (stocks, ETFs, and so on), these AI tools offer great research and analytical power for any serious investor:

» AI Invest by StockInvest.us: https://stockinvest.us/ai-analysis-offer

» Candlestick: https://candlestick.ai/

» Composer: www.composer.trade/

» Fin Chat: https://finchat.io/

» Kvants AI: https://kvants.ai/

» LevelFields: www.levelfields.ai

>> Stocked AI: www.stockedai.com/

>> STRATx AI: www.stratxai.com/

>> Trade Station: www.tradestation.com/

>> Trade UI: https://tradeui.com/

Personal Finance AI Tools

The following AI tools are for general money management such as budgeting and financial planning:

>> Consumer AI: https://consumerai.deeprose.eu/

>> Expense Sorted: www.expensesorted.com/

>> Monarch: www.monarchmoney.com/ai

>> Truewind: www.truewind.ai

Tax and Budgeting AI Tools

The following AI tools are among the early entrants for taxes and budgeting, and more will come as AI changes the dynamics of money management:

>> AiTax: www.aitax.com

>> FlyFin: www.flyfin.tax

>> Keepertax: www.keepertax.com

>> TaxGPT: www.taxgpt.com

>> Taxly: https://taxly.ai/

>> WellyBox: www.wellybox.com

>> ZeroTax AI: www.zerotax.ai

Robo-Advisors

Please note that the robo-advisor landscape may have evolved since the time of writing, and new players may have entered the market. It's essential to conduct further research and review each robo-advisor's offerings, fees, and services to find the one that best aligns with your investment needs and preferences.

Additionally, visiting the respective websites provides you with the most up-to-date information on their services and offerings. Before you drill down on the following robo-advisors, head over to Chapter 7 to discover the pros and cons as well as the features.

» Acorns: www.acorns.com/

» Ally Invest Managed Portfolios: www.ally.com/invest/managed-portfolios/

» Axos Invest: www.axosinvest.com/

» Betterment: www.betterment.com/

» Ellevest: www.ellevest.com/

» Empower: www.empower.com

» E*TRADE Core Portfolios: https://us.etrade.com/what-we-offer/our-accounts/core-portfolios

» M1 Finance: www.m1finance.com/

» Schwab Intelligent Portfolios: www.schwab.com/intelligent-portfolios

» SigFig: www.sigfig.com/

» SoFi Invest: www.sofi.com/invest/

» Stash: www.stash.com/

» Vanguard Personal Advisor Services: https://investor.vanguard.com/advice/robo-advisor

» Wealthfront: www.wealthfront.com/

» WiseBanyan: https://api.wisebanyan.com/

ChatGPT Alternatives

Lots of great AI tools rival ChatGPT, and some surpass it in a given area, so take some time and review the following list to find an optimal choice for you personally:

>> AnonChatGPT: https://anonchatgpt.com/

>> Bing Chat: www.bing.com/search?q=Bing+AI&showconv=1

>> Character GPT: https://beta.character.ai/

>> ChatPDF: www.chatpdf.com/

>> Chatsonic: https://writesonic.com/chat

>> Copy.AI: www.copy.ai/

>> Flawlessly.ai: https://flawlessly.ai/app

>> Google Bard: https://bard.google.com/

>> iAsk.ai: https://iask.ai/

>> Phind: https://phind.com

>> You.com: https://you.com

Directories of AI Tools

Behold! A bevy of AI tool and app directories that will help you find any tool or app that is AI-related — and I mean anything:

>> AI Seeker Directory: https://aiseeker.io/

>> AIscout: www.aiscout.net

>> Futurepedia: www.futurepedia.io/

>> Futuretools: www.futuretools.io/

>> Super AI Tools: www.superaitools.io/

Other Finance-Specific Tools Using Generative AI

And, finally, an extensive list of additional AI tools for your investment and financial research needs:

>> Alpha Sense (www.alpha-sense.com/): This site provides market research and intelligence for investors on companies, industries, and markets.

>> Amenity Analytics (www.amenityanalytics.com/): This Natural Language Program (NLP) investing platform can be customized to extract and classify the information most relevant to you, capturing key business events, sentiment, context, and temporal relevance consistent with your research strategy.

>> Babbl.dev (www.babbl.dev/): Babbl uses language models to detect bullish versus bearish sentiment indicators across stocks, topics, and market-wide.

>> BlueFire AI (https://bluefireai.com/): This tool performs financial statement analysis, behavioral profiling, and market data analytics.

>> Boosted.ai (https://boosted.ai/): Boosted uses finance-specific machine learning algorithms to identify patterns based on your unique inputs.

>> Docalysis (https://docalysis.com/): You can upload PDFs of filings or earnings transcripts and ask questions about them like "List all risk factors in bulleted form" or "Give a summary of all legal issues facing this company."

>> Hila.ai (http://hila.ai/): Hila provides question answering for specific documents (for example, for a specific earnings transcript or 10-K annual report).

>> New Constructs (www.newconstructs.com/): This site provides market research on more than 10,000 stocks and funds.

>> Nosible AI (https://nosible.com/): This tool makes it easy to demonstrate what your portfolio looks like and how it's different/unique. They have visualization and data libraries.

>> Roic.ai (https://roic.ai/): This tool provides ten years of financial statement data in one, easy to use screen.

>> Sentieo (https://sentieo.com/): Sentieo provides a searchable database of public and private company data, documents, and news from relevant sources, along with integrated modeling tools.

>> UpTrends (www.uptrends.ai/): This site tracks AI trends for investing.

Appendix C

General Investing Resources

No matter how much artificial intelligence you're using or consuming, the more knowledgeable you are about investing (artificial or otherwise), the better you will be informed and the better you will be as a user of AI. You can use these resources in conjunction with the strategies and tools covered elsewhere in this book to become a great investor.

General Investing Sites

The following are some of the best news sources and financial site aggregators online:

» Bloomberg www.bloomberg.com

» Dollarcollapse.com www.dollarcollapse.com

» For Dummies www.dummies.com

» Investopedia www.investopedia.com

» Kiplinger www.kiplinger.com/

- » Market Sanity www.marketsanity.com
- » Market Watch www.marketwatch.com
- » Nasdaq www.nasdaq.com
- » Seeking Alpha www.seekingalpha.com
- » Think Advisor www.thinkadvisor.com/
- » Value Walk www.valuewalk.com/
- » Zero Hedge www.zerohedge.com

Specialized Investing Sites

Here are a few sites that dig deeper into particular investing topics:

- » Goldsilver.com www.goldsilver.com
- » Howestreet www.howestreet.com
- » Trends Journal www.trendsjournal.com

Investing Books

Yes, some of these books I authored, but that's how I know that they will help you!

- » ***Stock Investing For Dummies***

  By Paul Mladjenovic, published by Wiley

  This book focuses on helping both beginners and intermediate investors successfully navigate the world of stock investing.

- » ***Factor Investing For Dummies***

  By James Maendel and Paul Mladjenovic, published by Wiley

  Factor investing coupled with AI is a powerful combination. Factor investing is an investment strategy that many pros use to select stocks (and ETFs) based on factors such as quality, momentum, and so on, that tend to outperform the general market over the long term.

>> *High-Level Investing For Dummies*

By Paul Mladjenovic, published by Wiley

This is considered an advanced or "high octane" version of *Stock Investing For Dummies*. This book goes into not only stocks and conventional exchange-traded funds (ETFs) but also inverse ETFs and options trading. Couple these "turbo-charged" speculative approaches with AI, and you add another dimension to your investing pursuits.

>> *The Intelligent Investor: The Classic Text on Value Investing*

By Benjamin Graham, published by HarperCollins

The more the stock market changes, the more investors should heed the stock market wisdom in this classic investing book from one of the greats.

>> *Security Analysis: The Classic 1951 Edition*

by Benjamin Graham and David L. Dodd, published by the McGraw-Hill Companies

Another classic from Mr. Graham on fundamental analysis (which I discuss in Chapter 8).

LinkedIn Groups

The following groups have seasoned investors and financial professionals involved, and they are a great learning environment for budding investors:

>> Accredited Investor Club https://www.linkedin.com/groups/46460/

>> Austrian School of Economics; Finance and Investing https://www.linkedin.com/groups/2351030/

>> Personal Finance Bloggers https://www.linkedin.com/groups/1913084/

>> Trading and Investing the Financial Markets https://www.linkedin.com/groups/2580474/

Investor Clubs and Organizations

Investing is one of those pursuits where you may be alone, but you shouldn't feel isolated. These clubs offer support and you can learn along with others having the same concerns:

>> American Association of Individual Investors www.aaii.com

>> National Association of Investment Clubs www.betterinvesting.org

Government Agencies

All public securities are subject to review and regulations, so these agencies have their place. Moreover, they have guidance and education for the general public that's useful from a regulator's point of view.

>> Commodities Futures Trading Commission (CFTC) www.cftc.gov

>> Securities and Exchange Commission www.sec.gov

>> For reports on public companies (such as 10K reports), go to https://www.sec.gov/edgar

Index

A

actively managed portfolios, 53
adaptability, 124
adjustable-rate bonds, 111
advance healthcare directive, 207
advertisements, 148
ADX (average directional index), 83
agricultural commodities, 101–102, 103
AI. *See* artificial intelligence
AI Practical Guide, 11
AI Tool Guru, 27
AI Tool Report, 27
AIForumHub, 263
AI Tools Report, 262
alerts, market, 97
Alpha Sense, 269
Amazon, 35
Amenity Analytics, 269
AnonChatGPT, 21
Apple (AAPL), 34, 35
artificial intelligence (AI). *See also* resources; tools, AI
  educational resources, 11
  financial planning with, 11
  general discussion, 7–8
  impact on career, 153–156
  investing alternatives, 10
  overview, 7
  potential problems
    bias, 230
    faulty predictions, 233–234
    fraud, 231
    inaccuracy and errors in, 229–230
    information versus wisdom, 232
    input versus AI output, 233
    job displacement, 153–154, 231–232
    overreliance on technology, 232
    privacy, 234
    using right tools, 232–233

prompts
  at basic level, 241
  for Chat GPT, 17–20
  comparisons of performance, 240
  complex questions, 236
  in different languages, 240–241
  document analysis, 241
  formulas, 237
  lists, 237–238
  overview, 235
  personal scenarios with goals in mind, 237
  pros and cons, 238–240
  for retirement planning, 201–203
  second opinions, 238
  simple questions, 236
  for small-cap AI stocks, 45
strategies
  for commodities investing, 106–107
  for precious metals, 97–98
  for real estate investing, 137–138
  stock investing, 9–10
  for taxes, 222–223
two types of, 8–9
Artificial Intelligence For Dummies (Mueller & Massaron), 273
asset class concentration, risk of, 134–135
asset inflation, 175
audio-to-text function, 25–26
automated portfolio management, 70
automated rebalancing, 70
average directional index (ADX), 83
average true range (ATR), 82

B

Babbl.dev, 269
backwardation, 95
Baidu, 36
Baker, Pam, 273

About the Author

Paul Mladjenovic was a Certified Financial Planner (CFP) from 1985 to 2021 and is a national speaker, educator, author, and financial coach. Since 1981, he has specialized in investing, financial planning, and home business issues. During those 40-plus years, he has helped hundreds of thousands of students and readers build wealth through his nationwide seminars, workshops, conferences, and coaching program.

Besides this book, Paul has written all previous editions of *Stock Investing For Dummies*, *High-Level Investing For Dummies*, *Micro-Entrepreneurship For Dummies*, *Zero-Cost Marketing*, *Precious Metals Investing For Dummies*, and *The Job Hunter's Encyclopedia*. He also co-authored *Affiliate Marketing For Dummies* and *Factor Investing For Dummies*. His national (and online) seminars include "The $50 Wealth-Builder," "Ultra-Investing with Options," and the "Home Business Goldmine," among others. The full details on his (downloadable) financial and business startup audio seminars can be found at www.RavingCapitalist.com. A page at this site (www.RavingCapitalist.com/AI) provides resources and views to help readers with AI. His online courses can also be found at educational venues such as Udemy.com, Skillshare.com, Freeu.com, MtAiryLearningTree.org, and MoneyClipsU.com, among others.

You can view Paul's profile at www.linkedin.com/in/paulmladjenovic/, and you can check out his author's page at www.amazon.com/author/paulmladjenovic. Readers can email questions or inquiries directly to paul@mladjenovic.com or at the bio page at www.RavingCapitalist.com.

Author's Acknowledgments

First and foremost, I offer my appreciation and gratitude to the wonderful folks at Wiley. It has been a pleasure to work with such a top-notch organization that works so hard to create products that offer readers tremendous value and information. I wish all of you continued success! Wiley has some notables whom I do want to single out.

A very special thanks to Georgette Beatty, my project editor, who is an amazing person and a magnificent professional whom I have had the pleasure and honor of working with on several books. I thank you for being so good to me and with me!

The technical editor, James Maendel, is a top financial advisor whose detailed and constructive input made sure that the content was second to none. He was also a superb co-author with me on *Factor Investing For Dummies*.

With deep and joyful gratitude, I thank Tracy Boggier, my amazing acquisitions editor. Thank you so much for being my champion at Wiley and shepherding yet another *For Dummies* guide for me to author, and I can't express enough appreciation for all that she does. *For Dummies* books are great, and they appear on your bookshelf only through the planning and professional efforts of publishing pros like Tracy.

My sincere thanks to Kelly Dobbs Henthorne, a copyediting pro who did an amazing job turning my mangled words into top-notch prose.

I dedicate this book to my wife, Fran, on the occasion of our 30th wedding anniversary . . . Lipa Zyenska, may God bless us with many more years! I also thank my boys, Adam and Joshua, with all my heart for their support throughout the writing of this book. I thank God for you, and I love you beyond words!

Lastly, I want to acknowledge you, the reader. Over the years, you've made the *For Dummies* series the popular and indispensable books they are today. Thank you, and I wish you continued success!

Publisher's Acknowledgments

Senior Acquisitions Editor: Tracy Boggier

Development Editor: Georgette Beatty

Copy Editor: Kelly Dobbs Henthorne

Technical Editor: James Maendel

Production Editor: Pradesh Kumar

Cover Image: © Tiago Zegur/Alamy Stock Photo